+CT21 .G3 1985

HISTORY
AND
HISTORIOGRAPHY

A THIRTY-ONE-VOLUME FACSIMILE SERIES
OF CLASSIC BOOKS FOR BOTH HISTORIANS AND STUDENTS
ON THE NATURE OF HISTORY,
HOW HISTORY IS COMMUNICATED,
AND HOW TO DO HISTORICAL RESEARCH

EDITED BY
ROBIN WINKS
YALE UNIVERSITY

A GARLAND SERIES

THE NATURE OF BIOGRAPHY

John A. Garraty

Garland Publishing, Inc., New York & London
1985

31273

For a complete list of the titles in this
series see the final pages of this volume.

© John A. Garraty, 1957
Published by Alfred A. Knopf, Inc.
Reprinted by permission of Alfred
A. Knopf, Inc.

Library of Congress Cataloging in Publication Data

Garraty, John Arthur, 1920–
 The nature of biography.

 (History and historiography)
 Reprint. Originally published:
New York : Knopf, 1957.
  Bibliography: p.
  Includes index.
  1. Biography (as a literary form)
I. Title. II. Series.
CT21.G3   1985   808'.06692   83-49165
ISBN 0-8240-6363-5 (alk. paper)

The volumes in this series are printed
on acid-free, 250-year-life paper.

Printed in the United States of America

BOOKS BY
John A. Garraty

THE NATURE OF BIOGRAPHY
[*Alfred A. Knopf, 1957*]

WOODROW WILSON: A GREAT LIFE IN BRIEF
[*Alfred A. Knopf, 1956*]

THE HISTORIAN AND THE BARBER
The Correspondence of George A. Myers and James Ford Rhodes
[*Ohio Historical Society, 1956*]

HENRY CABOT LODGE: A BIOGRAPHY
[*Alfred A. Knopf, 1953*]

SILAS WRIGHT
[*Columbia University Press, 1949*]

The Nature of

BIOGRAPHY

The Nature of
BIOGRAPHY

by

JOHN A. GARRATY

New York: Alfred · A · Knopf

1 9 5 7

L.C. catalog card number: 57–10559

© John A. Garraty, 1957

THIS IS A BORZOI BOOK,
PUBLISHED BY ALFRED A. KNOPF, INC.

COPYRIGHT 1957 by JOHN A. GARRATY. *All rights reserved. No part of this book may be reproduced in any form without permission in writing from the publisher, except by a reviewer who may quote brief passages in a review to be printed in a magazine or newspaper. Manufactured in the United States of America. Published simultaneously in Canada by McClelland & Stewart Ltd.*

FIRST EDITION

The lines by T. S. Eliot quoted on page 11 are from THE CONFIDENTIAL CLERK, *copyright, 1954, by T. S. Eliot. Reprinted by permission of Harcourt, Brace and Company, Inc.*

TO THE MEMORY OF

Benjamin P. Thomas

A GREAT BIOGRAPHER

The story of illustrious men cannot be too often retold. Like great outstanding mountain-peaks, these men invite description but elude definition; they provoke examination but defy exhaustion. . . . We grasp so much of the spirit as we can comprehend—and as there are infinite gradations of comprehension, so there are infinite varieties of portrayal."

DAVID SAVILLE MUZZEY,
Thomas Jefferson

Foreword

This book has had a long and complicated history. The story of how it has developed will be interesting, I believe, to readers of the following pages. In 1952 I received a fellowship from the Fund for the Advancement of Education in order to study psychology. I chose this subject because in earlier work I had come to realize how much of a biographer's success depends upon his understanding of human motivation and of such processes as rationalization, sublimation, and repression. It seemed to me that a biographer might profit particularly from an understanding of how psychologists study human personality. So I tried to find out about all the techniques—Rorschach tests, personality inventories, and so on—that modern students of personality find useful in their work. In my very superficial study of these methods I asked of each the question: "Can this method be used to study the personality of a subject who is dead?" If the answer was in the negative, and of course this was usually the case, I discarded the method, however important it might be in psychology. But eventually I collected a considerable number of methods that *could* be used on dead subjects. These devices are described in Chapter IX of this book.

I was aware of the fact that a psychoanalytical approach had already been employed by some biographers. On the basis of past reading of psychoanalytical biographies I did not expect much from this line of investigation, but I felt obligated as part of my general survey of methods to consider psychoanalysis from the biographer's viewpoint. While more impressed than I had anticipated, I was not, as readers of these pages will see, overwhelmed by the possibilities of psychoanalysis as a tool of biography.

But my interests had been shifted somewhat from the study of psychology to the study of biography. The psychoanalytical was one type of biography. There were others. Could a definitive system of classification be set up to cover every kind? I was soon digging into all the literature *about* biography that I could find. I now planned a manual on biography as a literary and historical form, describing the types of biography, the relation of biography to history, the sources commonly available to biographers together with the special problems entailed in using them, and the methods of research and writing employed by successful biographers of all kinds.

In 1954 I received a three-year Faculty Research Fellowship from the Social Science Research Council to continue my investigations. Eventually I had what I thought was a complete manuscript covering the subjects just described, but criticisms by other scholars, particularly Howard Mumford Jones, convinced me that the manuscript dealt too exclusively with the present, that it should be expanded to include some account of the development of biography over time. As a historian I was responsive to this line of argument, and set out to study the history of biography. What was originally designed as a single chapter has become half

Foreword [xi

this book. (And it is still the barest survey of a vast subject.)

In any case this book has evolved gradually over the past five years. Along the way parts of it have appeared, in different form, as articles in the *Saturday Review*, the *Centennial Review*, *Social Education*, the *South Atlantic Quarterly*, and the *Psychological Bulletin*. Many persons have helped me by reading all or part of this work and giving me the benefit of their knowledge. I can only list them here, but I do so with deep gratitude, and, of course, without suggesting that any of them is responsible for whatever errors or inadequacies the book contains: Harry Brown, Richard M. Dorson, Carlton J. H. Hayes, Charles Hirschfeld, Howard Mumford Jones, Alfred A. Knopf, Russel B. Nye, Arthur M. Schlesinger, Jr., Richard E. Sullivan, and Herbert Weinstock. On specific points I have been aided by Gordon W. Allport, Frank Freidel, Walter Johnson, and the late Benjamin P. Thomas. The aforementioned grants from the Fund for the Advancement of Education and the Social Science Research Council have eased the burdens of my work immensely. Finally, I wish again to pay tribute to my wife, Joan Perkins Garraty, whose encouragement has sustained my spirits over the years and whose careful criticisms have greatly improved this work at every stage in its composition.

JOHN A. GARRATY

East Lansing, Michigan
February 17, 1957

CONTENTS

		PAGE
I.	*The Nature of Biography*	3

DEVELOPMENT

II.	*Biography in the Ancient World*	31
III.	*The Development of Biography*	54
IV.	*Biography Reaches Maturity*	76
V.	*Nineteenth-Century Trends*	97
VI.	*The "New" Biography and the Modern Synthesis*	121

METHOD

VII.	*Choosing a Subject*	155
VIII.	*The Materials of Biography*	177
IX.	*The Problem of Personality*	215
X.	*The Writing of Biography*	241

| ESSAY ON SOURCES | | 261 |
| INDEX | *follows page* | 289 |

The Nature of

BIOGRAPHY

CHAPTER I

The Nature of Biography

BIOGRAPHY, to begin with a very simple definition, is the record of a life. It is thus a branch of history, each life a small segment in a vast mosaic, just as the story of the development of a town, a state, or a nation may be thought of as an element in a larger whole. The word "biography" has often been used loosely. Marquis James called his history of a great insurance company *The Biography of a Business*. George Gamow has written a *Biography of the Earth* from the time it "was born from the Sun, its mother, as the result of a brief but violent encounter with a passing star" to its "violent thermal death in the far-distant future." Others have written "biographies" of buildings, of books, even of ideas. But these books are biographies only by analogy, and perhaps the simplest accurate definition of biography should read: "The History of a Human Life."

In addition to representing history in microcosm, biography is related to history in another, much more complicated way. One cannot segregate an individual from his surroundings and study him, as one can analyze an unknown chemical in a test tube. Men interact with other men, and they are influenced by vague but vital social, cultural, and economic forces in their environment. To tell the story of any man, one must say something about the stage on which he acts out the drama of his life. Biographers call this kind of material "background," and there have been great variations in the amounts of it which they have employed. At one extreme, for instance, are the "psychographs" of Gamaliel Bradford, in which the protagonists sometimes seem to float almost like disembodied spirits in a vacuum. At the other pole is such a massive, multi-volumed "life and times" as Douglas Southall Freeman's *George Washington*. But if no one has yet concocted a universal recipe describing how much "background" a biographer should use, all writers agree that some is absolutely necessary if a man's life story is to be made intelligible to the reader.

Generally, the emphasis that a biographer places on his subject's surroundings will reflect his over-all view of the importance of individual intelligence and character in determining the course of events. This question has been debated through the ages, but it still lacks a final answer.

Some writers have gone so far as to argue that individual men are significant only because the times in which they live make them so. A sociologist, Joseph Schneider, after an elaborate study of the lives of English botanists from 1700 to the present, concluded that certain periods of history had proved favorable to the development of many plant specialists, whereas in other times, few important ones had appeared. "It is the cultural situation which produces famous men," he concluded. V. F. Calverton, writing in the 1920's, also denied the importance of the individual. "The

1. *The Nature of Biography*

idea of looking upon greatness as a mystery or an accident is . . . absurd," Calverton wrote in *The Newer Spirit*. The "peculiar manifestations" of "circumstances" provided the opportunity which "made it possible for certain men to become great." Shakespeare, according to Calverton, was great only because he "came in contact with those stimuli . . . that, reacting on his nature, could inevitably make him the man and author he was," while a proper study of George Washington would show "not how Washington rose above conditions to success, but how conditions . . . rode him to success." In the same vein, Stephen Vincent Benét once wrote a short story, "The Curfew Tolls," describing what a nonentity Napoleon would have become if he had been born a few years before his time and had thus been too old for the role he actually played in the denouement of the French Revolution.

Even a "great man" like Goethe spoke of the individual as a reflection of his times, intimating that any man born a decade earlier or later than he was in fact, would have "become quite a different being." And Professor Edward P. Cheyney, in his presidential address to the American Historical Association in 1923, without denying to man a limited freedom of action, concluded that every person "is controlled at every turn by the natural laws of the world in which he dwells."

But other writers have insisted that forceful individuals can often change the trend of events. Thomas Carlyle, of course, carried this theory to its logical extreme. Carlyle was a "hero-worshipper"; he insisted that history was no more than the sum of innumerable biographies. The biographer Sidney Lee emphasized "those aspects of men's lives which affect the movements of the crowd." And William

6] THE NATURE OF BIOGRAPHY

Roscoe Thayer urged his fellow historians to "try to discover how the human will—that force more mysterious than electricity—shapes and directs the deeds of men."

A third group has argued that neither the man nor the time in which he lives really controls what happens in history. "In the queer mess of human destiny," wrote William E. Woodward, one of Washington's biographers, "the determining factor is Luck. For every important place in life there are many men of fairly equal capacities. Among them Luck decides who shall accomplish the great work . . . and who shall fall back into obscurity and silence." Oscar Handlin wrote an entire book, *Chance or Destiny?*, in which he examined a series of critical events in American history and concluded that in each case the fate of the individuals concerned and of the nation as a whole was determined by pure chance. Whether this force be called luck, chance, or fate, those who stress it are in essential agreement that neither men nor great social forces control historical development.

It would be difficult to write a biography without having a definite opinion on the importance of the "hero" in history, and whatever one's theory, it must inevitably influence the kind of book one writes. The extreme position of Carlyle, though challenging, is exaggerated. For history deals with societies as well as individuals, and any society is far more than the sum of its parts. Vast economic, social, and cultural forces which obviously transcend the lives of individuals are basic elements in history. And luck too plays a part.

But the biographer had better avoid any oversimplified theory of historical development. The individual makes history; so does chance; so do social forces. One need not look

1. The Nature of Biography

beyond his daily experience to observe the operation of all three elements. Each of us makes decisions that influence the lives of others; each is controlled and limited by the world we live in; each is affected by the caprice of fortune. It is the biographer's job to determine the relative importance of each factor throughout his subject's career. Thus Gilbert Chinard wrote, in *Thomas Jefferson: The Apostle of Americanism:* "Jefferson . . . could have followed the line of least resistance and enjoyed the good things of life. . . . Such would have been Jefferson's destiny, had he been born in the Old World." In this way he illustrates the role of determinism and of chance in life. But Chinard added: "Had he been made of weaker stuff he would have become one of the fox-hunters, horse-racers and card-players of the Virginia gentry." Here the subject is seen overriding both fate and his environment. Taken as a whole, the passage shows that Chinard considered all the possibilities and arrived at his own judgment of their relative importance in a particular case. Whether one deals with small incidents or entire careers, the three major points of view should be always kept in mind—for they are all persistently operative.

But aside from this essentially philosophical question, the biographer must decide how to place his subject in his environment. Even the confirmed hero-worshipper must describe the world his protagonist is shaping.

David S. Muzzey put the problem well when he compared the individual to the waist of an hour-glass, standing "at the apex of a pyramid whose base broadens downward through descendants and at the apex of a pyramid whose base broadens upward through ancestors." In Muzzey's image, every historically significant man is "focal," gathering the experience of the past into himself and sending forth "widening rays of influence" into the future. "The task of the biographer," he concluded, is "to calculate the resultant of the forces," which consist of the personality of the subject and "the problems of the times in which he lived."

In his own biographical work, Muzzey never applied this idea fully. But the English scientist Angus Armitage did so in his life of Copernicus, *Sun, Stand Thou Still.* Armitage was handicapped in writing a biography of Copernicus, for almost nothing is known of the great astronomer's personal life. He overcame this difficulty by stressing the development of the science of astronomy and Copernicus's contributions to it. His book has three parts, corresponding to the waist and the two pyramids of Muzzey's hour-glass. "Astronomy before Copernicus" traces the history of man's knowledge of the stars down to the last quarter of the fifteenth century. "The Man and His Work" explains the subject's contributions and details the limited knowledge of his life which has survived, and "The Triumph of the Copernican Theory" describes the "widening rays of influence" (to use Muzzey's term) of Copernicus on the later development of astronomy.

THE BIOGRAPHER, however, must not deal only with the facts of his subject's career, with what he did, why he did it, and how he influenced his times and was in turn affected by them. He must also describe the man himself—his personality and character, his individuality. This aspect of biography is of fundamental importance; indeed, it explains the enduring popularity of the biographical form.

For people are interested primarily in people. They have never had to be persuaded that "the proper study of mankind is man." And the convincing description of personality involves problems distinct from the accurate description of facts. It is this which makes the writing of biography a technique apart from that of history.

Biographical writing, therefore, concerns itself with two separate yet related tasks. This is not to say that the historical part of biography is "scientific," or that the personal part is "artistic." A purely "scientific" biography can be deeply concerned with personality, as the examination of any psychiatrist's notebook would make clear, while no one would deny the artistic merit of many of the great histories from Herodotus and Thucydides to Macaulay and Parkman.

Nevertheless it is true that the *portrayal* as distinct from the understanding of personality involves an extremely difficult problem which is chiefly artistic in nature. Allan Nevins, long both a champion and practitioner of the artistic expression of historical information, once said that the ability to describe character "is primarily a literary gift; it has little to do with erudite grubbing . . . in tons of manuscripts." Psychologists themselves have found this to be true. In a paper entitled "Personality: A Problem for Science or a Problem for Art?" Gordon W. Allport writes:

> It *is* true that the giants of literature make psychologists, who undertake to represent and to explain personality, seem ineffectual and sometimes a bit foolish in comparison. Only a pedant could prefer the dry collections of facts that psychology can offer regarding an individual mental life to the glorious and unforgettable portraits that the gifted novelist, dramatist, or biographer can give.

Dr. Henry A. Murray, attempting to present the results of his exhaustive psychological study of fifty men of college age, was also made aware of the futility of his work unless it could be effectively presented. He solved the dilemma by partially sacrificing science to art, frankly seeking to utilize the techniques of the novelists in the effort to make his characterizations "real." "A psychologist who believes that he can tell the truth without being 'literary' has only to try writing a case history or biography, and then compare what he has done to a character sketch by any novelist of the first order," Murray concluded.

The best novelists have excelled and indeed outdistanced nearly all biographers in describing personality, setting a standard almost impossible of attainment for writers of lives. Naturally, therefore, the novel has had great influence upon biography, and has made the average biographer possibly more aware of the role of art in his field than the historian is in his.

The secret of the novelist's success lies in his unrestricted imagination. He may create what seems to be a very complicated character, but the character is never more complicated than the creator wishes to make it. He is never confronted with the need to select the typical from a maze of trivial or contradictory actions, nor is he bothered by the absence of evidence: his imagination can supply whatever detail his artistic sensibilities require.

The biographer, however, has at once more and less to draw upon. He has mountains of evidence from which to extract the essence of his subject. He has also the advantage of reality—he need not convince his readers that he is dealing with an actual person. And his imagination is constantly stimulated as each new fact falls into place. On

1. The Nature of Biography

the other hand, his "facts" do not always yield their meanings easily, and he must choose among them with discernment. Also, no matter how much evidence he has, he never has it all, and often lacks the most vital elements in the edifice he is trying to reconstruct. Yet he is bound by what he has. He can bring great artistry to the selection and interpretation of his evidence, but if he is to perform his proper function, the sources must be there, and all the relevant sources must be considered.

At the heart of the matter is the fact that in describing personality, the biographer is dealing with qualities that defy absolute analysis. The historian Charles A. Beard was so awed by the complexity of human personality that he could not bring himself to write a biography. "I cannot be sure enough about human character and human motives to write the life of anyone," he explained. The picture of a personality can be no more than convincing. Absolute certainty in interpreting character is something that even the psychologist does not claim to achieve. As one of T. S. Eliot's characters says in *The Confidential Clerk*:

> There's always something one's ignorant of
> About anyone, however well one knows them;
> And that may be something of the greatest importance.

The infinite complexity of the mind of man gives the biographer a tremendous power, but also burdens him with a great responsibility. When he describes a personality, no one can be certain that he is right, but it is almost equally difficult to prove that he is wrong. If he says that his hero wrote a particular letter, or was at a certain place at a specific time, his accuracy can be checked. But when he deals with motives, feelings, and other aspects of personality, he is dealing, essentially, with matters of opinion. The records, for example, may indicate over and over again that Mr. A was egotistical, competitive, and aggressive. Yet some will read from them that he was a self-confident extrovert and others that he was a timid soul "compensating" for some obscure feeling of inferiority. None can say with complete assurance that *his* view of Mr. A is correct.

Furthermore, the average man is so contradictory and complicated that by selecting evidence carefully, a biographer can "prove" that his subject is almost anything. "A little reflection," a writer in the *Southern Literary Messenger* remarked in 1856, "will show that half a dozen different narratives of the same life may be constructed, each of which shall contain facts and facts only, while none of them shall furnish . . . a true account."

Even when he is dealing with directly observable actions the biographer's ability to select from among many different facts gives him a tremendous power. Suppose one were writing a life of Harry S. Truman. One might emphasize Truman's failure as a haberdasher, his connection with the corrupt Pendergast machine in Missouri, the devious circumstances of his selection as Roosevelt's running-mate in 1944, his early fumblings with the complexities of his job after Roosevelt's death, his overdependence upon certain unsavory cronies, his temper (as expressed, for example, in a letter to a certain music critic), the failure of his China policy, the "softness" toward Communism in his administration, and many similar aspects of his career. On the other hand, one might play down or ignore all these things, and stress Truman's fine service as an artillery officer in World War I, his liberal record as Senator from Missouri during the New Deal era, the way he championed civil-

1. *The Nature of Biography* [13

rights legislation as President, the high caliber of so many of his appointees in the foreign-policy field, his courageous stand in the Korean crisis, and other incidents that show him in a friendly light. All the *facts* used in either of these approaches might be accurate, but the resultant stories would be very different. Anyone who considers these accounts impossibly exaggerated should look into two lives of Andrew Jackson, one written by his friend Amos Kendall, the other by Davy Crockett.

Indeed, there is no need to resort to hypothetical cases to demonstrate the effectiveness of selectivity. A glance at the various lives of any important historical personage makes the point clearly. To take an example almost at random, let us consider some biographies of Alexander Hamilton. Hamilton was probably the most convinced nationalist of his age, a man to whom the separate sovereignty of the individual states was at best a necessary evil. Yet during the Civil War a Southern sympathizer named C. J. Riethmuller wrote a biography of Hamilton designed to "prove" that Hamilton would have supported the right of secession. In the eighties, Henry Cabot Lodge produced a *Hamilton* that made it clear that the first Secretary of the Treasury would have been a loyal member of the Republican party if he had been alive at that time, and in the 1920's Arthur Vandenberg argued that this would still have been true after World War I. A later biographer, Robert Warshow, pictured him as "The First American Businessman." In all these cases, a particular impression was created by the selection of certain evidence and the avoidance of contradictory facts.

But the unscrupulous selection of evidence is most effective when applied to the description of personality. Take the case of Andrew Carnegie. Little is known about the great steel baron's early career aside from what he himself wrote of it in his *Autobiography*. But his biographers, by selecting only part of what he said about himself and modifying the facts they pick out, have produced radically different images of the man.

In discussing his life as a Western Union messenger boy, Carnegie wrote:

> One great excitement of this life was the extra charge of ten cents which we were permitted to collect for messages delivered beyond a certain limit. These "dime messages," as might be expected, were anxiously watched, and quarrels arose among us as to the right of delivery. In some cases it was alleged boys had now and then taken a dime message out of turn. This was the only cause of serious trouble among us. By way of settlement I proposed that we should "pool" these messages and divide the cash equally at the end of each week. I was appointed treasurer. Peace and good-humor reigned ever afterwards.

Carnegie's unfriendly biographer, J. K. Winkler, translated this into:

> The youngsters got an extra dime for delivering messages beyond a certain limit. Andy was greedy for these assignments. Bickerings and quarrels broke out. Finally the extra money was pooled and divided equally at the end of the week.

Every statement in this paragraph can be verified in Carnegie's own account. But Winkler neglected to point out that Carnegie's greed was shared by all the other boys, and that the money "was pooled" at Carnegie's suggestion, a fact that would have undermined the impression he was creating of Carnegie's greed and unpopularity.

At another point in his autobiography, Carnegie stated:

1. The Nature of Biography

> My life as a telegraph messenger was in every respect a happy one, and it was while in this position that I laid the foundation of my closest friendships. The senior messenger boy being promoted, a new boy was needed, and he came in the person of David McCargo. . . . "Davy" and I became firm friends at once. . . . A short time after "Davy's" appointment a third boy was required, and this time I was asked if I could find a suitable one. This I had no difficulty in doing in my chum, Robert Pitcairn. . . . Hon. H. W. Oliver, head of the great manufacturing firm of Oliver Brothers, and W. C. Morland, City Solicitor, subsequently joined the corps. . . .

Winkler mentioned McCargo, Pitcairn, Oliver, and Morland, but merely said they also worked with Carnegie in the telegraph office, ignoring the friendship angle completely, but Burton J. Hendrick, a friendly biographer, used selection in the opposite direction:

> It was characteristic of Andrew that, after finally establishing himself in this new world, he should seek to find a similar opportunity for his friends. In a brief period a considerable part of Rebecca Street crossed the river and took up its headquarters in the Pittsburgh telegraph office. . . . As soon as an opening offered, Andrew came forward to name a candidate, and in this way Robert Pitcairn, David McCargo and Henry W. Oliver presently joined the staff.

The fact that Carnegie did not know McCargo until *after* the new boy joined the staff is here obscured, and the single instance in which the future steel tycoon was actually responsible for the hiring of a friend is made to look like a common practice. Thus (for these are but two illustrations of hundreds of subtle alterations in these books) Winkler was able to present a picture of Carnegie as a greedy, unpopular personality and Hendrick could portray him as friendly and generous—both drawing upon the same "facts."

Biographers also influence the pictures they present by the ways they interpret evidence. In extreme cases they have been known to give facts a meaning exactly opposite to their obvious one in order to create a particular impression. Winkler, for instance, in his effort to prove that Carnegie was an avaricious man, had to get around the well-known fact that the steel tycoon was a prominent philanthropist who had devoted the last twenty years of his life to giving away his money. To do this he pointed out that Carnegie had no sons. But for this, "would Carnegie have held to his dictum: 'I would as soon bequeath my son a curse as the almighty dollar'?" Winkler asked.

> Could he have resisted the temptation to place *his* son among the world's super-rich and super-powerful? One doubts.
> For Andrew Carnegie came of a tribe clannish and jealous of its privileges, eager for glory, and with both eyes peeled for the main chance.

Winkler dismissed the fact that Carnegie did have a *daughter* as beside the point!

Most biographers, of course, are not so foolish as to resort to this kind of distortion. If they draw conclusions opposite to the superficial meaning of the facts they usually have some common-sense reason. Thus Lloyd Lewis, in his fine biography of General Sherman, cannot be taken seriously to task for writing of his hero's promotion to Major General: "The promotion . . . comforted Sherman far more than he pretended when he wrote to [his wife] Ellen, 'I know not why it gave me far less emotion than my old commission as 1st Lieutenant of Artillery.'" But whenever

1. The Nature of Biography

a biographer begins a sentence with "Despite the fact that," or "Strange to relate in view of his opinion that," or "Paradoxically," the reader can be reasonably sure that he is about to indulge in a bit of reverse interpretation.

However, interpretation is usually more logical, though not necessarily more accurate. Examine for a moment the interpretation given to a simple biographical detail in a man's life, in this case Abraham Lincoln's hesitancy in joining the Republican party in 1855 and 1856. The facts are clear: the party existed; Lincoln was attracted to its principles; yet he held back until shortly before the Presidential election of 1856. Why? Biographers have supplied answers which reflect their over-all predilections.

One way to "interpret" this incident is to ignore it as Ward Hill Lamon did in his *Recollections of Abraham Lincoln*. This is a form of selection rather than interpretation, however. Another is to deny it. Thus Emil Ludwig, who subtitled the section of his life of Lincoln that deals with this period, "Fighter," and who therefore could not see Lincoln holding back from anything, writes: "In his own State of Illinois, Lincoln was naturally in the fore in the foundation of the new party. Indeed, there was some feeling that it was in large measure his creation. . . ." But most biographers use the incident to interpret Lincoln's character. According to Nathaniel W. Stephenson: "It was inevitable that he should go along with the anti-slavery coalition which adopted the name of the Republican party. But his natural deliberation kept him from being one of its founders." In Albert J. Beveridge's account, "Lincoln had been gradually tending toward the new party; yet his obstinate mind yielded slowly," while the unfriendly Edgar Lee Masters, in *Lincoln: The Man*, explained: "He did not know what to do; and there was no fire in him to burn up and light the way."

Some authors, aware of the power of interpretation, have consciously sought to avoid it, but they have never succeeded completely. In the preface of her life of George Washington, Shelby Little stated: "I have tried to set down with complete detachment the record of Washington's life, based on his words and actions and on the words and actions of his contemporaries." Yet before she has written two dozen pages she had ventured into interpretation and judgment. In dealing with Washington's reasons for accepting General Braddock's offer of a position on his staff in the ill-fated campaign against Fort Duquesne, she dutifully quoted Washington's own statement that he was volunteering only to serve his country and "merit . . . the good will" of his friends, "having no prospect of attaining a commission, being well assured it is not in Gen'l. Braddock's power to give such an one as I would accept of." But then she added:

> This was the situation—or was it? Washington's heart was set on a King's commission, and if General Braddock could not confer it, he had influence in London. It was worth trying.

On another occasion, Mrs. Little even resorted to mind-reading. She was discussing Washington's reaction to the wave of speculation in government securities which accompanied Hamilton's funding of the national and state debts in 1790.

> Such thoughts as he gave to the public indignation over "speculation" were probably impatient ones. Was there anything wrong in shrewd men buying what other men considered worthless? Had he not bought dozens of the

1. The Nature of Biography

1754 land claims? . . . But, he was careful to express no opinion.

Mrs. Little may well have been correct in these interpretations, but what had happened to her "complete detachment," her exclusive dependence upon contemporary "words and actions"? And, of course, these interpretations color the portrait of Washington she presented.

Instead of steering clear of interpretations, instead of stifling his imagination, instead of attempting the impossible task of refusing to select the important from the trivial in the interest of an unattainable objectivity, the biographer must interpret, imagine, and select constantly if he is to approach the reality he seeks. But he must remember that it is reality that is his object, not a mirage. He is, as the critic Desmond MacCarthy once said, "an artist who is on oath."

Scrutinize these excerpts from two widely read biographies. The first, from Lytton Strachey's sketch of Florence Nightingale, seems completely straightforward and factual:

> Why, as a child in the nursery, when her sister had shown a healthy pleasure in tearing her dolls to pieces, had *she* shown an almost morbid pleasure in sewing them up again? Why was she driven now to minister to the poor in their cottages, to watch by sick-beds, to put her dog's wounded paw into elaborate splints as if it was a human being?

The second, from Benjamin P. Thomas's *Abraham Lincoln*, seems much less solidly grounded upon fact:

> The lonely man in the White House had time for meditation while he waited for news night after night. With his strong sense of fatalism, he felt a Power beyond himself shaping the nation's destiny, and in an hour of anxiety he solemnly penned his thoughts.

Strachey's obvious purpose in the first passage was to show that in childhood Florence Nightingale exhibited almost as an obsession the passion for nursing that was to become her chief interest in life. But his statements, "based on" Sir Edward Cook's *Life of Florence Nightingale*, are distortions and outright perversions of the facts as Cook reported them. The dog, for example, was not hers, its leg was not "put into elaborate splints," and Florence merely assisted the local parson in the first-aid that was actually administered. The source that Strachey "translated" into the sister's "tearing her dolls to pieces," actually reads "[Florence] used to nurse and bandage the dolls which her elder sister damaged," a remark that clearly indicates no more than ordinary childish wear and tear. Further, the whole passage ignores Cook's explicit warning that most stories about Florence's early interest in nursing are unauthenticated, probably representing no more than an *ex post facto* exaggeration of traits common to most little girls. "Florence Nightingale is not the only little girl who was fond of nursing sick dolls or mending them when broken," Cook wrote. "Other children have tended wounded animals." Strachey interpreted the evidence; he used his imagination; but he violated his "oath" as a biographer.

Thomas's description of Lincoln, however, while more imaginative, is truthful. Fortunately, he has described the reasoning behind his reconstruction of Lincoln's thoughts and feelings:

> Sometime during the late summer of 1862, when Lee and his army were thrusting into Maryland, Lincoln wrote a memorandum. . . . "The will of God prevails. In great contests each party claims to act in accordance with the will of God. Both *may* be, and one *must* be wrong. God

1. The Nature of Biography

cannot be *for*, and *against*, the same thing at the same time." Then he goes on, wondering why God, who, by his mere quiet power over the minds of men, could stop the war at any time, allows it to continue; trying to find out what God's purpose is. Those are all the facts we have. But here is where the imagination comes in.

Lincoln must have been alone. He couldn't have thought out and penned such a memorandum except in solitude. But he was an extremely busy man. If he was alone, he must have written it late at night. Why was he up late and not working? He must have been waiting for news. What was his mood? Solemn, obviously, from the nature of the memorandum. Anxious, inevitably, with the enemy on Northern soil and a great battle impending.

As a result of this reasoning, Thomas wrote the above-quoted lines. "These sentences are largely imaginative," he admitted, "yet I am convinced that they portray the situation accurately, and that something would have been lost in the telling without the use of imagination."

The novelist can use imagination the way Strachey used it, for the truths he seeks to describe are universal and non-specific. The biographer's imagination must be *controlled*, for his truth is individual and specific. Marchette Chute, who has managed to write biographies of men like Chaucer and Shakespeare (whose personal lives can only be reconstructed imaginatively) without violating the canons of her profession, has put it this way: "There is no fun in a thing unless you play the game according to the rules. . . . The basic restriction upon any biographer is that he must be trying to tell the truth."

But the dangers involved in the overfree use of imagination and the reckless misuse of selection and interpretation are scarcely more serious than those resulting from the attempt to suppress these devices completely. Lytton Strachey must be forgiven many of his failings, if only for the lively attack which he aimed at all dull and uninspired biographical compilations in his *Eminent Victorians*:

> Those two fat volumes, with which it is our custom to commemorate the dead—who does not know them, with their ill-digested masses of material, their slipshod style, their tone of tedious panegyric, their lamentable lack of selection, of detachment, of design? They are as familiar as the *cortège* of the undertaker, and wear the same air of slow, funereal barbarism. One is tempted to suppose, of some of them, that they were composed by that functionary, as the final item of his job.

In his assault upon conventional biography Strachey in one sense went too far. He was complaining of the inordinate length and artlessness of so many Victorian biographies. His own works were brief and compact—and malicious. Yet he conveniently forgot works like John Morley's life of Voltaire, Lord Bryce's biographical sketches, James Parton's *Famous Americans of Recent Times*, and many other examples of nineteenth- and early twentieth-century biography that were brief, lively, and far more honest than his own.

But in another sense, Strachey did not go far enough. He failed to stress the weakness of so many biographies which, though unbiased in judgment and well expressed in form, showed a lack of understanding of the dual nature of biography. Since the publication of *Eminent Victorians* in 1918 the bulky "commemorative" biography which Strachey scorned has generally disappeared, victim of the increasing cost of bookmaking and (it may be hoped) an improvement in public taste. But many present-day works, particularly those which represent the greatest investments of time and scholarly effort, those whose authors may be best

1. The Nature of Biography

trained professionally for the task at hand, have failed to deal with the problem of personality in any coherent, organized way. Too often the writer, an academic person trained in history, say, or literature, has been interested only in describing minutely the significance of X's role in the fight over the Tariff of Abominations, or in advancing some new interpretation of the poetry of Y. The result is poor biography, and perhaps it is not even good history or good criticism.

In 1750 Dr. Johnson complained that "biography has often been allotted to writers who seem very little acquainted with the nature of their task." This continues to be true. On the one hand there have been the glib and careless popularizers, those whom Addison called the "Grub-street biographers, who watch for the death of a great man, like so many undertakers, on purpose to make a penny of him." On the other hand there have been the plodding collectors of facts, to whom the need for artistry or even technique has never occurred. As Edmund Gosse once complained: "The popular idea seems to be that no one is too great a fool, or too complete an amateur, or too thoroughly ignorant of the modes of composition, to undertake the 'life' of an eminent person." Occasionally (but only occasionally) a biographer has appeared who has appreciated the nature of his task. When this happens, first-rate biography may be the result.

IF BIOGRAPHY is to be compounded of career and character, what is the recipe, what the balance? According to Gosse, "there should be some relation between the size of [a subject's] portrait and the effect which he produced in public life." But there must be room for different tastes and purposes. A satisfactory study may be very short, in which case career is probably subordinated to personality, or it may just as logically run to several volumes with greater stress laid upon the historical setting and a detailed record of the subject's activities. The danger is that the former will be long on unsupported generalizations, and that the latter will lose its subject in a maze of detail. This is not to disparage the longer works, which, from John Morley's *Gladstone* and Albert Bigelow Paine's *Mark Twain* to such modern behemoths as Freeman's four volumes on *R. E. Lee* and the still uncompleted works of Arthur S. Link on Wilson, Frank Freidel on Franklin D. Roosevelt, and Dumas Malone on Jefferson, have served a useful purpose. It does often seem, however, that all of these books and others of the type are closer akin to history than to biography. In his mammoth *George Washington*, Freeman devoted one hundred and ten pages to a description of the Virginia society in which Washington grew up, scarcely mentioning his subject's name in the process. He even covered a full page with a description of the state of the world during the months Washington spent in his mother's womb—a passage which included a select list of important figures recently deceased and soon to be born, and the ages and contemporary status of George II, Sir Robert Walpole, Montesquieu, Handel, Bach, Frederick of Prussia, Kant, William Pitt, and half a dozen others.

In truth, for a literary form with a long history, biography has produced fewer recognized masterpieces than any other type of writing, and many of these gems have been special cases, lucky accidents rather than the result of the application of sound principles of biographical writing. Nearly all our outstanding biographies, from Einhard's *Charlemagne*, to Vasari's *Lives of the Painters*, to Boswell's *Life of Johnson*, and down to such recent classics as Ernest Jones's *Life of Sigmund Freud*, have been written by men who have known their subjects personally.

Most of the authorities on biography have believed that intimate acquaintance with the subject is a prerequisite of great biography. Dr. Johnson certainly thought so, and Boswell's experience in writing *his* life seems to bear his judgment out. So did Voltaire, who wrote: "'tis a monstrous piece of charlatanry to pretend to paint a personage with whom you have never lived." Waldo H. Dunn, in his important history of English biography, came to the same conclusion. The German scholar Georg Misch wrote that "great works of biographical art . . . are always made possible only by a living relationship between the biographer and his subject." More recently, Harold Nicolson pointed out the advantage of personal acquaintance in providing "a system of triangulation enabling the author to fix the position of his hero with greater accuracy than would ever be possible were he writing about people whom he had never personally known."

But there have been dissenting opinions. The merit of such lives lies chiefly in the pictures they present of their subjects' personalities, which not only look "real," but, because of the special circumstances, may be presumed to be so. Contemporaries are not likely to excel in descriptions and evaluations of their subjects' careers, or in estimations of their subjects' place in history. Since both career and character are vital in biography, most biographies by contemporaries have serious defects, however interesting they may be. Even Boswell's *Johnson*, certainly the most universally admired biography in any language, suffers from grave faults when judged as a biography. Boswell has been justly praised for his brilliant use of anecdote and conversation, for his subtle synthesis of materials, and for his masterly presentation of character. But his book is all out of proportion, with its heavy emphasis on the last years of Johnson's life, and it is dependent for that period chiefly on the observations of one man, the author. Where Boswell was forced to make use of sources other than his own keen eye and acute ear for dialogue, his book is hardly more than pedestrian in quality. It may be the world's best biography, but it is not a model biography.

Indeed, the great virtue of all the classic biographies written by authors who were intimates of their heroes has really been autobiographical rather than biographical. And despite superficial similarities, the two forms are intrinsically quite separate. Autobiography results from remembrance, biography from reconstruction.[1] Boswell's *Johnson* is, essentially, one man's recollections of another. (Or at least its lasting interest depends upon the personal relationship that existed between the two men and Boswell's ability to describe that relationship vividly and honestly.) It is not that books like the *Life of Johnson* are unimportant. Of course they are far superior to the general run of biography. But to discuss them in a consideration of the nature of biography is not very profitable. They have been unique personal successes.

Admittedly there is no reason why Boswell, for instance, could not have written a biography of someone he had not

[1] In his thoughtful study of English autobiography, Wayne Shumaker wrote: "Whatever the similarity of their purposes biography and autobiography are, materially speaking, often nearly as widely separated as history and the novel. The one draws facts from reading, observations, and interviews; the other raises memories into consciousness."

1. The Nature of Biography

known. He was a close student of the form. If he had, it might have been a great book—but it would have been quite unlike his *Johnson*. Johnson's own biography of the unfortunate friend of his youth, Richard Savage, is a much sharper portrait than most of the later *Lives of the Poets* to which it was eventually appended. So is Carlyle's brilliant sketch of his friend John Sterling superior (as portraiture) to his mammoth lives of Cromwell and Frederick the Great. But few would argue that Johnson's estimate of Savage as a poet, or even Carlyle's judgment of Sterling's *career*, are comparable either to similar judgments in these authors' other biographical works, or to the critical evaluations of Savage and Sterling made by later students.

In short, those who stress the importance of personal knowledge are thinking in terms of character rather than of career. If, by its nature, biography must encompass both, the life written by a contemporary is not likely to be perfectly balanced. Further, if great biography must await the chance congruence of a worthy subject and a talented observer, it has only a limited future, and many important individuals can never hope to be chronicled adequately after they have passed on.

Perhaps the nature of biography places perfection beyond attainment. To describe the *man* one really ought to know him intimately; to evaluate his *work* one needs perspective, and access to records seldom available to contemporaries. But fortunately for the practicing biographer, who deals chiefly with figures out of the past, it is at least possible to overcome the absence of personal acquaintance, whereas perspective (by definition) can come only with time. The problem of re-creating a personality one has never known is great, but should not be insurmountable.

The serious biographer, baffled by the imponderables of personality, may be tempted to limit his activities to describing and explaining his subject's career, which is concrete and definable. But he should resist this temptation. He may never be able to know his man as Boswell knew Johnson. But he must try to do so. The end is understanding; the means are sympathy, scholarship, and sensitivity.

In sum, biography is the reconstruction of a human life. It attempts to describe and evaluate one individual's career, and also to reproduce the image of his living personality, analyzing its impact upon his actions and the world in which he lived. All biographies must be historical and scientific in that they aim at truth and depend upon verifiable evidence. At the same time they must be imaginative and artistic, because insight and felicity of expression are essential if the full three-dimensional truth is to be transferred to the flat surface of a printed page. The biographer's responsibility is large. He assays the role of a god, for in his hands the dead can be brought to life and granted a measure of immortality. He should, at least, then, seek to emulate the more reliable divinities in his zeal for truth, his tolerance of human frailty, and his love for mankind.

DEVELOPMENT

❖❖❖❖❖❖❖❖❖❖

TO TRY *to tell the story of the development of biography over the centuries in the course of one hundred-odd pages may seem presumptuous or even futile. The span of time and the number of works that must be encompassed by a historian of the form are each so large that only a lifetime of effort and a volume of major proportions could do them justice. What follows, however, does not pretend to be a comprehensive history of biography. It is, instead, a discussion of the biography of the past from the point of view of the present. It seeks to mark out only the broad trends of development and of these to emphasize only the ones that seem to have led most directly to modern English and American biography. The focus, as broad as the civilized world at the start, grows gradually narrower as the argument approaches the present. The question I have attempted to answer is not: "What has been the story of biography since man first recorded the history of an individual life?" but "What are the sources from which our modern biography has drawn inspiration and precept?"*

CHAPTER II

Biography in the Ancient World

THE roots of biography lie buried in man's search for immortality. Five thousand years ago Egyptian kings left in their tombs records of their fame along with the symbols of their wealth in order to insure their safe passage to eternity. These first crude accounts were not biographies by the standards of modern times, for they made no pretense at describing either the careers or the characters of their subjects. But their purposes were biographical—they sought to preserve, on earth and in heaven, the reputations of individual men.

Though they were autobiographical in form, their almost total lack of individuality makes it clear that they were actually biographies prepared as part of burial ceremonies. The "biography" of the magnate Inni, dating from the era of the New Kingdom (B.C. 1580–1350), represents the type in its most complete form. Inni was a functionary under four pharaohs. His tomb contained an account, carved on stone, of his services, and its walls were decorated with pictures showing him superintending a harvest, visiting his estate, receiving gifts from the king, and performing other functions. From these remains, one learns little of Inni, but a great deal about life in the New Kingdom.

While all the early biographical fragments portrayed types rather than men, they nonetheless displayed a flamboyant egotism. "Self-glorification has never since appeared with such naïveté," Georg Misch remarked in his comprehensive survey of ancient autobiography. "Some of the documents confront us with immoderate, even brutally vigorous, self-glorification, to a degree unique in history." By depicting themselves only at the high points of their careers, by idealizing their achievements, the Egyptians produced images as flat and distorted as their pictographs. Of the judge it is said that he "excelled the tongue of the balance in accuracy," of the slave-owner that he was kindly and tolerant. "I went forth from the door of my house with benevolent heart," one potentate of the twelfth dynasty declared. "I stood there with benevolent hand." How gullible they must have thought the deity they sought to supplicate!

In Assyria and Babylonia the development of biography followed a more secular path than in Egypt. By B.C. 1400 it had become customary there to record the deeds of kings in the form of chronicles. As in Egypt, these records were phrased in the first person, as though the king was telling his own story, but it is almost certain that they were not actually autobiographical. Etched on clay tablets, or chiseled on stone slabs, these accounts are full of blood and battle and the vain vaporizings of absolute potentates.

II. Biography in the Ancient World

Pride, hatred, and brutality run through them endlessly, but behind the bombast looms the primitive terror of the unknown that characterizes the human animal scarcely removed from the stone ax and the cave. "I am the king, I am the lord, I am the exalted, the great, the strong; I am famous, I am prince, I am the noble, the powerful in war; I am a lion, I am a hero of youthful strength; Assurnasirpal, the mighty king." Shelley caught the spirit of these ancient records in "Ozymandias"—"Look on my works, ye Mighty, and despair!"

But with the passage of time, these ancient biographies grew more sophisticated. The egotism remained, but virtues other than courage and strength assumed more importance, and development as well as mature power was occasionally described. By the time of Darius the Great, after the Persian conquest of the Middle East, the records had begun to deal with the constructive as well as the destructive side of leadership, and to show some sign of the ruler's concern for the ruled. The imposing monument that Darius carved beside the road that ran from Babylon to the East to commemorate one of his triumphs was full of the conventional self-glorification. "I am Darius, the great king, king of kings, king in Persia, king of the lands." And the bulk of the record consisted of a routine description of his heroic accomplishments. But there were glimmerings of a more mature view. "These lands gave me service and tribute. . . . I cherished him who was friendly to me, punished him who was hostile to me. Ahuramazda granted me dominion, gave me help."

One might expect Greek civilization to have produced a great corpus of outstanding biographies. After all, it was the Greeks who supposedly liberated the individual from the mass and gave him a real awareness of himself and his limitless potentialities. The rationality, subtlety, and curiosity of the Greeks would seem to have provided an ideal breeding ground for biography; so would their secular spirit and their interest in history. But the Greek lives that have come down through the ages are few, fragmentary, and disappointing.

Of course, Greek biography went well beyond the naïve vainglory of Egyptian and Babylonian lives. But the Greeks simply were not interested in writing biography. For one thing, although they believed in the worth of the individual man and in the importance of developing his talents fully, they were also preoccupied with the idea of man's helplessness before the mysterious force of Fate, as a reading of any of their great tragic poets makes clear. Some Greek writers also depreciated man's ability to rise above his environment. Hippocrates, for example, explained the physical and mental differences between Asiatics and Europeans in terms of varying climatic conditions. "The human body and character," he wrote, "vary in accordance with the nature of the country." People who lived in well-watered, mountainous regions where the extremes of temperature were wide—people, that is, like the Greeks—tended, according to Hippocrates, to be physically powerful and courageous to the point of ferocity and brutality. Those who inhabited temperate lands where the seasonal variations were small usually suffered from a "deficiency of spirit and courage." Herodotus was expressing a similar view when he praised the Persian King Cyrus for discouraging those of his subjects who wished to migrate to the rich lands of a conquered foe. "Soft countries," Cyrus said, "invariably breed soft men." Such a philosophy, discounting the im-

II. *Biography in the Ancient World* [35

portance of individuals, naturally discouraged the writing of biography.

In addition, the Greeks were not particularly concerned with the perpetuation of the self beyond death. Until relatively late in the development of their civilization, they did not produce formal prose memorials of individual heroes. The Athenians memorialized soldiers who fell in battle, but they did so collectively—the band was praised, not the single patriot. It was part of their view of virtue that, as Aristotle said, the "magnanimous" man was sufficient unto himself; he neither talked about himself nor expected others to speak in his behalf.

Consider Pericles' eulogy of the Athenians killed in the Peloponnesian War, as recorded by Thucydides. The orator begins by disparaging the very idea of using mere words to commemorate worthy actions. "Worth which has displayed itself in deeds would be sufficiently rewarded by honors also shown by deeds." And when he nonetheless conforms to custom and delivers his speech, he speaks chiefly of the virtues of Athenian democracy and of the value of courage, not of the individual merits of the fallen.

Further, Hellenic civilization valued "ideal" men. Just as (at least until the time of Praxiteles) Greek sculpture strove to fabricate perfect types rather than individuals, so Greek biography was concerned with the question of how well individuals conformed to a preconceived pattern of ideal behavior. Similarly, the biographers were aiming at the perfect form of *biography*. They tested their subjects against a rigid standard of values and they did so in a standardized manner. They were more eager to produce a perfectly organized and polished essay than to achieve a truthful portrait; indeed, they might deliberately sacrifice accuracy to make their prose conform to the "ideal." For example, Isocrates, who developed the *encomium* [1] with his speech in praise of Evagoras, King of Salamis, ignored the fact that Evagoras was assassinated and implied that he died a happy death, simply because he believed that the "form" required it. Encomiasts also frankly adopted the role of advocate. They were out to make a plausible case, not necessarily to tell the whole truth. *Encomia* were sometimes written about purely legendary characters. Polycrates even wrote one on mice. Inaccuracies aside, a great emphasis on form meant that the biographies were incomplete. In his *encomium* on Agesilaus, Xenophon considered his subject's character under the headings of piety, justice, self-control, courage, wisdom, urbanity, and patriotism; he ignored other aspects of the man because they were not required by the form with which he dealt.

Finally, to the Greeks, the ideal man was the mature man. They were aware that character developed over time, but felt that the development itself was unimportant. Like the Egyptians, who pictured their heroes at the peaks of their careers, ignoring their failures and the dull routine of life, the Greeks studied man only in maturity, discarding as trivial the steps which led to his "final" form.

The earliest Greek biographical fragments to have survived are the memoirs of the poet Ion of Chios, dating from the fifth century before Christ. These were casual sketches of such famous men of that day as Pericles, Sophocles, and Aeschylus. Ion portrayed his subjects wholly from the outside, catching their impact on society rather than their personal points of view, but adding descriptive details, such as

[1] The encomium was originally a verse form used to celebrate the achievements of victorious athletes.

personal appearance, that were new to biography at the time. Early in the next century Xenophon attached biographical appendices to his epic account of the Persian Wars in the *Anabasis*. He also wrote a defense of his friend Socrates (the *Memorabilia*) and the already mentioned *encomium* on Agesilaus. But even the most elaborate of these works, the *Memorabilia*, was far from being a complete biography. It was not written as a single work, being rather a collection of separate pieces dealing with Socrates which were brought together and named by later scholars. The first section was produced as a reply to the accusations that had led to Socrates' condemnation and to slurs against the master's character made after his death by his enemies. In another part, written about B.C. 385, Xenophon assumed the offensive with a series of Socratic dialogues. "In order to support my opinion that he benefited his companions, alike by actions that revealed his own character and by his conversation, I will set down what I recollect of these," Xenophon wrote. The third part, a loosely connected collection of dialogues and aphorisms, and the fourth, dealing with Socrates' educational views, were also separately written. Taken all in all, the *Memorabilia* summarized Socrates' philosophy, and contained many vivid personal anecdotes (of dubious authenticity, however). But it lacked a connecting narrative, and there were vast gaps in the story. "I have described him as he was," Xenophon boasted at the end of the last section, but he did not actually make good this boast.

Yet, however disjointed and incomplete, the *Memorabilia* was the most elaborate biographical work produced up to that time. The intellectual ferment begun by Socrates and carried on by Plato and Aristotle was developing a climate favorable to biographical writing. The controversy that raged for generations over the execution of Socrates produced a great deal of literature about the man and stimulated interest in his emphasis on close, rational self-examination. Plato's effective use of concrete illustrations to "prove" generalizations (as when he justified his argument that Athens had never possessed a "good" statesman by describing the careers of Pericles and other prominent leaders) also played a part. By the middle of the fourth century, although interest in form, types, and argument for its own sake had not disappeared, writers were beginning to feel that an individual was worthy of study in his own right. Even the *encomium,* although excessively formal, abounded in graphic detail. It introduced anecdotes of the subject's childhood in order to demonstrate the seeds of his future greatness, and it established firmly the idea that a great man's deeds should be preserved in words. Significantly, Isocrates was the first Greek to write a real autobiography (the *Antidosis*), designed, he said, to "serve as a monument . . . more noble than statues of bronze."

Aristotle provided another important stimulus to biography. From Plato's postulate that the only true reality was the ideal, he conceived the theory that the ideal could be observed and understood perfectly only in action, that is, while performing its proper function. A man's life could be described, Aristotle said, not by listing his "characteristics" but by placing "the man's acts . . . on record so that his character and nature were revealed by them." This idea led Aristotle's protégé, Theophrastus, to write his famous *Characters,* which, while still designed to illustrate "types," did so by piling up examples of specific behavior. Consider, for example, this delightful picture of vanity:

II. Biography in the Ancient World   [39

> When ambition is the ruling passion of a vulgar mind, it shows itself in the eager pursuit of frivolous distinctions. The vain and vulgar man strives always to gain a place at table next to the master of the feast. . . . He takes vast pains to be provided with a black servant, who always attends him in public. If he has a considerable sum of money to pay, he provides himself with new coin for the purpose. . . . When his favorite dog dies, he deposits the remains in a tomb, and erects a monument over the grave. . . .

Theophrastus was not describing a particular person, but he was developing a technique that others were to adopt for biographical purposes. Instead of forcing a man into a preconceived mold, he proved that a man's actions could be used to generalize about his personality. "I have long been an attentive observer of Human Nature," he wrote in his introduction to the *Characters*. "I am now in the ninety-ninth year of my age;[2] and during the whole course of my life I have conversed familiarly with men of all classes. . . . With these qualifications I have thought myself fitted for the task of describing those habitual peculiarities by which the manners of every one are distinguished."

Theophrastus became, after Aristotle's death, the leader of the so-called Peripatetic school, which Aristotle had founded. Angered by Theophrastus' success, another Peripatetic named Aristoxenus of Tarentum turned to biography for revenge, and produced what were probably the first "debunking" lives ever written. Little of Aristoxenus' work has been preserved, but references to it in the works of later writers make it obvious that his role in the development of biography was important. He attacked not only

[2] Note, however, that the traditional Greek disregard for accuracy led Theophrastus, who died at eighty-five, to exaggerate the length of his experience in order to add force to his argument!

Aristotle, but also Socrates and Plato. According to Aristoxenus, Socrates was sensual, ignorant, selfish, temperamental, and a bigamist. Aristoxenus had been influenced early in his career by a follower of Pythagoras named Xenophilus; in his life of Plato he claimed that the *Republic* had been plagiarized from Pythagoras. He also wrote lives of Pythagoras and some of his disciples, these in a friendly vein. The quality of his biographical work was probably poor (certainly it was completely subjective), but its significance is clear. Aristoxenus was the first biographer to write unified treatises on particular individuals designed to defend or attack a particular point of view by exemplifying it in the person of one man.

A whole school of Peripatetic biographers developed from Aristoxenus. Little of their work remains, but its basic nature can be reconstructed from fragments and commentaries. These writers thought of themselves primarily as biographers. They were professional compilers and critics, and placed great emphasis on telling their stories in readable form. They sought to present their subjects from as many points of vantage as possible. Peripatetic biographies, in addition to dealing with the mature man, described his origins, family background, and education. Besides discussing his career, they dealt with his appearance, mannerisms, and disposition. They began with birth and ended with death.

It is true that most of the Peripatetics were poor critics. They indulged in the traditional Greek disregard for accuracy, and, either out of naïveté or out of an understandable desire to tell a good story, they did not hesitate to make use of legends and other unreliable sources. Sometimes they deliberately falsified facts, and they reveled in sensationalism. One of the later Peripatetics, Hermippus of Smyrna, who wrote a huge work on famous writers and philosophers, made a specialty of graphic death scenes, which he evidently composed entirely out of his imagination when the truth was not known, prosaic, or difficult to come by. The Peripatetic method was also discursive and anecdotal. But if their works were second rate, these writers were important in the development of biography. Hermippus, for example, influenced Plutarch. They made biography a literary genre, and a popular one. They advanced the methods and polished the style of biographical writing, even though they did so carelessly and with little regard for truth.

The most extensive example of Peripatetic biography that has survived is a life of Euripides by a Greek named Satyrus. This work shows that Peripatetic biography had not entirely escaped from the Greek emphasis on form and patterned arrangement. The beginning and the end are chronological, but the body of the life is broken down under broad captions dealing with Euripides' career as a dramatist, his personality, and his philosophy. The emphasis is on the mature man considered topically. The work has unity and organization, but little consciousness of development except in the first section dealing with the early years.

The line of Peripatetic biographers had died out by the third century before Christ. Greek writers in succeeding generations, chiefly scholars working in the great libraries of Alexandria, reacted against the slipshod inaccuracies of the Peripatetics, but in doing so they also lost the Peripatetic concern for literary artistry. Antigonus of Carystus, writing his popular *Lives of the Philosophers* about B.C. 240, evidently combined reliability with a good style, but most of the Alexandrian biographers were merely pedantic. They devoted themselves to correcting the factual errors of Peripatetic biographers like Satyrus, and to writing routine introductions to the works of the great Greek authors. Where the Peripatetics had been artistic but inaccurate, the Alexandrians were exact but dull and disorganized.

The Roman conquest of the Mediterranean world meant, of course, the spread of Greek culture westward, but the Romans had biographical traditions of their own that also influenced the writing of lives. The early Roman nobility had a vast respect for ancestors. The typical upper-class home contained portrait masks of the owner's forebears and inscriptions describing the offices and honors each had held. The traditional Roman funeral oration, the *laudatio funebris,* delivered by a close relative or friend of the deceased was also well established long before Greek literature was known in Italy.

When a member of an important family died, the body was borne in a great procession to the Forum. Actors impersonated the famous ancestors of the deceased. In the Forum the body was placed on a pyre, but before the torch was applied, the orator mounted the rostra. The "ancestors" sat on ivory seats facing the corpse, but the speaker addressed himself to the populace, gathered around the pyre. Typically his speech was full of ancestor-worship, and was of course completely uncritical, but it also dealt in detail with the official career of the subject, and sometimes contained a narrative account of important events in his life. It was common for prominent families to preserve written copies of these speeches, which they used both to recall past glories and as source material when later funerals required a repeat performance. Since these orations were usually prepared by amateurs, and prejudiced amateurs at that, they were seldom accurate. Cicero said of them: "By these laudatory speeches our history has become quite distorted; for much is set down in them that never occurred—false triumphs, too large a number of consulships, false relationships. . . . [It is] as if I, for example, should say that I was descended from Manius Tullius the patrician, who was Consul . . . ten years after the expulsion of the kings."

Roman pride in family and love of fame, so clearly reflected in the funeral orations, also led to the writing of "authorized" lives of powerful magnates by slaves or retainers. The life of the dictator Sulla was fabricated by one of his freedmen, and Tiro prepared a life of Cicero. Such works were common throughout the late Republic, and became formalized under the Empire. While purely Roman in origin, they were of course influenced by Greek biography. Cornelius Nepos, whom Gibbon praised highly, wrote a life of the wealthy art patron, Pomponius Atticus, in the first century before Christ, which dealt with Atticus' character in a topical fashion quite similar to the *encomia* of Isocrates and Xenophon. Indeed, by the time of Nepos the distinction between Greek and Roman biography was rapidly disappearing.

The supreme figure of ancient biography was Plutarch, who was born about the middle of the first century of the Christian era in Boeotia. Plutarch represented the blending of Greek and Roman culture at the apex of its development, and his *Lives of the Noble Grecians and Romans* was in many ways a summary of that culture. He wrote his biographies in pairs, always matching a Greek with a Roman. Thus he compared great generals like Alexander and Caesar, and great orators like Demosthenes and Cicero. His impartiality is attested by the fact that it is still doubtful whether he was trying to convince the Greeks that there had been Romans who were their equals, or to convince the Romans that they were no better than the Greeks. The organization of Plutarch's biographies was not unusual. Most of them dealt first with the ancestry, birth, and early life of the subject, then outlined his character, and then considered his career, which was used to illustrate in concrete terms the operation of his personality. Like Theophrastus and the Peripatetics, Plutarch used the specific to prove the general, and placed great stress on personal anecdotes. He made little contribution to the form or technique of biography, although he excelled all his predecessors in his masterful execution of traditional methods. But he was the first great exponent of a new point of view.

First of all, he escaped almost completely from the argumentative element of Greek biography and the panegyrical element of Greek *encomium* and Roman *laudatio* alike. It was not that he was coldly objective. "It was for the sake of others that I first commenced writing biographies," he admitted in a famous passage in his life of Timoleon. "But I find myself proceeding and attaching myself to it for my own; the virtues of these great men serving me as a sort of looking-glass, in which I may see how to adjust and adorn my own life." Neither was he strictly impartial. He was a hero-worshipper who looked upon the great Greeks and Romans as a race apart from the general run of mankind, and a moralist who sought to model his own life on those of his heroes and to teach others to do likewise. But his ultimate goal was always *understanding,* and he realized that it could be achieved only by sympathy, insight, and hard work.

II. Biography in the Ancient World

Plutarch explained his point of view clearly in writing of the Roman General, Lucullus. Lucullus had, before Plutarch's time, been instrumental in saving Plutarch's native city, Chaeronea, from being charged by the authorities with harboring an outlaw who had murdered a Roman officer. In gratitude the Chaeroneans had erected a statue of Lucullus in the market place. In writing his biography, Plutarch wished to defend himself against the charge that personal feeling would make him overly friendly to Lucullus. He frankly admitted that he was prejudiced in favor of the General, but, he added, he would not consider "swerving from the truth." Lucullus himself, Plutarch went on:

> . . . would not thank us, if in recompense for a service which consisted in speaking the truth, we should abuse his memory with a false and counterfeit narration. For as we would wish that a painter who is to draw a beautiful face, in which there is yet some imperfection, should neither wholly leave out, nor yet too pointedly express what is defective, because this would deform it, and that spoil the resemblance; so since it is hard, or indeed impossible, to show the life of a man wholly free from blemish, in all that is excellent we must follow truth exactly, and give it fully; any lapses or faults that occur . . . we may regard rather as the shortcomings of some particular virtue, than as the natural effects of vice. . . .

Similarly, in his life of Alcibiades, Plutarch, while leaving no doubt that he abhorred and condemned his subject, also described his charm, brilliance, and military skill, and explained his weaknesses in terms of these very virtues, which brought success to him too easily. He offered a wonderful anecdote pointing up the complex character of Alcibiades, which is worth repeating, for it illustrates Plutarch's approach perfectly:

Alcibiades had a dog which cost him seventy minas, and was a very large one, and very handsome. His tail, which was his principal ornament, he caused to be cut off, and his acquaintances exclaiming at him for it, and telling him that all Athens was sorry for the dog, and cried out upon him for this action, he laughed, and said, "Just what I wanted has happened then. I wished the Athenians to talk about this, that they might not say something worse of me."

Plutarch also excelled other classical biographers in the profundity of his scholarship. One authority counted two hundred and fifty Greek authors among the writers quoted by him, some eighty of whom are known today only through Plutarch's references. Plutarch was not always accurate; modern biographers of many of his subjects have found dozens of errors in his work. Indeed, he lacked the modern scholar's concern for tracing information back to its ultimate source. Sometimes he made use of secondary accounts even when primary sources were readily available to him, and he did not always try to distinguish between fact and hearsay, or reality and legend. But he usually made it clear what his sources were, and he readily admitted his doubts when evidence was missing or contradictory.

Plutarch always emphasized character over career. He was weak when he tried to explain the political significance of the events in his narratives. Though his knowledge of the past was encyclopedic, he was interested in people rather than in history. While from the modern point of view this approach makes his lives incomplete, it would be wrong to criticize him for it. He was conscious of what he was doing. "As portrait-painters are more exact in the lines and features of the face, in which the character is seen, so I must be

II. Biography in the Ancient World

allowed to give my more particular attention to the marks and indications of the souls of men," he explained.

His method was to describe his characters in action. No other biographer, not even Boswell, has excelled him in the masterly handling of anecdotal material. His stories are more than merely clever or interesting; like the incident of Alcibiades' dog, they never lack a point and always illuminate the personality. In his life of Alexander, he placed great stress on what he called Alexander's "passion for pre-eminence." Time after time, in a dozen different circumstances, he illustrated this characteristic with telling anecdotes. He recounted, for instance, the story of how Alexander, campaigning in Asia, learned that his teacher, Aristotle, had published some philosophical treatises. "Alexander to Aristotle, greeting," the hero wrote at once. "You have not done well to publish your books of oral doctrine, for what is there now that we excel others in, if those things which we have been particularly instructed in be laid open to all?" Later in his narrative, Plutarch described an incident between Alexander and one of his lieutenants, Parmenio. It was during the Persian campaign, after Alexander had defeated the army of Darius and captured most of the Persian ruler's family. Darius sent intermediaries offering a vast ransom and a section of his kingdom if Alexander would free the captives and make peace. "These propositions," Plutarch wrote, "[Alexander] communicated to his friends, and when Parmenio told him that, for his part, if he were Alexander, he should readily embrace them, 'So would I,' said Alexander, 'if I were Parmenio.'" Whether the prize was knowledge, wealth, or power, Plutarch made clear that Alexander must possess it wholly.

Finally, Plutarch was startlingly "modern" in his techniques for catching and holding the interest of his readers. A contemporary writer of profiles, Lincoln Barnett, has claimed that there is nothing in that type of sketch that Plutarch did not anticipate. He made brilliant use of the clever introduction, or "lead." Sometimes he began with a broad generalization, setting the theme of his interpretation:

> It is no great wonder if in long process of time, while fortune takes her course hither and thither, numerous coincidences should spontaneously occur. (Sertorius)

On other occasions he began with a provocative anecdote:

> Caesar once, seeing some wealthy strangers at Rome, carrying up and down with them in their arms and bosoms young puppy-dogs and monkeys, embracing and making much of them, took occasion not unnaturally to ask whether the women in their country were not used to bear children; by that prince-like reprimand gravely reflecting upon persons who spend and lavish upon brute beasts that affection and kindness which nature has implanted in us to be bestowed on those of our own kind. (Pericles)

Or with a tantalizing suggestion:

> What Titus Quintius Flamininus . . . was in personal appearance, those who are curious may see by the brazen statue of him, which stands in Rome. (Flamininus)

Or with a clever quotation:

> Cato Major, hearing some commend one that was rash and inconsiderately daring in battle, said, "There is a difference between a man's prizing valor at a great rate, and valuing life at little"; a very just remark. (Pelopidas)

Or with some personal reference, as in the already quoted passage from his Timoleon.

II. Biography in the Ancient World

Plutarch was one of the greatest biographers of all time, and one of the most influential. His influence, however, was not really felt until the Renaissance. In the centuries immediately following his death, his work had little impact. As with his contemporary, Tacitus, whose life of Agricola was the first biography in which the discussion of the hero's personality was effectively fused with the chronological account of his career, his reputation became established only long after his passing. The "important" biographer during the period of Rome's decline was Gaius Suetonius Tranquillus.

Suetonius was Plutarch's contemporary, and his *Lives of the Caesars* was packed with anecdotes. There, however, the similarity ends. Where Plutarch was an artist, Suetonius was a compiler. He recounted the lives of the first twelve Caesars, recording their deeds, personal and professional, with little comment or inspiration. He followed the traditional pattern of the Alexandrian scholars, dividing his chronological narrative into two parts separated by what Professor Duane Reed Stuart has called "a huge parenthesis" which described the character of each subject.

Suetonius crammed a great deal of information into his works. As secretary to the Emperor Hadrian, he had access to the official records of the early Empire. But he had all of the vices and few of the virtues of the closet scholar. He grubbed for facts, seldom stopping to consider what the facts meant. On the surface at least, his biographies were impartial; good qualities were listed along with bad. But through all the wealth of anecdote and graphic detail, no consistent portrait ever emerged.

Nothing points up Plutarch's genius so well as a comparison of his sketch of Julius Caesar with Suetonius'. Both writers drew upon essentially the same sources, and there is relatively little difference between them so far as facts are concerned. But how different their treatment of these facts! Suetonius, the pedant, often parades his sources before the reader in dull and repetitious quotations of the authorities. Plutarch usually indicates the specific origin of his information only where the evidence is doubtful or contradictory. Both men record tales of miraculous and supernatural events in Caesar's life, yet where Suetonius credulously parrots every legend he has heard, Plutarch more often than not prefaces his account with "It is said" or with such a comment as: "This Livy positively states for truth."

Frequently, in dealing with the same event, Plutarch shows vastly greater insight into the situation than Suetonius. Both men, in discussing Caesar's divorce of Pompeia, recount the story of her suspected liaison with Publius Clodius. Disguised in female attire, Clodius had stolen into Caesar's house during the celebration of the rites of the goddess of fertility, from which all men were barred. He had been apprehended, but when he was brought to trial Caesar refused to testify against him on the ground that there was no evidence of wrongdoing. When questioned as to why, then, he had divorced Pompeia, Caesar replied with the famous remark that *Caesar's* wife must be above even suspicion. Suetonius treats this incident as an example of Caesar's mercy and self-restraint, but Plutarch comments shrewdly: "Some say that Caesar spoke this as his real thought; others, that he did it to gratify the people, who were very earnest to save Clodius. Clodius, at any rate, escaped."

But Plutarch is most obviously superior in his handling

II. Biography in the Ancient World

of dramatic incidents. Here is what Suetonius makes of Caesar's decision to cross the Rubicon:

> Overtaking his cohorts at the river Rubicon . . . he paused for a while, and realizing what a step he was taking, he turned to those about him and said: "Even yet we may turn back; but once cross yon little bridge, and the whole issue is with the sword." As he stood in doubt, this sign was given him. On a sudden there appeared hard by a being of wondrous stature and beauty, who sat and played upon a reed. And when . . . many of the soldiers left their posts, and among them some of the trumpeters, the apparition snatched a trumpet from one of them, rushed to the river, and sounding the warnote with one mighty blast, strode to the opposite bank. Then Caesar cried: "Take we the course which the signs of the Gods and the false dealings of our foes point out. The die is cast."

Plutarch's story is both more credible and more exciting:

> When he came to the river Rubicon . . . his thoughts began to work, now [that] he was just entering upon the danger, and he wavered much in his mind, when he considered the greatness of the enterprise into which he was throwing himself. He checked his course, and ordered a halt, while he revolved with himself [sic], and often changed his opinion one way and the other, without speaking a word. This was when his purposes fluctuated most; presently he also discussed the matter with his friends . . . computing how many calamities his passing that river would bring upon mankind, and what a relation of it would be transmitted to posterity. At last, in a sort of passion, casting aside calculation, and abandoning himself to what might come, and using the proverb frequently in their mouths who enter upon dangerous and bold attempts, "The die is cast," with these words he took the river.

Caesar's murder is so inherently dramatic that any account of it would be exciting, but Plutarch provides extra touches and insights that Suetonius misses. When Casca strikes the first blow, Suetonius carefully describes exactly where the blade enters Caesar's body. Plutarch, although less definite, remarks that the wound was not serious, "coming from one who at the beginning of such a bold action was probably very much disturbed." Then he puts the reader inside Casca's heart in that brief moment when the conspirator stands alone committed before the outraged symbol of the majesty of Rome. As Caesar, grasping the offending dagger by the hilt, shouts: "Vile Casca, what does this mean?" his terrified assailant cries out: "Brother, help!"

The murderers close in, and the moment passes. Then, after describing Caesar's fall before the massed attack of the conspirators, Plutarch adds without further comment: "The conspirators themselves were many of them wounded by each other, whilst they all leveled their blows at the same person." Without denying Caesar's faults or the patriotism of his attackers, Plutarch thus points up the discreditable side of the action—a score of armed men against a lone and unsuspecting victim.

Yet if he was no Plutarch, Suetonius was always immensely popular, and the reason is not hard to come by. He told all, and the "all" of the early Roman emperors was both fascinating and titillating. Suetonius' *Lives* were saturated with tales of lust, brutality, and perversion. Consider this passage from his *Tiberius*:

> In his retreat at Capri there was a room devised by him dedicated to the most arcane lusts. Here he had assembled from all quarters girls and perverts, whom he called *Spintriae,* who invented monstrous feats of lubricity, and defiled one another before him, interlaced in series of threes, in order to inflame his feeble appetite.

II. Biography in the Ancient World   [53

Sex and scandal made the *Lives of the Caesars* popular, and the formula was adopted repeatedly in later ages with the same success.

But if Suetonius had little that was original to offer aside from sensationalism, he was at least hard-working and honest. Those Roman recorders of emperors' lives who took him as a model (men like Marius Maximus and Junius Cordus, whose works are now lost, and the various authors of the still-extant *Scriptores Historiae Augustae*) had neither of these virtues. The *Historiae Augustae* were composed about the year 300 by half a dozen authors. These men adopted whole Seutonius' scheme of organization, but possessed neither his interest nor his access to the sources. Where they lacked facts they filled their pages with trivial anecdotes. Suetonius had occasionally included letters and documents from the imperial archives in his *Lives*; his successors, unable to tap such sources, simply manufactured documents to fill up space and to disguise their ignorance. They often strung their materials together without art or reason, and with equal frequency they permitted their narratives to degenerate into servile flattery and uncritical panegyric. Biography flourished under the later emperors as never before, but along with the rest of classical culture it lost all originality and vitality as a once great civilization crumbled into the depths of the Dark Ages.

CHAPTER III

The Development of Biography

THE main impetus to biography in medieval times came from the Church. Christianity had its heroes, the martyrs and saints, and their lives became the source of a great deal of biographical writing. In the beginning a young and struggling institution naturally revered and commemorated its departed leaders, and drew inspiration and courage from the memory of their accomplishments. By the third century most local churches had developed menologies (calendars of saints' days), which were gradually elaborated into accounts of the lives, or at least of the sufferings and miracles, associated with each saint.

As the Church rose in power, extending its influence all over Europe, the habit of writing saints' lives became firmly established. Before the ninth century the lives were written in Greek or Latin and were read chiefly by members of the clergy, who passed them on to the faithful in the form of

III. *The Development of Biography*

sermons. Probably they were often used as primers to teach the classical languages to novices in the monasteries. The great monastic centers like Fulda in Germany and St. Gall in Italy developed large collections of lives of their leaders, and these books played a vital unifying role in the development and preservation of monastic traditions, especially among those orders which established widely scattered branches in the course of their missionary work.

Beginning about the ninth century, saints' lives were sometimes translated into the vernacular. Since they were among the earliest of vernacular writings, they greatly affected the development of all the modern European languages. The most popular vernacular lives were cast in verse. In this form their influence extended far beyond the churches. Minstrels sang them all over Europe, and their popularity is attested by the fact that some two hundred verse lives still exist in French alone, dating from the ninth to the fifteenth centuries. But whoever the saint, whatever the language, the pattern was essentially the same. Not the whole life but a few key incidents, not the man but the way he reflected the universal faith—these are the common threads of all hagiography. As Waldo H. Dunn put it: "The Church and its work were the important matters; man was only an instrument." Furthermore, since the authors of all these works were motivated primarily by a desire to inculcate piety in their readers, they made little effort to find out the truth. Catering chiefly to the simple tastes of an uneducated audience for whom their words provided entertainment as well as spiritual edification, the writers of saints' lives developed a formula that experience soon proved effective. Around the barest outline of facts about each holy man they clustered miraculous tales of sin punished, illness cured, pagan converted, and faith restored, always through the sanctity of the protagonist of the story.

The earliest biographies of any saint were usually the most accurate, and it is easy to understand why this was so. Since record-keeping was expensive and therefore seldom pursued systematically, reliable facts were often difficult for later writers to unearth. The "truth," passed verbally from generation to generation by a credulous and generally unschooled people, graded insensibly but steadily into legend. For medieval man there was a perpetual confusion between history and legend. "History," as C. H. Talbot said, "was what one told you." The soon-familiar pattern was, therefore, easily accepted by the faithful. "There is a casual sequence in the order of events, which gives the most unveracious lives considerable verisimilitude," Gordon H. Gerould wrote in his study of saints' legends. "Certain miracles follow certain others in traditional and almost necessary order."

It would be unfair to judge any saint's life by the skeptical standards of modern scholarship. Naturally the hagiographers accepted the possibility of miracles, and told as truth stories no present-day biographer would dare to record. But scarcely any of them even bothered to make sure that the miracles they described had been attributed to their particular subjects, or to search out available facts, few as these might be. That the level of saintly biography in the Middle Ages was very low is proved by the existence of a handful of superior examples of the form.

The passage of time constantly accelerated the trend from reality to legend. For the good of the cause, first the probable and then the possible were added to the known.

III. *The Development of Biography* [57

Miracles attributed to one saint gradually were transferred to others. One copyist's error became the next man's source. Entirely fictitious "saints" found their way into the collections. A practice that had begun as a means of commemorating the spiritual achievements of individual heroes was thus converted into a naïve educational tool for the teaching of piety to the illiterate multitudes.

Although devoted to the veneration of more worthy heroes, most saints' lives were not entirely unlike the lives of the Roman emperors collected in the *Scriptores Historiae Augustae*. Like the emperors' lives, they were inaccurate, dull, formula-ridden, and overly flattering. It would be fruitless to discuss them in any great detail, but a typical one (the life of Willibrord by the monk Alcuin) may be worth summarizing. The tale begins with a description of Willibrord's father, a man, according to Alcuin, who was so holy that he married only so that he could beget a future saint. An account of Willibrord's birth, heralded by a number of miracles, is followed by a brief and very vague summary of his education. At the age of thirty-three—we are not told the year—Willibrord goes to Germany as a missionary. The bulk of the life deals with this missionary work—in the main by describing the miracles performed by the subject. These tend either to be extremely crude (four separate incidents tell of antagonists who either die or become violently ill after conflicts with Willibrord) or to be based on well-known stories from the Gospels, such as the miracle of the loaves and the fishes, some form of which is attributed to Willibrord on three occasions. A physical description and a summary of Willibrord's character (energetic, forbearing, holy, charitable) come next, and then there is an account of his death and the miracles associated with that event. A final miracle relating to Willibrord's father closes the life.

On the rare occasions when some insight into personality and some respect for accuracy crept into a saint's life, the author usually possessed special sources of information or had known his subject well. In one of the earliest English biographies, the *Life of Saint Columba*, written about 700 by an Irish abbot named Adamnan, a glimmer of Columba's crusading spirit and simple godliness shines through the mass of miracles and moralizing. Adamnan was the head of the monastery of Iona, which Columba had founded, and must have had access to important records, for his book is full of circumstantial details. A generation later, the ecclesiastical historian Bede wrote a life of St. Cuthbert in which miracles, while still the dominant subject, were treated with some respect for the laws of probability. Bede's patent belief in miracles did not prevent him from discarding the less plausible legends that clustered about his hero. Bede was England's first great historian and the leading scholar of his age; anything from his pen was sure to be superior to the general run.

A few other exceptional lives of saints stand out from the unimaginative and uncritical mass. The monk Jonas, a missionary in northern Italy, wrote a superior account of St. Columban, founder of the monastery of Bobbio in the Apennines. For this work, written early in the eighth century, Jonas gathered material from people who had known Columban, and while much of his text dealt with miracles, the tales were seldom fantastic. He described Columban selecting a site for a well, directing a fisherman whose net had been empty to a new location where it was soon over-

III. The Development of Biography

flowing, performing minor surgery on an injured finger, and so on. The reader closes this brief life with the feeling that Jonas was neither drudge nor credulous gossip, but a sensitive and sophisticated scholar. Another unusual saint's life was Willibald's life of St. Boniface, the famous missionary to Germany. Willibald's book, based on an earlier account now lost, was both accurate and circumstantial. Naturally he idealized his portrait, but he held close to chronology, explained the saint's ideas and teaching methods, and left his readers with a reasonably clear impression of the man's nature. Eadmer of Canterbury wrote a life of St. Anselm early in the twelfth century which Harold Nicolson has called "the first 'pure' biography" produced by an Englishman. Eadmer appreciated the dual nature of the biographer's task. "Not only will I record the events of his life," the monk explained, "but also whatever it contains which seems of importance regarding his private conversation, his own distinctive traits, or the display of his miracles." Eadmer used letters and his own recollections of Anselm's conversations to illustrate the man's personality, and he showed an almost Plutarchian talent for delineating character. Similarly, the fourteenth-century *Little Flowers of St. Francis of Assisi*, written in Italian by an unknown author, while weak on details and packed with the conventional miracles, offered a warm and convincing picture of "the most lovable of medieval saints."

But the religious mainspring of most medieval biography restricted the development of objective, individual-centered lives. In Russia, where the Church was more subordinated to the State than in western Europe and where, after the Tartar invasion, patriotism could find expression only through the Church, the saints' lives emphasized military feats rather than religious miracles. As a result, the best Russian saints' lives, while still didactic in purpose and stereotyped in form, were more graphic and realistic. For example, the eleventh- and twelfth-century narratives that clustered around the names of Boris and Gleb, the martyred sons of Vladimir, were full of concrete details. The heroes were carefully described, their adventures and trials vividly portrayed, and the spiritual element was confined to accounts of miracles performed at the tombs of the saints. The thirteenth-century *Life of Alexander Nevsky* portrayed its subject as an ideal prince and warrior, and emphasized his strength, wisdom, and courage. The miracles it described were of a military nature, and they were disassociated from Alexander's person—during a great battle, for example, an archangel appears and slays many enemy soldiers.

But there was little comparable development in western Europe, where most secular biography derived from annalistic chronicles rather than from saints' lives, and consequently tended to lack unity and to bury the individual beneath a mass of unrelated facts. However, the relatively rare biographies of individual lay figures, while marked by faults (chiefly the desire to glorify their subjects), were somewhat more likely to present truthful accounts and rounded portraits than were the lives of the saints.

One of the finest medieval lives was the sketch of Charlemagne written in the ninth century by Einhard, a monk who lived at the Emperor's court. Einhard wrote in imitation of Suetonius, in that after a short preface, he divided his work into accounts of Charlemagne's "exploits at home and abroad" and his "private life and character." But he far exceeded his model in both discrimination and reliability.

III. *The Development of Biography* [61

"It would be foolish of me to say anything about his birth and infancy, or even about his boyhood," Einhard wrote. "For I can find nothing about these matters in writing, nor does anyone survive who claims to have personal knowledge of them." Such self-control was indeed rare in Einhard's day, and of course it adds to the confidence that we can place in his work. Einhard's description of Charlemagne's career was not particularly outstanding,[1] but his sketch of the Emperor's personality showed a real insight into the man. His picture of the Emperor struggling late in life to learn to write, carrying a writing tablet on his campaigns and practicing his letters in spare moments snatched between battles, demonstrated an awareness of the importance of Plutarch's "matter of less moment"; his wry admission that Charlemagne "made little advance in this strange task" indicated his essential regard for the truth. Nor, despite the generally flattering tone of his book, was Einhard above subtle criticism of his hero. He praised the Emperor for his devotion to his family, but pointed out that his overprotective attitude toward his daughters was responsible for their scandalous behavior, and he indicated that Charlemagne's lavish hospitality, however admirable, burdened the state with heavy expenses.

Another exceptional medieval biography was Jean de Joinville's *Life of St. Louis*, probably written early in the fourteenth century. Since Louis was both a king and a saint, this work is somewhat difficult to classify. It was definitely not a conventional "saint's life" despite its emphasis on Louis's saintlike qualities. Like Einhard, Joinville excelled

[1] It should be noted that this is a good example of the generalization offered in Chapter I that biographies by contemporaries tend to be weak on career and strong on character.

in describing personality. He pictured Louis as the ideal Christian man and stressed his piety, humility, charity, and simplicity, but he did not hesitate to point out an occasional fault. "I had then been five years with the king," Joinville wrote after introducing an example of Louis's neglect of his family, "and never before had he spoken to me, nor, so far as I ever heard, to any one else, of the queen and his children; and, so it appears to me, it was not seemly to be thus a stranger to one's wife and children." Joinville also knew how to use the anecdote effectively, and quoted copiously from his own conversations with Louis, striving to show the man in action. Thus, despite a certain discursiveness and the disorganized state of his manuscript, he created a vivid picture of the King.

But biographies like Einhard's and Joinville's were the exception in the Middle Ages. Even writers who escaped from the miraculous by dealing with non-religious figures made very little effort to unearth facts and report them objectively. In the earliest English chronicle of a king, Bishop Asser's life of Alfred, written about 893, the author traced the King's ancestry back to Adam, and later royal lives were scarcely more accurate. These works did, however, play one important role in the development of biography. They shifted the emphasis from moralizing to narrative. They were usually devoid of interpretation and perspective—the typical king's life was, as Burckhardt wrote in his *Civilization of the Renaissance in Italy*, no more than a "contemporary narrative, written without any sense of what is individual in the subject"—but they did tell their stories in proper chronological order.

Beginning in the fourteenth century, however, the rise of humanism provided a great impetus to the writing of biog-

III. *The Development of Biography* [63

raphy. First in Italy and then throughout the Continent the humanists began to re-examine Greek and Roman culture and to show great interest in what Henry Osborn Taylor called "the profound and inclusive consideration of human life."

The situation in Italy was particularly suited to the development of biography. People of all classes recognized and prided themselves on their Roman heritage; and, at the same time, the age was marked by "the thirst for glory and the worship of ability." Achievement rather than high birth became man's first claim to distinction; to leave one's mark as the subject of a biography or a portrait was the highest Italian ambition.[2]

Of course there was no sudden or drastic change-over from the medieval point of view. Petrarch, probably the first humanist, wrote a collection of lives of famous Romans that, while representing the start of the revival, was still primarily devoted to illustrating virtues and vices common to all men. His book was designed, like the saints' lives, to teach a lesson rather than to describe character. Petrarch's contemporary, Giovanni Boccaccio, wrote a life of Dante that was almost as full of "arbitrary fancies" as the most credulous menology. Boccaccio was sometimes wildly inaccurate and always violently prejudiced. He interrupted the flow of his narrative with long digressions on the weaknesses of the female sex, the ingratitude of the citizens of

[2] Biographical writing was also stimulated by the humanistic *historians'* arbitrary restriction of their work to political events. "The exclusion of literature, learning, and art from their formal historical work was part of the price paid by humanists for the valuable guidance of their classical models," writes Wallace K. Ferguson. "For the history of culture they were forced to utilize other media less well adapted to the purpose. One of the most common was the biography or series of biographies of writers and artists."

Florence, and the nature of poetry. His tone of reverent worship resembled that of the hagiographers, as did also his disregard of chronology. His *Dante*, however, showed unmistakable signs of the new spirit of the Renaissance. It contained many direct references to classical works, and its organization reflected the influence of Suetonius. It also treated Dante's emotional problems and the details of his personal life with a frank interest foreign to the Middle Ages. The book was a clear indication that curiosity was undermining the didactic element in biography, and that individuals were beginning to emerge instead of types. By the end of the fourteenth century a writer like Filippo Villani was producing, in his *Lives of Illustrious Florentines*, brief sketches of artists, scholars, soldiers, and statesmen that were all recognizable as distinct persons. And by the middle of the fifteenth century, along with a great increase in the number of run-of-the-mill lives, some really incisive studies had been written. The influence of Plutarch and Suetonius was strong in these works, but above all they demonstrated an increased concern for the individual personality. The analysis of character became a subject of interest in itself, as, influenced by Theophrastus, the Italians of the early sixteenth century began to produce treatises on such ideal types as the perfect courtier and the perfect householder. Machiavelli's masterpiece, *The Prince* (1514), was the most famous of these works. John Addington Symonds perhaps exaggerated when he said that among Italian Renaissance biographers "the desire for edification and the fire of fancy had yielded to an influence more strictly scientific, and to a curiosity more positive," but the best of their works were far more accurate and lifelike than what had gone before.

III. The Development of Biography

Typical of the better sort of Italian Renaissance biography was Giorgio Vasari's *Lives of Seventy Most Eminent Painters, Sculptors and Architects*, first published in 1550. Vasari's work bore the stamp of classical and medieval origins. He began each sketch with some broad generalization which the story was supposed to illustrate, and included relatively little material designed to illuminate character. He approached the artists with a frank admiration not particularly suited to a sound critical evaluation of their work, often failing to distinguish, as Wallace K. Ferguson has said, "between the *vero* and the *bene trovato*." But his interest in the individual was obvious in every paragraph. The loving detail with which he described both the artists' goings and comings and their masterpieces reflected this interest. And upon occasion he made excellent use of personal anecdotes. Thus his biography of Giotto contained a brief but intensely human account of the painter's humor, including the famous story of the realistic fly he painted on the nose of one of the portraits his master was working on.

The Italian enthusiasm for personality and for classical models spread throughout Europe in the fifteenth century as Italian writers traveled and settled in other countries and as their works were translated. The sixteenth century found the new movement in full flower. The revived interest in Plutarch, for example, led the Frenchman Jacques Amyot to the manuscript collections of Venice and Rome. By 1559 he had produced his brilliant translation of the *Lives*. Amyot caught the spirit of Plutarch perfectly, chiefly because, like Plutarch, he was fascinated by human personality. "*L'histoire*," he wrote in the preface of his translation, "*est à la vérité le trésor de la vie humaine*." Even earlier the *Lives* had been translated into Italian, German, and Spanish, and in 1579 Sir Thomas North translated Amyot's version into English. Suetonius also began to appear in the modern tongues; over forty editions of his *Lives of the Twelve Caesars* were published between 1470 and 1820 in all the important European languages. Even Tacitus' *Agricola* had been rendered into English by the end of the sixteenth century. These new translations stimulated the writing of contemporary works. Amyot's Plutarch created a vogue for collective biography in France, for example, and if most of these collections were either dull digests or slavish imitations, an occasional writer captured something of the new spirit.

Besides reviving the classics, sixteenth-century writers also translated some of the "new" Italian works and wrote biographies of their own in the new style. The Dutch humanist Erasmus wrote brief sketches of Sir Thomas More and John Colet which were full of the fascination with personality and the love of specific detail that characterized the period. Even historians absorbed with great events frequently allowed themselves to be diverted from their narratives into the description of interesting people. Pierre Matthieu's *Histoire des derniers troubles de France* (1596) contained many such digressions, the most notable being his graphic description of Henri de Guise. Throughout the *Histoire*, Matthieu's frequent references to the Duc de Guise were contrived to illustrate his gradually developing ambition. Then, after describing the Duke's assassination in 1588, Matthieu presented an extended portrait in which he compared him to another ambitious man, Julius Caesar. The parallel shows clearly the influence of Plutarch and of Suetonius.

Perhaps the most important of the Continental writers

III. The Development of Biography

who were influenced by the Renaissance interest in personality was Pierre de Bourdeilles, Seigneur de Brantôme. Closely associated with the court of the Valois princes, Brantôme was ideally situated for developing his interest in what he called the *"particularitez"* of the great figures of his age. Although he was something of a court gossip, and absolutely fascinated by scandal, his brief sketches of lords and ladies show a real talent. He had a flair for physical description, rhapsodizing, for instance, over the charms of Anne of Brittany or Marguerite de Valois, and he knew the value of concrete illustration in creating vivid images. "It is not enough to say that people are beautiful, wise, virtuous, valiant, . . . splendid, or perfect," he wrote. "One must specify everything." Brantôme seldom penetrated very deeply into the minds and hearts of his subjects; nevertheless he possessed a rare technical mastery and he typified the growing interest of the men of the Renaissance in the complexities of the human character.

One can also see the spirit of the Renaissance at work in sixteenth-century English biography. The *History of King Richard the thirde* (1515), probably written by Sir Thomas More, showed in its terse style the influence of Tacitus and reflected the new search for the inner man in such paragraphs as this one describing King Richard after the infamous murder of the princes in the Tower:

> . . . after this abhominable deede done, he never hadde quiet in his minde, hee never thought himself sure. When he went abrode, his eyen whirled about, his body privily fenced, his hand ever on his dager. . . . He toke ill rest a nightes, lay long wakying and musing, sore weried with care & watch, rather slumbred then slept, troubled wyth fearful dreames. . . .

Works like William Roper's life of More and George Cavendish's brilliant study of Cardinal Wolsey demonstrated by their very length and detail the growing interest in individual lives, although neither biography was noticeably marked by the classical influences that marked most Renaissance lives.

For nearly twenty years before his death in 1552, John Leland traveled widely in search of old records in his position as "king's antiquary." He collected old coins, church records, and a mass of biographical material on English writers. In the eighteenth century nearly six hundred of his short lives were published. These proved to be scarcely superior to the collections of saints' lives gathered in medieval times; they were carelessly thrown together and almost completely uncritical. But unlike the older collections, they contained accounts of all kinds of writers, not merely of ecclesiastics. And even purely religious collections, such as John Foxe's *Acts and Monuments* of the Protestant martyrs, displayed more graphic detail and personal interest than their medieval prototypes. The increasing number of such collections and the wide audience reached by some of them, like Foxe's martyrology, illustrated the steady development of interest in the individual among the reading public.

However, even the great literary artists among the biographers of this period were not entirely successful in portraying their subjects as whole men. One reason for their failure lay in the fact that there was still no real appreciation of the nature of biography as we understand it. Medieval "biographers" were not really aware that their *lives* were any different from their *histories*. Bede, for example, incorporated his life of St. Cuthbert into his *Ecclesiastical*

III. The Development of Biography

History without altering the material in any significant way. To him, as Donald A. Stauffer pointed out, "biography . . . was only history viewed more closely." Stauffer made a very thorough study of early English biography, and the first example of any clear discrimination between history and biography that he could find did not appear until 1599, when John Hayward distinguished between accounts of "the government of mighty states" and "the lives and actes of famous men" in his *Life and raigne of King Henrie IIII*.

The failure of biography to develop as a special form of literature and history handicapped it seriously. In France, for example, the seventeenth century produced a combination of factors that should have led to great biography. The scope of classical learning was ever widening, writers of all kinds were fascinated by the human personality, and the French language was rapidly becoming a subtle and artistic tool for the expression of ideas. There was a great deal of writing about people, but little *biography* because no one formalized the genre. The great memoir-writers of the age of Louis XIV often painted brilliant pictures of their contemporaries, combining psychological understanding and literary polish. In the 1650's there was a fad for "portraits" —brief characterizations of one's friends and associates— that were often charmingly frank and vivid. But there was no firm line between truth and fiction in them. Apocryphal memoirs were as common as real ones, and were judged by the same standards. Imaginary portraits in such novels as Madame de Scudéry's *Grand Cyrus* were not clearly distinguished from genuine ones such as appeared in the memoirs of Cardinal de Retz or La Rochefoucauld. The practice of publishing these sketches with false names substituted for the real ones (sometimes accompanied by "keys") did not usually add to their accuracy. When La Bruyère, late in the century, translated Theophrastus, he published along with the translation a large collection of *caractères* of his own. However, he not only combined all sorts of general observations on society, religion, and other matters with his sketches, but also admitted that in the *caractères* he had *sometimes* "taken one trait from this man, and another trait from that man." Yet many of his sketches obviously described real people. It is significant that the words "biography," "*biographie*," and "*biografia*" did not exist in England, France, and Spain until well into the seventeenth century. As the modern French medievalist Marc Bloch once wrote: "The advent of a name is always a great event even though the thing named has preceded it; for it signifies the decisive moment of conscious awareness."

This "awareness" of biography as a separate form grew far more rapidly in England than elsewhere, which probably explains why English biography, although continuing to draw upon French and other sources, clearly outstripped that of the rest of Europe in the seventeenth and eighteenth centuries. However, even in England the development was slow. Francis Bacon, writing in 1605, divided histories into three classes, dealing with "a time, or a person, or an action." "The first we call chronicles," he said, "the second lives, and third narrations, or relations." But it was not until the 1660's that the word "biography" appeared, and only with Dryden's introduction to his well-known translation of Plutarch (1683) was a clear definition of the new word offered.

Further, the growing realization that biography could be a special and distinct form of writing did not produce at once—indeed, it still has not produced—any agreement as

III. *The Development of Biography* [71

to its nature and methodology. In his *Worthies of England* (1662), Thomas Fuller illustrated both the new trends in biography (he was one of the first writers to use the word) and the continuing confusion associated with biographical writing. Fuller was an antiquarian in the Leland tradition; he collected a hodgepodge of information on the counties of England, including, along with each county's "worthies," its manufactures, famous buildings, and agricultural products. He compared England to a house, and the shires to the rooms in it. His purpose was "to describe the Furniture of those *rooms.*" Like the medieval writers, he sought to "preserve the memories of the Dead," to "gain some Glory to God," and to "present Examples to the living." But he also recognized that biography should be entertaining in itself. In addition, he excoriated his predecessors for their uncritical acceptance of legends, and he set himself high standards of accuracy. In words that have a modern ring, he criticized the hagiographers of the Middle Ages for their carelessness and dishonesty. But he regarded chronology as a "surly little animal," he was overly concerned with "the rules of charity," which often kept him from telling the whole truth, and he had no feeling at all for the portrayal of character.

Bishop Gilbert Burnet's work typified the best of the new ideas about biography that were developing in the seventeenth century, yet he too could not escape entirely from the confusions of the past. He praised Plutarch's virtues and condemned the general run of contemporary biography. "There is no sort of history worse done," he complained in his *Lives and Actions of James and William, Dukes of Hamilton and Castleherald.* He attacked both the "gross partiality and flattery" of panegyrical lives, and (in a later book) the "spite" of unfriendly biographers. "Certainly Resentment may make the writer corrupt the truth of History, as much as Interest," he said. Burnet was a great believer in scholarship, being influenced by the careful French school of the sixteenth century. "People desire to see Papers, Records, and Letters published at their full length," he wrote. But he remained a moralist despite his regard for truth, always seeking to make his biographies teach a lesson, and he tended to mix too much history with his account of a man's life, or rather, to see history through an individual's eyes, as in his well-known *History of His Own Time,* written in imitation of Jacques De Thou's *Historia sui temporis.* He also believed that personal matters were not a proper concern for biography. He would "draw a Vail over all these . . . and avoid saying anything . . . but what may afford the Reader some profitable instruction." Despite his strictures about honesty and impartiality, he belonged to what Stauffer called "the polite school." In his *Life and Death of Rochester,* clearly his best biography, marked by eminent fairness and a simple, effective style, he repeatedly missed opportunities to bring his subject to life. For example, after explaining in detail Rochester's bitter criticism of the hypocrisy of middle-class morality, he added anticlimactically: "In detestation of these Courses he would often break forth in such hard Expressions concerning himself as would be indecent for another to repeat." Samuel Johnson saw the essential weakness of Burnet's approach when he said to Boswell, in commenting on the vivid death scene in the *Life and Death of Rochester*: "A good *Death*: there is not much *Life.*"

The lack of a definite concept of biography in the seventeenth century is well illustrated in the *Athenae Oxonienses,*

III. The Development of Biography

a collection of lives of distinguished graduates of Oxford. This work was prepared by Anthony Wood. It epitomized the virtues of ruthless honesty and meticulous scholarship, but lacked the warmth and sympathy which good biography must possess. Wood made a thorough search of all the available records: he waded through the Oxford archives, read every scrap he could find written by or about his subjects, dug up old church records, and pored over wills, genealogical tables, and tombstones. But he presented the fruit of his researches without attempting to *understand* the men he wrote about. He was so absorbed in facts and dates and so coldly impersonal in his determination to be accurate and complete that he was a poor biographer. Wood was assisted in his work by John Aubrey, who represented the opposite extreme. Aubrey had a wonderful feeling for character and an insatiable curiosity about the quirks of personality that distinguish every man from his fellows. Where Wood grubbed in dusty records, Aubrey searched his own memory and interviewed friends of his subjects, collecting masses of gossip and countless anecdotes of questionable veracity. Aubrey's disorganized notes and brief sketches were bursting with vivid descriptions and character-revealing details: Milton's peculiar pronunciation of the letter *r*, Ben Jonson's wall eye ("like Clun the player; perhaps he begott Clun"), Thomas Hobbes's temperance ("I have heard him say he did beleeve he had been in excesse 100 times which, considering his great age did not amount to above once a yeare"), Sir Walter Raleigh's "getting up one of the Mayds of Honour against a tree," and so on. But for all his ability to describe personality, Aubrey lacked the diligence to ferret out information that was not readily available, and he could not organize his materials or distinguish between fact and legend. Like his employer, he understood only part of the biographer's task.

The seventeenth-century writer who came closest to encompassing the new trends in a unified biographical technique was Izaak Walton. In his five biographies he combined extensive research, respect for truth, feeling for character, and a good measure of literary artistry. He used his subjects' published works, their letters, wills, and other papers. He collected the impressions of surviving friends and searched his own memory, since in most cases he was dealing with men he had known himself. But Walton was no mere compiler; he knew the value of concrete illustration in portraying personality and the effectiveness of showing a character through his actions rather than through generalized description. Walton was also a self-conscious literary craftsman concerned with the over-all unity of his work, with felicity of expression, and with heightening the sense of reality through such literary devices as suspense. He constantly revised and polished his biographies as each new edition appeared (and there were many, even in his own lifetime).

"I . . . resolved that the world should see the best picture . . . my artlesse Pensil (guided by the hand of Truth) could present to it," he wrote in his *John Donne*. He produced books that portrayed real men, related the men to their work, and preserved the sense of chronology and growth that distinguishes biography from the character sketch and the analytical study alike.

Of course Walton committed many "sins" that would outrage the modern historian. He was careless when quoting, say, from Donne's or Herbert's poetry; he interpolated material into letters; he reported as direct discourse statements for which he had no specific source. He even presumed to describe his subjects' thoughts. Critics have suggested that all his characters were drawn in his own image, and they have accused him of suppressing evidence that might seem to contradict the impression of calm saintliness which permeated all the books he wrote. It is true that Walton had little to say about Donne's driving ambition and fiery spirit or about diplomat Henry Wotton's cynicism. But Walton did not lie about such qualities or consciously distort them. Perhaps he hinted where he should have been direct and blunt. But his limitations were those of his own kindly and placid disposition. They did not derive from bad motives or misconceived purposes. He emphasized those aspects of his heroes' lives which seemed important to him. In short, he was not afraid to interpret as well as to describe. One can quarrel with his interpretations without denying the great contributions he made to the development of biography.

Walton came closer to being a professional biographer than any writer since Plutarch; he foreshadowed the great English biographers of the next century, who, like Samuel Johnson, admired his work at the same time that they rejected his eulogistical attitude. Indeed, he may be thought of as a bridge between the old and the new. He embodied both the medieval characteristics of piety and moralizing and the modern ones of honesty, artfulness, and feeling for character. It is fair to say that when Walton died in 1683, a new age in biography was being born.

CHAPTER IV

Biography Reaches Maturity

Of the eighteenth century, Donald A. Stauffer writes: "The classical and medieval theories of the stable social and religious order in which man was a subordinate part had not yet been completely supplanted by the introspective individualism of the Romantics. For a short period during this transition, man as an individual, and the world in which he lived were both realities. Out of this fortunate moment, reflecting the interplay of old and new conceptions, rose the biographies of the eighteenth century in vigor and variety that have not been surpassed." Stauffer may have overstated his case when he claims that later ages have not improved on the lives of the eighteenth century, but certainly no earlier period equaled that century in the quality and quantity of its biographical writing.

Alexander Pope gave the age its slogan when he wrote in 1733:

IV. Biography Reaches Maturity

> *Know then thyself, presume not God to scan;*
> *The proper study of mankind is man.*

Under the impact of this philosophy, simple curiosity challenged the desire to moralize as a motive for the writing of lives, and every man became a possible subject for a book. Biography reached out to draw upon other literary forms like the drama and the novel at the same time that it influenced these forms itself; the market for all kinds of biographies increased rapidly; and for the first time a considerable body of critical literature on biography appeared. In England particularly, Grub Street scribblers, gifted amateurs, careful scholars, vulgar scandalmongers, pious hero-worshippers, and most of the great literary figures of the century, from Defoe to Samuel Johnson, wrote biographies, read biographies, and discussed the form in endless detail.

The interaction of biography with plays and novels is one of the most fascinating aspects of eighteenth-century literary history. Biographies were written of prominent actors, and brief pamphlet lives of the heroes of historical plays, which Stauffer called "biographical mistletoe growing on the tree of the drama," were also common. Samuel Richardson wrote his *Pamela* in the form of a biography, and Tobias Smollett included a lengthy memoir of a real viscountess in his *Adventures of Peregrine Pickle*. Purely fictional "biographies" of historical personages vied with accounts of imaginary characters written, like *Robinson Crusoe*, in careful imitation of matter-of-fact lives. Many writers hopelessly confused biography and the novel, singing the praises of the former while filling their pages with the most fantastic flights of the imagination. Defoe, for example, began by turning out hack biographies of recently deceased worthies. Finding himself frequently at a loss for accurate information, he invented anecdotes and "characteristic" details, and gradually developed into a full-fledged novelist.

The theater taught biographers the value of dialogue in portraying character and that of vivid scenic and personal details in conjuring up reality in the mind. Shakespeare's marvelous insights led biographers to seek to duplicate his success in their own accounts. The novelists' ability to create "real" people stimulated biographers to scan the records for evidence of small personal characteristics and idiosyncrasies. The fiction-writer's "habit of psychological observation" (like Shakespeare's) was a further challenge.

As in earlier years, the confusion of biography with other literary forms was particularly noticeable in France. François de Fénelon's *Dialogues des Mortes* (1712) indiscriminately mixed accounts of French kings and Greek legendary characters, and the average *mémoire* of the period was so hopeless a blend of history, autobiography, fiction, biography, and scandal that Richard Steele wrote in the *Tatler*: "I do hereby give notice to all booksellers and translators whatsoever, that the word 'Memoir' is French for a novel; and to require of them, that they sell and translate it accordingly."

But in this case confusion was a sign of health and of growth. Biography, drawing sustenance from the most implausible sources, was constantly developing in every direction. The classical influence continued. In England alone there were probably a dozen editions of Theophrastus in the eighteenth century, and the popularity of La Bruyère's *caractères* continued unabated on both sides of the Channel. Plutarch also remained a perennial favorite, and

IV. *Biography Reaches Maturity* [79

modern parallel lives, comparing, for example, Lord Chesterfield and Samuel Johnson, found a ready market. But an astounding variety of new forms sprang up. One man wrote a biography in alternate chapters describing first his hero's actual career and then his life as he should have lived it. Another described the life of a Greek satirist in the form of an interview conducted in heaven. Still others wrote biography wholly in dialogue, in verse, or as a series of letters.

Many more kinds of people were considered suitable subjects for biography. Whereas medieval writers had dealt only with kings and saints, in eighteenth-century England, as Stauffer put it:

> Neither the living nor the dead were safe, and now, not even the humble. No flowers were allowed to blush unseen, no gems to remain in dark, unfathomed caves; and the short but simple annals of the poor appeared monthly, annually, systematically. . . .

A volume entitled *The history of the lives of the most noted highway-men, foot-pads, house-breakers, shop-lifts and cheats* appeared in 1714, and shortly thereafter came a four-volume collection of *The lives of the most eminent persons who died in the years 1711, 1712, 1713, 1714, 1715.* Biographical dictionaries poured from the presses. Collections of lives of clergymen, doctors, naval officers, philosophers, and actors were topped finally by the tremendous eighteenth-century edition of the *Biographia Britannica,* which expired in a sea of type after fifty years of labor without passing the letter *F.* Biographers not only wrote of every conceivable type of person; they also rifled the records of all history in search of subjects. No age or nation was immune. Outstanding examples like Middleton's *Cicero,* Voltaire's *Charles XII,* Mallet's *Francis Bacon,* and

Johnson's *Richard Savage* demonstrate the way hundreds of eighteenth-century biographers ranged over time and space in their work. The vitality that produced masses of trivia and oddities and shelves of inaccurate and sensational lives led other writers to improve their standards of scholarship. There had been earlier careful researchers like Anthony Wood, but in the eighteenth century the scholar really came into his own. This typical scholar placed tremendous emphasis on accuracy and detail; he refused to accept secondary authorities; sometimes he seemed more interested in commenting learnedly on the mistakes of his predecessors than in drawing true-to-life portraits of his subjects. Frequently his strength was his length; literary artistry and imagination fell before his all-consuming interest in minutiae and his tendency to digress into a dozen obscure byways. In the hands of such biographers the footnote flourished, not merely as a means of indicating sources, but also as a vehicle for the discussion of fine points and contradictory evidence. Edward Malone began his life of Dryden (1791) by saying: "John Dryden . . . is supposed, on no satisfactory evidence, to have been born on the 9th of August, 1631," and then launched into an extended explanation of the difficulty of determining "the precise time of his baptism" because of the loss of church records. More than a thousand involved footnotes marred Malone's pages, overpowering the reader with unimportant and often immaterial erudition. In William Harris's *Life of James I*, the footnotes had footnotes of their own, and on one occasion Harris produced a footnote to a footnote to a footnote.

But the best of the scholarly biographers did not become

IV. Biography Reaches Maturity

bogged down in the chaotic masses of facts they collected. Instead, in Voltaire's words to Mme du Châtelet, they "made of this chaos a general and well-arranged picture." They sought out small truths not as ends in themselves but as a means for constructing large generalizations. They tore down the work of the past not for the joy of destroying but to build anew on firm foundations. "The enlightened spirit which now reigns among the principal nations of Europe," said Voltaire, "requires that we should go to the bottom, where in former times a historian barely thought it worth while to skim the surface." This new spirit led Voltaire to doubt even the authority of Tacitus. It also led Voltaire's English contemporary, Conyers Middleton, to base his life of Cicero chiefly on Cicero's own writings, and to question the accuracy of the great Plutarch. The scholars also heightened the growing distrust of biographies designed only to praise dead heroes and to provide lessons for the edification of the living. Sometimes, sad to relate, they carried objectivity to the point at which they refused to make judgments of any kind, and produced works devoid of interpretation and therefore of meaning. More generally, even when they did not entirely abandon the moral purposes so common in earlier days, they managed to subordinate didacticism to truth. They realized that if their subjects were to be set up as models, they must not be made to appear impossibly perfect. The scholars' creed was well summed up by David Mallet in his life of Bacon:

> Whoever undertakes to write the life of any person . . . ought to look upon this law as prescribed to him: He is fairly to record the faults as well as the good qualities, the failings as well as the perfections, of the Dead: with this great view, to warn and improve the Living.

In their search for the whole truth, eighteenth-century biographers labored mightily to understand the inner natures of their subjects. The influence of the novelists and of the French memoir-writers was strong here, but even more powerful was the example set by contemporary autobiographers, who bared their souls with ever-increasing frankness. Of course autobiography was not a new thing, and occasional writers had dealt candidly with themselves. St. Augustine's analysis of his inner conflicts, Jerome Cardan's scientific self-examination, and Cellini's naïve account of his sins were outstanding examples from earlier times. But eighteenth-century writers perfected the autobiographical form and made it immensely popular. Wayne Shumaker, a recent student of English autobiography, suggests that the development of introspective autobiography may have resulted from the increasing ascendancy of inductive over deductive habits of thought—"the view that Truth, instead of being already known in its essentials, could be discovered only by the slow accumulation of particulars." At least in England, the rise of Quakerism and Methodism, with their great emphasis on the individual and his inner feelings, was a further stimulus to the writing of autobiography. John Wesley, for example, called upon his followers to write out accounts of their lives and particularly of the conditions of their conversions, and he published some of these in his *Armenian Magazine*. The introspective nature of these autobiographies, with their careful reconstruction of psychic states, was bound to influence biographers.

In any case, in an age intensely curious about mankind, any man's account of himself, if honestly told, was likely to find an audience. And most serious autobiographers

IV. *Biography Reaches Maturity* [83

sought to be honest. They achieved varying degrees of success in widely differing forms and styles, from the urbane Gibbon's polished and masterfully controlled revelations to Rousseau's self-debasing yet boastful confessions. "In the presence of the heart-searching God," wrote Thomas Scott, whose *Authentic Narrative* appeared in 1779, "I have given without one wilful misrepresentation, addition, or material omission, an history of the great things God hath done for my soul."

The effectiveness of such accounts stimulated biographers to try to get within the very minds of their heroes. Many, of course, simply put imaginary thoughts and words into their subjects' mouths. But the best writers substituted careful and perceptive study for pure imagination, and in the Plutarchian tradition found inner truth by massing many small facts into logical and revealing unities. Works like Boswell's *Johnson*, Condorcet's *Voltaire*, and La Beaumelle's *Madame de Maintenon* are monuments to the success of such methods.

To reach the inner man without losing contact with demonstrable fact, biographers made increasing use of personal documents. The value of an individual's letters was appreciated at last. While an occasional author had quoted from letters as far back as the twelfth century, little reliance was placed upon them until the time of Conyers Middleton's *Cicero*, and only in 1775 with the appearance of William Mason's life of Thomas Gray was the use of letters in biography properly explained and illustrated. The period was also marked by the increased use as source material of diaries, journals, and other personal jottings. Except for travel journals and wills, however, there was little interest in publishing such documents themselves until the nineteenth century. In his studies of English diaries, Sir Arthur Ponsonby located only four published before 1800. Whether derived from personal documents or from interviews, remembrance, or conventional historical sources, the chief key to the inner man was the anecdote. In ancient times, Plutarch had demonstrated the effectiveness of the illuminating incident, and many subsequent biographers had followed his lead, but in the eighteenth century the anecdote flourished as never before. "It is a trite but true observation," Henry Fielding wrote in *Joseph Andrews* (1742), "that examples work more forcibly on the mind than precepts." In part the popularity of anecdotes reflected the increasing tendency to write lives purely to entertain (for almost by definition an anecdote was expected to be enlivening, if not actually humorous). But the anecdote aimed above all at re-creating reality by capturing an incident complete with backdrop, character, and action.

In some hands the anecdote lost all serious purpose and served only as a kind of funny story. In a biography anecdotes are worthless unless they are typical and true. When derived, as they often are, from sketchily recalled conversations, distorted and exaggerated by constant retelling, and told with more regard for eccentricity than for insight, they are most questionable, and their illustrative value is nil. A Boswell, with his keen ear, his dedication, and his journals, might be trusted to use anecdotes judiciously; others collected stories indiscriminately and reproduced them pointlessly. Toward the end of the century, the telling of anecdotes became a literary form in its own right, and the popularity of *-ana* (Walpoliana, Johnsoniana, Addisoniana, Swiftiana) carried the mania to the extreme. Haphaz-

IV. Biography Reaches Maturity

ard assortments of trivia, devoid of organization and often of truthfulness, these collections were indicative of the boundless vitality of rapidly evolving biography. But they were mutations not destined to contribute much to the eventual development of the form. However, when the fad for anecdotes ended, a residue of true value remained. The importance of Plutarch's "matter of less moment" had become a permanent tenet in the biographer's creed. Biographer's also became far more careful (and far more successful) in their physical descriptions of their subjects. Engraved portraits appeared in books, adding visual images to those created by words.

The eighteenth century was also marked by a shifting point of view toward style and organization. Classical lives were carefully patterned, and there certainly was a medieval "type." By comparison, eighteenth-century biographies were formless. But their seeming lack of structure actually reflected the interest of authors in the unique nature of the individual. Writers sought not general rules, but particular techniques suitable for special cases. At their best, they aimed to be interesting, to portray individuals, and to tell the truth. Style and organization were only means to these ends.

Many biographers, failing to keep these aims in balance, produced distorted works. Some, like Defoe, sacrificed everything to entertainment, and ended by writing novels. Others, like the collectors of anecdotes, became submerged in quirks of personality, and lost sight of chronology, unity, and the humdrum truth. Many scholars became obsessed with facts, finding in them a fascination that escaped the average reader. Like Edward Malone, they devoted more space to describing their problems as biographers confronted with the *lacunae* and the contradictions in the evidence than to judging the meaning of the evidence. Felicity of style, artfulness of form—such things they blissfully ignored.

But most eighteenth-century biographers were at least stumbling toward graceful forms of expression. As the obligation to improve the living by the example of the dead declined, and biography developed as a device for whiling away dull hours, biographers necessarily paid more heed to style. The novelists made a great contribution in this direction. When a writer of fiction like the Abbé Prévost turned to biography, he brought with him not only a fine command of words, but also a wish "to reconcile all the advantages of truth with that agreeable illusion which arises from surprise, from suspense, and [from] impatience." His object, the Abbé wrote in his *History of Margaret of Anjou* (1755), was to make his biography "differ little from the most interesting works of imagination."

The first significant literature *about* biography also appeared in the eighteenth century, as writers began to speculate on the form in prefaces, in separate essays, and in reviews of the work of others. Fumbling beginnings in the seventeenth century have already been noted; later generations carried the word forward rapidly. Little general agreement developed from such discussions. While most writers conceded that biography was different from history, many did not distinguish between the two in their own works. An author of the life of a British duke claimed to have "omitted nothing that might give an exact idea of the state of Europe for these fifty years past." Another biographer, lacking data on his hero's early life, decided to "fill up this chasm" with "a view of the age in which he was born." A third, desperately trying to combine the general and the particular, concluded a section of intimate detail by writing: "While the business I have described engaged all the attention of the Parisians, nothing very interesting occurred in the affairs of Europe." Similarly, the growing dissatisfaction with biographies that were primarily moral tracts did not lead to the disappearance of this type. Honest and sophisticated biographers like Samuel Johnson, who rejected panegyric, nonetheless saw biography largely in moral terms. Oliver Goldsmith, editing Plutarch in 1762, wrote that the biography of a good man was the best possible reading for the youth of the nation, and that even the life of a scoundrel had value as a teaching device.

Diversity of opinion was common to most areas of biographical criticism. While publishers responded to the intense inquisitiveness of the period by flooding the market with accounts of scandal, vice, and crime, many commentators insisted upon the importance of restraint and the sacredness of private affairs. Early in the century Addison complained:

> This manner of exposing the private concerns of families, and sacrificing the secrets of the dead to the curiosity of the living, is one of those licentious practices which might well deserve the animadversions of our government.

And in 1788 the same argument was being used by another essayist, Vicesimus Knox, who wrote that biography was "every day descending from its dignity" in order to gratify "impertinent" and "malignant" curiosity. "There are certain foibles and weaknesses," Knox pontificated, "which should be shut up in the coffin." Again, most writers recognized the importance of impartiality and the danger involved in too close identification with one's subject. But some, like Johnson and Roger North, believed that an accurate portrayal could be drawn only by a writer who had known his subject personally, while others sided with Addison in the belief that no life should be written "till envy and friendship are laid to sleep."

Thus it must be said that the great expansion of biographical writing in the eighteenth century failed to produce a unified body of biographical theory. But amid the welter of conflicting points of view, certain trends did stand out. These, at some sacrifice of subtlety and detail, may be studied most simply in the work of three men: Samuel Johnson, Conyers Middleton, and James Boswell.

Dr. Johnson was surely the greatest figure in eighteenth-century biography. Not only did he himself write lives and analyze the problems of writing them, but also his own life was the inspiration for many biographies. His tremendous prestige lent special force to his strongly stated opinions on all literary matters, and since his heart belonged to biography above all other forms of writing, his expressions on that subject were especially influential. He stressed the practical value of biography, which, he said, reached the average reader more directly than history because all people are essentially alike and can therefore identify themselves with any person of whom they read. For this reason he felt that biography need not concern itself exclusively with great men; anyone's story, properly told, would be interesting. "The prince feels the same pain when an invader seizes a province, as the farmer when a thief drives away his cow. Men thus equal in themselves will appear equal in honest and impartial biography." But honesty and impartiality were vital. "The value of every story depends on its being true. . . . If it be false, it is a picture of nothing."

IV. Biography Reaches Maturity

And uncritical praise was the biographer's most serious crime. "If a man is to write *A Panegyrick*," Johnson once told Boswell, "he may keep vices out of sight; but if he professes to write *A Life*, he must represent it really as it was." "If we owe regard to the memory of the dead," he wrote in one of his *Rambler* essays, "there is yet more respect to be paid to knowledge, to virtue, and to truth."

In esteeming biographies of obscure persons Johnson both reflected and advanced the interest of the age in the individual; indeed he epitomized the zeal of the period for all knowledge. "There is nothing so minute or inconsiderable, that I would not rather know it than not," he admitted to Boswell. He also contributed to the trend toward writing biographies of non-political and non-religious figures with his great collection of *Lives of the Poets*, and in that same masterpiece he expanded the scope of biography farther by blending a critical evaluation of the poets' works with his accounts of their characters and activities. Here again his chief loyalty was to the truth as he saw it. Neither friendship nor current popular opinion could keep him from giving his candid opinion of each poet's verse; his opinions might occasionally be dogmatic or difficult to reconcile with his intelligence, but they were always his own, and sincerely held.

Beyond all else, Johnson exemplified the urge to understand. This drive was common to all his productions, but most notable in his *Life of Richard Savage*, first published in 1744. Although Savage, an engaging but irresponsible, dissolute, and thoroughly second-rate poet, had been Johnson's friend, Johnson told Savage's story without disguising or omitting his weaknesses. But he told it with compassion. He did not pass over the poet's "irregular and dissipated manner of life" or his incredible vanity. ("He could not easily leave off when he had once begun to mention himself or his works; nor ever read his verses without stealing his eye from the page, to discover in the faces of his audience how they were affected with any favourite passage.") From bitter experience Johnson knew that Savage made a poor friend, quick to take offense, vindictive, and malicious. But he tried to understand and explain Savage's faults. He described his unfortunate origins, the years of struggle against poverty and obscurity (a struggle that Johnson had also experienced), the tender sense of dignity that substituted futile defiance of fate for humility. "The reigning error of his life," Johnson wrote with his usual insight, "was that he mistook the love for the practice of virtue, and was indeed not so much a good man, as the friend of goodness." And he summed up his subject's tragic life in these words:

> The insolence and resentment of which he is accused were not easily to be avoided by a great mind, irritated by perpetual hardships, and constrained hourly to return the spurns of contempt and repress the insolence of prosperity.... Those are no proper judges of his conduct who have slumbered away their time on the down of plenty; nor will any wise man easily presume to say, "Had I been in Savage's condition, I should have lived or written better than Savage."

Johnson's frankness was much in advance of his age—when his *Lives of the Poets* was published, one reviewer claimed that his subjects might have received as much "brotherly kindness" from the infidel Turk as Johnson afforded them. But even at the time some observers appreciated what he was trying to do, and later generations have converted his postulates into biographical axioms. He did

IV. Biography Reaches Maturity

not escape entirely from old traditions. He was an indefatigable moralizer: biography must be *useful;* however understandable Savage's frailties, they must serve as a warning. But he never pointed a moral by blunting the sharp edge of truth.

If Johnson stands for the eighteenth century urge to understand human nature, Conyers Middleton stands for the development of scholarly methods of investigation. Of course Johnson was also a scholar, but his biographies were written from a broad base of general knowledge, not from intense research into the particular careers he described. Sorting out "the rubbish of antiquity" was to him a "tedious and troublesome" business. He seldom inconvenienced himself to verify a date or track down a fact "in books and pamphlets not always at hand." Middleton, however, was a thorough and at least superficially scientific investigator. In the preface of his *History of the Life of Marcus Tullius Cicero* he described his method of research.

First he read all of Cicero's works, noting down every passage of possible biographical importance. Next he studied other Greek and Roman authors, culling material relating to Cicero and filling up the "interstices of general history" neglected or passed over lightly in his hero's writings. Only after completing his first draft did he turn to secondary sources. He feared to do so earlier "lest they should fix any prejudice insensibly upon me before I had formed a direct judgment of the real state of the facts, as they appeared to me from their original records." In general, he found these secondary sources of little value. Most were either "trifling panegyrics" or "imperfect abstracts of [Cicero's] principal acts." But they served a useful purpose in making him reconsider some of his own judgments. Occasionally, a statement in these books also reminded him of some incident that he had omitted or slighted in his first draft.

Middleton tried to weave Cicero's own writings directly into the text rather than to attach them, "*sewed on . . . like splendid patches*," in the form of appendices. He was fully aware of the difficulty of translating from Latin into English without sacrificing either accuracy of meaning or the eloquence and antique character of the classical authors. "I have endeavoured to take the middle way," he wrote, "and made it my first care always to preserve the sentiment; and my next to adhere to the words, as far as I was able to express them in an easy and natural style." Scholar that he was, Middleton printed the Latin for all his translated passages in footnotes, so that others could judge of his success.

Before beginning his labors, Middleton had been at a loss to see why no earlier writer had undertaken a full-scale life of so interesting and important a figure as Cicero. Later, in a touching and revealing passage, he explained that he now understood the reason: "The tediousness of collecting an infinite number of testimonies scattered through many different volumes; of sorting them into their classes, and ranging them in proper order; the necessity of overlooking many in the first search, and the trouble of retrieving them in a second or third; and the final omission of several through forgetfulness or inadvertency; have helped to abate that wonder."

In short, Middleton seems the model of the perfect scholar. He mastered every possible source. ("My head, indeed, is . . . full of antiquity," he announced with honest pride.) He arranged his materials carefully, cited his sources conscientiously, and wrote clearly and with a dig-

IV. Biography Reaches Maturity

nity and polish worthy of his great subject. He had also the scholar's concern for objectivity. Aware that the inclination to write a life "is generally grounded on prepossession and an affection already contracted for the person whose history we are attempting," and that most biographers tended toward prejudice and partiality, he sought to keep his own opinions out of his pages by letting Cicero tell his own story.

In this last aim, however, he failed. Awareness of the problem did not lead to its solution; his book, despite his good intentions, was completely one-sided in its portrayal of the "shining character" of its hero. "It is not possible to excite an affection for Cicero," he wrote, "without instilling an affection at the same time for every thing that is laudable." Middleton was not dishonest. He admitted frankly his own belief in Cicero's perfection, and he tried to be fair. But just as his careful scholarship points up the chief weakness of Johnson as a biographer, so his inability to see and report the whole truth points up Johnson's strength. For writing a biography is like constructing a mosaic from a mass of many-colored tiles. Johnson would select his tiles carelessly, taking what was at hand rather than rummaging through the pile for the perfect piece. Middleton would painfully segregate the pieces, sorting them by color, size, and shape. Yet Johnson's final picture, however crude or distorted the details, would have a verisimilitude that Middleton's neatly arranged image would lack. There is more to knowledge than hard study, more to clarity of vision than good intentions.

In one sense, James Boswell, whose *Life of Samuel Johnson* (1791) has become *the* classic biography, was not typical of anything. He was unique, and his book has no parallel. What other biographer has dogged his subject's footsteps, ever alert for the chance remark, the new insight? Boswell time and again plied Johnson with complicated and embarrassing questions designed simply to provide material for the *Life*. Deliberately, and through an exercise of guile that Edmund Burke said was without equal "in the whole history of the *Corps Diplomatique*," he arranged a meeting between Johnson and his known enemy, John Wilkes, merely to watch the sparks fly. He began to collect material on Johnson's life on first meeting him in 1763, and he devoted a major part of his time to the task for nearly thirty years.

But Boswell did bring together the main elements of modern biography, elements which had been developing over the years. He was widely read in the field—nearly one hundred biographies are mentioned in his *Johnson*. Johnson taught him to worship truthfulness and to approach his task with sympathy and understanding. The scholars instilled in him a passion for accuracy and completeness. Plutarch and the anecdotal writers showed him the importance of the small fact, and William Mason's life of Thomas Gray taught him how to use letters in his work. To all these elements he added his own particular genius, for if he was neither a great stylist nor an intellect of the first rank, he was nonetheless a genius.

Boswell's method was extremely simple and unimaginative. "I do it chronologically," he explained to a friend in 1788, "giving year by year his publications, if there were any; his letters, his conversations, and everything else that I can collect." "Year by year"—indeed in some sections day by day—he traced Johnson's path. No detail was too tiny to be included, no labor too great to track down a date or validate a conclusion. His own copious journals were his chief sources; to these he added correspondence, the recollections and memoirs of others, Johnson's writings, and facts gleaned from earlier biographies. But he was no mere drudge. Although his pages lacked over-all organization, he was a master at arranging diverse information relating to a particular incident and in telling each story in a clear and fascinating manner.

His accuracy was amazing. "Perhaps no book so rich in opportunities for error has ever come through . . . minute study and criticism with so little damage to its reputation," wrote the great Johnson authority, Sir Walter Raleigh. But it was not the nearsighted accuracy of a Middleton, correct in details but distorted in total effect. No one could have recorded the long conversations of Johnson without varying from his exact words, and comparison of the *Life* with Boswell's journals shows that he frequently amended, elaborated, and even rearranged some of this material when he came to transfer it from the journals to the biography. Boswell aimed for, and reached, a higher truth. His memory (prodigious as it was) might fail in recalling the exact word, but it did not lose the exact sense.

Boswell had his faults. His book should be called *Boswell's Johnson*, not Boswell's *Life of Johnson*, for the author's relationship with the subject assumes a significance out of proportion with the facts of Johnson's life. It also lacks not so much unity as cumulative effect and a comprehensive estimate of its subject and his importance. A reader can pick it up at almost any point, read a few dozen pages, and get almost as clear a view of the bluff, intense, yet kind-hearted Doctor as he would from a careful study of the whole. But Boswell—assiduous, inquisitive, honest—

loved life in all its aspects. While he did not manage his own life very well, he lived it to the full, tasting all its pleasures, delving into the meaning of existence with all his powers, observing everything and everyone he came in contact with. He managed to transmit this zest to the pages of his *Johnson*. As a result, he produced a great work of art, not merely the greatest eighteenth-century biography, but the culmination of centuries of development. Hero-worshipper, moralist, scholar, philosopher, scandalmonger, and story-teller all contributed to his training.

No, James Boswell was not typical. But he was nearly everything that a biographer can be. Since his day biographers have refined and expanded his methods, sharpened and polished his tools. They have not really pushed much beyond him. Biography, after 1791, had reached maturity.

CHAPTER V

Nineteenth-Century Trends

The historian of biography in the century after Boswell's death can record few really significant developments. There were changing fashions, and some refinement of tools and techniques, and perhaps an improvement in the general level of biographical writing, but outstanding works were scarce. No startling methodological developments occurred until early in the twentieth century.

Romanticism, by its fascination with the unknown and the unknowable, its stress on introspection and intuition, its love of freedom and individualism, its vaunting ambitions, and its emotionalism, might have been expected to contribute a new dimension to biography. In fact, though it rose to prominence at a time when biography was flowering as never before, it added little to the form. Throughout the first third of the nineteenth century, while the romantic movement was at its peak, no one approached the level of

Boswell or Johnson. The romantics supplied admirable source material for later biographers. They wrote letters overflowing with self-revelation, ransacked the past for intimate diaries and journals (Pepys's diary was first published in 1825), and often lived the kind of uninhibited lives that have inspired later generations to biographical efforts, but they made little direct contribution to biography. Even Carlyle, despite his worship of the God-inspired hero, his conviction that biography was the only true history, and his eminently sensible criticism of so many of the biographies of his own day, furnished little in his own huge lives of Cromwell and Frederick the Great beyond great industry and careful scholarship. His best biography, the brief sketch of John Sterling, scarcely equaled Johnson's *Life of Savage* in sympathetic understanding, and was not a major element in his own development. It represented little more than Carlyle's protest against the growing reticence of the Victorian age.

Carlyle achieved his first great success in 1837, when he published his *French Revolution*. In the same year Victoria ascended to the British throne. Already the fiery reformist spirit of romanticism was degenerating into the smug moral earnestness of the era that bears her name. For biography it was a regressive age marked by the return to popularity of the panegyric and the commemorative life.

John Lockhart's *Life of Sir Walter Scott*, published in seven volumes between 1836 and 1838, provided a foretaste of what was to come. Lockhart wrote in the Boswellian tradition. Like Boswell he knew his subject from long years of association, drew on letters and other personal documents to buttress his own observations, and achieved his effects by piling up dozens of small incidents and permitting them to tell their own story. But perhaps because he was Sir Walter's son-in-law, he exhibited a reticence that, while not dishonest, would have been inconceivable to Boswell. "I consider no man justified in journalizing what he sees and hears in a domestic circle where he is not thoroughly at home," Lockhart wrote. "I think there are still higher and better reasons why he should not do so where he is." Contrast this attitude with Boswell's descriptions of Johnson's passionate absorption in his food and of dozens of the Doctor's other petty foibles. Yet despite what Harold Nicolson has called Lockhart's "consummate literary tact," his biography was criticized in its day for being too frank.

By the forties biography was rapidly descending into complete respectability. An age that invented the verb "to bowdlerize" and considered "leg" an indelicate word could not be expected to excel in biography. "Authorized" and "commemorative" lives proliferated. As they grew duller and more reserved, they also grew longer. The "Life and Letters" variety flourished in two or even three stout volumes—often with dashes substituted for the names of persons still living and "offensive" passages "modified" or entirely removed. (As Charles Dickens once said, many biographies of his day seemed to be written "by somebody who lived next door to the people, rather than inside 'em.") Of course such practices had existed even in the candid eighteenth century, and all Victorians were not so cautious. But in the earlier era the polite biographer was on the defensive; in the later he dominated the field. The poet Tom Moore, writing a biography of Lord Byron, suppressed evidence in Byron's memoirs and then evidently destroyed the source itself lest others less squeamish gain possession of knowledge he considered unfit for human consumption.

This happened in 1830; at the height of the era diarists were censoring themselves.

This attitude of mind grew out of a combination of Puritan morality, the new middle class's search for respectability, and the reforming zeal of the romantic idealists. It was not confined to England. In France it was far less dominant, but even there Baudelaire, writing in the sixties, complained of the "imbeciles of the Bourgeoisie who interminably use the words: 'immoral,' 'immorality,' 'morality in art' and other such stupid expressions." Baudelaire once took a "five-franc whore" to the Louvre to look at the statuary. The girl was embarrassed and outraged that "such indecencies could be flaunted in public."

In America, despite the coarse, easygoing nature of society, biography was as inhibited as in England. Early American biography had been dominated by the clergy. Being designed to inculcate piety and teach lessons, it was little influenced by the frank honesty of the age of Boswell and Johnson. The first "classic" American biography, Mason Locke Weems's life of Washington, published initially in 1800, was a mixture of fairy stories and outrageous panegyric. Washington "was never guilty of so brutish a practice as fighting," Weems wrote in describing his hero's school days. "If he could not disarm [his classmates'] savage passions by his arguments, he would instantly go to the master, and inform him of their barbaric intentions. The boys . . . were often angry with George for this, but he would say, 'angry or not angry, you shall never, boys, have my consent to a practice so shocking.'" Little wonder that the "Victorian reaction" hit America hard! Jared Sparks's *Life and Works of Washington*, completed in 1837, was perhaps typical. Sparks "edited" Washington's letters carefully, cor-

v. Nineteenth-Century Trends

recting his spelling and punctuation, changing "Old Put" to a dignified but flavorless "General Putnam," altering a statement that a certain sum "would be but a fleabite to our demands" to "totally inadequate," and so on. John C. Hamilton's life of his father, Alexander Hamilton, was marked by this same veiling of the truth. All evidence of Hamilton's illegitimate birth was suppressed, which was perhaps understandable in a biography by a member of the family, but so also was every sign of the sulphurous remarks that Hamilton had sometimes made about George Washington. To criticize Washington in mid-nineteenth-century America was to commit unthinkable blasphemy. To some minds it was scarcely less blasphemous to criticize any President, even by implication. For example, President Grant's Secretary of State, Hamilton Fish, out of consideration for his chief, deliberately refrained even in his diary from commenting upon the many unsavory events of the Grant Administration which he knew about and disapproved of.

Yet if the middle years of the nineteenth century were dominated by this priggishness, healthier biographical trends were also noticeable. For one thing, the habit of reading biographies grew stronger. The spread of literacy made this possible, and current taste gave it force. As a result the number of lives published continued to increase. "Thanks to the officious zeal of friendship and the active industry of literary undertakers," one English critic noted as early as 1821, "biographical memoirs have become as multitudinous, prolix, and veracious as epitaphs in a country churchyard." The period also produced much sound scholarship, especially when authors were dealing with non-contemporary figures, as in the cases of Carlyle's long biographies and of books like George Henry Lewes's

Goethe (which was widely read even in Germany), David Masson's life of Milton, and, to cite an American example, Washington Irving's *Christopher Columbus*. Even a writer like Jared Sparks, although he abused the scholar's rules, reflected the growing concern over source materials and thorough research.

Related to the growth of scholarship was the professionalization of biography. Johnson had stressed the importance of a special kind of training for writing lives, but only in the nineteenth century did a fair number of primarily biographical writers emerge. Sainte-Beuve in France (though he is best known as a critic), John Forster in England, and James Parton in America are three quite different examples of this type. Later in the century John Morley offered perhaps the best illustration of the professional, for in addition to editing the *English Men of Letters* series, he wrote brilliant short lives of Diderot, Rousseau, Voltaire, and Burke and a great "definitive" life of Gladstone.

The Victorian age also marked the development of uniform sets of lives, of which Johnson's *Lives of the Poets* was the prototype. The *Men of Letters* series, begun in 1877, was the best of these. Jared Sparks edited a *Library of American Biography* in the thirties and forties which ran to twenty-five volumes, and by the end of the century dozens of such series were in print. The publication of biographical dictionaries, whose roots ran back to the early antiquaries, also proceeded apace. The *Cyclopaedia of American Biography* and the more ambitious British *Dictionary of National Biography*, both products of the 1880's, were the best of many such works in English. Biographical criticism, particularly in the form of essay-reviews, also became more common, and in the hands of men like Sainte-

v. Nineteenth-Century Trends

Beuve, Carlyle, and Macaulay, was better done than ever before.

Nor did all the Victorians submit to the dominant prudishness of the age. Carlyle was unrelenting in his defiance. "How delicate, how decent is English biography, bless its mealy mouth," he sneered when timid souls attacked Lockhart's cautious criticisms of Sir Walter Scott. Biography, he wrote on another occasion, should reveal "all the inward springs and relations" of a subject. Walt Whitman commented to a friend: "I have hated so much of the biography in literature because it is so untrue: look at our national figures how they are spoilt by liars . . . who put an extra touch here, there, here again, there again, until the real man is no longer recognizable." When you write of me, he urged, "be sure to write about me honest; whatever you do, do not prettify me: include all the hells and damns." Abraham Lincoln made essentially the same complaint to William Herndon, his law partner. One day he tossed aside unfinished a life of Burke he had been trying to read. "It's like all the others," he said. "Biographies as generally written are not only misleading but false. The author of this life of Burke makes a wonderful hero of his subject. He magnifies his perfections—if he had any—and suppresses his imperfections. . . . Billy, I've wondered why book-publishers and merchants don't have blank biographies on their shelves, always ready for an emergency, so that, if a man happens to die, his heirs or his friends . . . can purchase one already written, but with blanks. These blanks they can at their pleasure fill up with rosy sentences full of high-sounding praise."

Of course an occasional crotchety biographer disregarded convention and wrote a scathing or even a scandalous life. Rufus W. Griswold's *Edgar Allan Poe* (1850) was a notorious example, but the most interesting specimen of the type was John Thomas Smith's life of the sculptor Joseph Nollekens. Smith had expected to be remembered in Nollekens's will, and when he was not, he took his revenge by writing a biography full of nasty anecdotes that emphasized Nollekens's stinginess and generally unpalatable nature. The sculptor (according to Smith) made a business of selling "botched antiques," and was so miserly that, although rich, he lived off butcher's scraps. The spirit of this book can best be understood through quotation:

> ... independent of his natural stupidity and ignorance in conversation, his bodily humours appeared in several parts of his person as well as his face, which was seldom free from scorbutic eruptions; particularly about his mouth. Indeed, poor man! his appearance and want of decent manners rendered it impossible for any one accustomed to tolerable society, to associate with him.

Such books, however, had little influence. Their obvious bias played into the hands of those who advocated restraint.

But by the eighties the worst of Victorian reticence was passing. Early in the decade James Anthony Froude published his life of Carlyle. It was written in the Boswellian manner, long, detailed, and frank. Carlyle had turned over his journals, letters, and other effects to Froude, instructing him to tell the truth. This Froude was determined to do. "The biographies of the great men of the past," he wrote, "are generally useless. They are idle and incredible panegyrics, with the features drawn without shadows, false, conventional, and worthless." He resolved to tell "all the truth so far as the biographer knows it."

v. *Nineteenth-Century Trends* [105

As a matter of fact, Froude's book was as warm and sympathetic in its view of Carlyle as Boswell's was of Johnson. Like Boswell, Froude was a disciple of his subject. But just as Johnson's uncompromising honesty reinforced Boswell's, so Carlyle's gruff, selfish, domineering personality left its mark on the writing of Froude. Froude once asked Carlyle whether he should eliminate one of Mrs. Carlyle's letters referring unflatteringly to a person of some eminence. Carlyle replied: "It will do him no harm to know what a sensible woman thought of him." Froude took the lesson to heart along with his master's other teachings. As a result, he did not hesitate to point out (some would say to overemphasize) how unhappy the self-centered Carlyle had often made his sensitive and intelligent wife, Jane Welsh. When his volumes appeared, they were bitterly assailed. Froude was accused of everything from mere bad taste to ghoulishness. Tennyson attacked him; respectables everywhere were outraged. The effect, however, was salutary. For if Froude's *Carlyle* did not herald a new era in biography, at least it set people to arguing about the nature of the form. A hot debate, which dragged on for years, raged in the pages of the periodical press. General opinion was critical of Froude, but the critics were on the defensive.

The most severe of Froude's detractors took a position little different from that dominant in the Middle Ages. There were, according to one commentator, only three motives for writing biography; one wished either to erect a monument to a departed loved one, or to set an example for future generations, or to make money. Only the last of these motives could justify the exposure of intimate details. "It is impossible . . . to defend the publication of such details even in a limited degree, except on grounds which few writers of respectability would willingly avow." Margaret Oliphant, the novelist, offered a more moderate opinion. While critical of Froude, she demanded only a decent respect for those still living. After, say, twenty years, a biographer might be frank. "The sentiment of the death-chamber is one thing," she wrote, "the judgment of history another." The biographer must be aware of his responsibility, for he fixes his subject's place in history. It was, according to Mrs. Oliphant, a question of "the ethics of biography."

This question of ethics persisted for years. In the nineties George Tyrrell, an Irish Jesuit (later excommunicated for "modernism"!), argued that in writing contemporary biography it might be a *duty* to suppress evidence. "Vulgar curiosity" did not give the biographer a right "to anticipate the Day of Judgment." However, like Mrs. Oliphant, Tyrrell tried to distinguish between contemporary biography and "the judgment of history," admitting that the historian must tell the whole truth.

But the defenders of greater freedom of expression were growing more vocal. Edmund S. Purcell, whose life of Cardinal Manning had been attacked for its frankness, defended his position in an article "On the Ethics of Suppression in Biography" in the *Nineteenth Century*. To withhold significant information was "almost a lie," he said. In 1896 Paul Leicester Ford published *The True George Washington*. Ford protested against the dehumanizing of the great figures of history. "In place of men . . . we have demigods, so stripped of human characteristics as to make us question whether they deserve much credit for their sacrifices and deeds." Ford did not get very far in his personal struggle to make a warm human being out of Washington, but his intentions were good, and they reflected the growing revolt against Victorianism.

One of the most effective of the "revolutionaries" was Edmund Gosse. He attacked Victorian biography on all fronts: it was too long; it was written too often by untrained authors; it was overly concerned with convention and with the feelings of relatives and friends of the subject. Seventeen years before Lytton Strachey's famous blast against biographical morticians, Gosse wrote: "We in England bury our dead under the monstrous catafalque of two volumes (crown octavo), and go forth refreshed, as those who have performed a rite which is not in itself beautiful, perhaps, but inevitable and eminently decent. . . . The two great solemn volumes . . . follow the coffin as punctually as any of the other mutes in perfunctory attendance." In a lecture delivered in 1910 Gosse lashed out at the biographer who was not an earnest seeker-for-truth. He shows his subject "in a tight frock-coat, with a glass of water in his hand, and one elbow on a desk, in the act of preparing to say, 'Ladies and Gentlemen,'" Gosse said. But Gosse was more than a critic. He wrote lives of Gray, Congreve, Donne, and other poets, as well as a number of short sketches. In 1907 he published *Father and Son*, a touching yet devastating account of his youthful relations with his father, the zoölogist Philip Henry Gosse. The elder Gosse had typified the fervent, evangelical piety of the Victorian Puritan. His son's brilliant dissection, done in the spirit of Johnson, had an even more powerful effect on public opinion than Samuel Butler's autobiographical novel, *The Way of All Flesh*, which had come out a few years earlier, for its frank discussion of a "taboo" subject was not disguised as fiction. Although the old guard continued to complain ("Nothing is too insignificant, nothing too private for narration," wailed Agnes Repplier), its day was over.

The movement so far discussed, which began with Froude and reached maturity with Gosse, might be categorized as an attempt to reform biography from within. But during the same period the form felt also the impact of many outside forces. One was the growing emphasis on scientific objectivity in the writing of history, which by the late nineteenth century was beginning to have a harmful effect on biography. Of course the critics of Victorian restraint were arguing for objectivity, but the scientists wished to remove from their work not only reticence, but also sympathy. Froude was objective about Carlyle's weaknesses, but his admiration for his master was apparent. The disciples of Leopold von Ranke, striving to make the study of the past completely scientific, attacked Froude not only for his many careless errors of fact, but also for his freely expressed feelings and colorful writing. The icy objectivity they advocated was destructive to the biographer's aim of *understanding* and to the whole task of portraying personality. The influence of Auguste Comte's Positivism, with its view that the way to both knowledge and wisdom lay in the undirected massing together of every possible fact, was also harmful. Scholarly biography, always prone to submerging itself too much in details, became more depersonalized than ever.

The emphasis on science in the study of the past also led to a search for the "laws" of history. Impressed by the tremendous progress made by nineteenth-century physical and biological scientists, historians tried to work out theories of historical action which would enable them to understand the past better and to predict the future course of

v. *Nineteenth-Century Trends* [109

human events. Since laws are general rules, applicable to all men alike, it was inevitable that this search should lead to the de-emphasis of biography, the study of individuals. "The tendency of historical research," Francis S. Seymour complained in his interesting volume on *Historic Personality* (1893), "has been to make the consideration of personal character more and more subordinate to the examination of . . . the great movements which constitute the landmarks in the development of civilization."

The influence of Hegel, with his theory of the rise and fall of civilizations, and of Darwin, with his idea that the environment exerts inexorable control over the development of species, gradually increasing during the nineteenth century, became predominant in the eighties and nineties. By the turn of the century the economic determinism of Karl Marx was also contributing to the belittlement of the individual. If man was a mere pawn, helpless before the sweep of a relentlessly evolving universe, or a selfish animal motivated only by his material interests, he was scarcely worth careful study in all the loving detail required of biographers.

Of course deterministic theories did not *automatically* require the subordination of the individual. Even Carlyle, glorifier of the Great Man, was a determinist in his belief that the rise of a hero to meet a crisis resulted from God's grand design, not from chance. But the determinism of nineteenth-century science, with its rejection of both chance and supernatural force, did discourage the study of the individual.

The one exception to this generalization was the new science of psychology, which, in the late nineteenth and early twentieth centuries, interacted with biography in ways stimulating to both disciplines. The psychologists were as interested in laws as any of the other scientists, and they were not particularly concerned with the individual in his own right. In fact, they tended to undermine every man's privilege to consider himself a unique being. But psychologists had to study people, and particularly in the early days of the discipline they made considerable use of biography. This was especially true in the debates which raged in the profession over the relative roles of heredity and environment in controlling human nature.

The influence of Darwin's *Origin of Species* was seminal in both camps. By stressing Darwin's idea of the survival of the fittest, some psychologists concluded that environment was the dominant factor; by stressing the inheritance of qualities that made adaptability possible, others assigned the major role to heredity. In general, the environmentalists were in the ascendancy around the turn of the century, but the arguments were hot, and both schools used biographical evidence freely in their debates. Francis Galton's *Hereditary Genius* (1869) provided ammunition for both sides, although Galton himself leaned toward the defenders of heredity. After studying works like Foss's *Lives of the Judges*, Lord Brougham's *Statesmen of the Reign of George III*, and "very many biographies" of individuals from all walks of life, Galton concluded that "men who are gifted with high abilities . . . easily rise through all obstacles," but that those upon whom the environment smiles cannot succeed "unless they are endowed with high natural gifts." William James, in an article on "Great Men and Their Environment," published in 1880, also defended the importance of the individual, chiding the determinists by

v. Nineteenth-Century Trends

asking them whether Shakespeare's plays would have been written by someone else if he had died in infancy.

But the weight of opinion was on the other side. It is significant that a historian, John Fiske, wrote the "Evolutionist's Reply to Dr. James." "One might learn all of Plutarch's Lives by heart and still have made very little progress toward comprehending the reasons why the Greek states were never able to form a coherent political aggregate," Fiske wrote. "Important as the 'great man' may be, it is not his individual thoughts and actions which primarily concern the sociologist." Historians, Fiske implied, should be sociologists, not biographers. Yet even Fiske made use of biographies in arriving at his conclusions. To prove that man is only a puppet, one must still study man.

The psychologists who turned to biographies for evidence were usually willing to assume the factual accuracy of the average life, but they were appalled by the prudishness and psychological ignorance of Victorian biographers. Their published comments, although rare, undoubtedly had a healthy impact on the form.

In working on his *Study of British Genius* (1904), which drew evidence from the *Dictionary of National Biography* and "over three hundred biographies of individuals," Havelock Ellis was shocked by the lack of psychological understanding in most lives. Indeed, as early as 1896 he had decried the unscientific nature of most biographical writing. Biography, he said, was really a branch of applied psychology, yet few biographers knew anything of the theories of men like Wilhelm Wundt, G. Stanley Hall, Hugo Münsterberg, and Joseph Jastrow, who "have taught us how to obtain by exact methods a true insight into the processes of the average human mind." The typical biographer, in describing what he "presumes to call 'Life'" did not even realize "that the rules of [his] art have in large part been laid down" by the work of such men. Instead, he produced "a figure that is smooth, decorous, conventional, *bien coiffé,* above all, closely cut off below the bust."

Being a scientist, Ellis was perhaps unduly optimistic about the value of "rules," and he grossly oversimplified the problem of depicting personality. "Biography," he wrote in 1900, "is, or should be, at least as much of a science as ethnography; it is a description of the life of an individual just as ethnography is the description of a race." But unlike most scientists, he was urging the reform of biography, not its dismissal as a dangerous misconception or a frivolous waste of time.

In 1900 another student of the mind published a book that was to rock the whole intellectual world and tumble the already tottering wall of Victorian reticence. This book was Sigmund Freud's *Interpretation of Dreams.* Freud's psychoanalytic view of man, with its stress on unconscious motivation and on sex, met with great resistance even among psychologists; its impact on biography was slight for some two decades. However, by the outbreak of the First World War the master himself had applied his theories to biography, and together with a few disciples had produced the first really important new development in the writing of lives since the eighteenth century.

To demonstrate the applicability of psychoanalysis to biography Freud chose a subject for whom a conventional approach was seriously handicapped by the shortage of evidence: Leonardo da Vinci. Only the bare outline of Leonardo's career was known; of his personality scarcely

v. *Nineteenth-Century Trends* [113

a vestige remained. Yet Freud's study published in German in 1910 attempted to penetrate the deepest recesses of the artist's soul. His book was totally unlike any earlier biography. After establishing (through the traditional method of quoting his subject's own words) that Leonardo thought sex "so disgusting that human beings would soon die out if it were not a traditional custom," he sought to explain both how and why the artist sublimated his libidinous impulses.

According to Freud, Leonardo converted his sex drive into the insatiable and all-pervasive inquisitiveness that made him the typical Renaissance Man. He did so unconsciously, and because of his illegitimacy. Because he lived the vital first five years of life alone with his mother, he had no father image with which to identify himself. His mother, seeking to compensate for both her own lack of a husband and his of a father, probably lavished too much affection on him "and robbed him of a part of his virility by maturing too early his erotic life." This startling analysis rested on a single childhood "memory" reported by Leonardo in later life: "When I was still in the cradle, a vulture came down to me, opened my mouth with his tail and struck me many times with his tail against my lips." Obviously, as Freud pointed out, this was a fantasy rather than a memory. He treated it therefore as a dream. Applying his psychoanalytic theories, he decided that the tail was a phallic symbol, the incident an unconscious wish for fellatio. (Poor Freud was painfully aware that this hypothesis would horrify most people. "Let the reader be patient for a while and not flare up with indignation," he begged. "It is quite certain that this indignation will never solve for us the meaning of Leonardo's childhood phantasy.") He then went on to explain that fellatio itself was only "the elaboration of another situation in which we all once felt comfort," namely, nursing. Leonardo was dreaming of nursing.

But why the vulture? All vultures were commonly believed in ancient times to be females who could be impregnated only by the wind. Using conventional scholarly methods, Freud demonstrated that Leonardo, an omnivorous reader, could scarcely have missed acquiring a knowledge of this bit of folklore. Since he was illegitimate, simple wish-fulfillment made it easy for him to imagine (in a day dream) that his mother, like the vulture, had conceived without male assistance. Given these unconscious feelings, it followed that Leonardo's dislike of sex resulted from too much mother love and from shame over his illegitimate birth.

Freud's book was full of such elaborately reasoned and challenging interpretations of the scraps of evidence at his disposal. A small slip of the pen in a journal entry became evidence that Leonardo suppressed his true feelings about his father; the Mona Lisa's enigmatic smile masked his pity for his mother. To the psychoanalyst, Freud said, "nothing is too trifling as a manifestation of hidden psychic processes."

But the significance of *Leonardo da Vinci* did not lie in Freud's particular interpretation of the artist's personality. As a matter of fact, recent critics have challenged his interpretation on a number of specific points. Freud's explanation of the symbolic meaning of the vulture, for example, has been exploded by the discovery that in reading Leonardo's account of this "memory" he mistranslated the Italian word *nibbio*, which means "kite," a bird quite unlike the vulture and lacking the vulture's mythological significance. However, Freud himself pointed out that his explanation was only a hypothesis. The real importance of the book lay in several assumptions and generalizations behind the specific conclusions about the special case, Leonardo. For one thing the book suggested a new technique for understanding personality and for gaining insights into the meaning of documents. "Psychoanalytic investigation," Freud wrote:

> has at its disposal the data of the history of the person's life, which, on the one hand, consist of accidental events and environmental influences, and, on the other hand, of the reported reactions of the individual. Based on the knowledge of psychic mechanisms, psychoanalysis then seeks to investigate dynamically the character of the individual from his reactions. . . . If such an undertaking, as perhaps in the case of Leonardo, does not yield definite results, then the blame for it is not to be laid to the . . . method, but to the vague and fragmentary material left by tradition.

Biographers should not "force psychoanalysis to furnish an expert opinion on . . . insufficient material," Freud warned. If they did, then they, not the method, were responsible for failures.

Secondly, the book explained why small, seemingly petty details supply "the clearest discoveries of virtues or vice in men." Plutarch had noticed this, but had not really explained it. All the great biographers had recognized intuitively the relationship among chance expressions, casual mannerisms, oddities of behavior, and a man's underlying character; only with Freud was this relationship given a theoretical basis.

Freud also made some interesting comments on the overly partisan biographer. Others had been aware of the danger of identifying too closely with one's subject. Freud explained this tendency by suggesting that writers often choose their subjects "for personal reasons of their own emotional life." To appreciate the value of his insight one need not accept wholeheartedly his rather pat explanation that these biographers "enroll the great man among their infantile models, and . . . revive through him . . . their infantile conception of the father." The great Plutarch had realized that he used his work as "a sort of looking-glass" into his own soul. Freud offered an explanation of how this process functioned.

Almost equally important was Freud's dry, scholarly, yet utterly candid treatment of the role of sex. Although he discussed homosexuality and many other abnormalities in the frankest language, he repeatedly made the point that he did so only to explain the nature of his subject. "If a biographical effort really endeavors to penetrate the understanding of the psychic life of its hero," he wrote, "it must not, as happens in most biographies through discretion or prudery, pass over in silence the sexual activity or the sex peculiarity of the one examined." Perhaps Freud made sex too important; nonetheless he forced people to see that it could not be ignored.

Finally, Freud reconciled (in one specific area) science's tendency to generalize with biography's tendency to particularize. The rise of the social sciences had harmed biography because the scientists had insisted that the individual was worthy of study only as a means of determining the "laws" of human behavior. Freud's own study of many individuals had led him to the "laws" of psychoanalysis. In his *Leonardo* he turned the process back on itself, using the "laws" to throw light on the individual. But (unlike many of his followers) he did not insist that the "laws" *determined* the actions of the single case. He felt reasonably sure that Leonardo's childhood experiences had led to sexual repression. But this reaction "did not have to take place; in another individual it would perhaps not have taken place." Physiological factors might have a role to play; certainly pure chance was also involved. Freud did not feel depressed at the thought that mere accident could alter the operation of the laws of human behavior. "I believe that no one has a right to feel so," he asserted. "If one considers accident as unworthy of determining our fate, one only relapses to the pious philosophy of life, the overcoming of which Leonardo himself prepared when he put down in writing that the sun does not move."

Thus Freud helped lay to rest the conflict between science and biography by showing that man was so complex that no simple determinism could explain him. If man was a slave to outside forces, the forces were so numerous that no two persons were affected by them in the same way. The biologist's microscope had given the lie to the seeming uniformity of cells and tissues; Freud's microscope exposed to view the same infinite variety in the tortuous passages of man's spirit.

While science was challenging biography from one side, imaginative literature was challenging it from the other. Like the scientists, creative writers both criticized traditional biography and provided it with new ideas. Throughout history the creative imagination of the literary artist had balked at biography's requirement that truth must be demonstrable, but for centuries the difference between what was "true" and what could be proved had been imperfectly understood. The French *mémoirs* and *caractères* of the seventeenth century illustrated this, as did the work of early English novelists like Daniel Defoe. But scholarship, with its unanswerable criticisms of careless research, had clarified the line between fact and imagination. Most serious nineteenth-century biographers were convinced that they must buttress their statements with footnotes and prove every conclusion with a mass of facts. Even the "rebels" took this position. Froude, for example, although himself attacked by the scholars, professed to have been "struck dumb with wonder at the facility with which men will fill in chasms in their information with conjecture."

But by the turn of the century a reaction had set in. The stupefying dullness of many Victorian lives was killing public interest in biographies. George Brett of the influential Anglo-American publishing house of Macmillan remarked to a popular lady novelist who was writing a life: "Nobody reads biographies," and demanded that she at least disguise her book behind a catchy title. The opportunity was ripe for imaginative writers to revitalize the form by sacrificing accuracy to entertainment and substituting intuition, or what they liked to call the "higher truth," for concrete fact.

It cannot be overemphasized that this point of view was very old. The second-century historian Arrian wrote in his *Anabasis of Alexander the Great*, after telling an anecdote of dubious validity: "If this was really done by Alexander, then I commend him for it; and if it merely seems credible to his biographers that he might have done and said these things, then on this basis too I commend Alexander." In all ages the Parson Weemses of biography, ignorant or contemptuous of scholarship, but with clear consciences, had recounted scraps of gossip and twisted evidence. Now, however, sophisticated authors began to do likewise.

Hilaire Belloc, of Anglo-French origins, Oxford trained,

v. *Nineteenth-Century Trends* [119

was one of the leaders of this trend. In books like his *Danton* (1899) and *Marie Antoinette* (1910) he invented evidence and supplied definite interpretations where the facts indicated only confusion or doubt. Belloc attempted "to stand in the chaos of time and see it as it must have been." He was contemptuous of footnotes. "If you put in details of the weather, of dress and all the rest of it," he wrote in an essay "On Footnotes," "but refuse to spoil a vivid narrative with the snobbery and charlatanism of these perpetual references, the opponent takes it for granted that you have not kept your notes and cannot answer him; and indeed, as a rule, you have not kept your notes and cannot answer him."

Other writers followed Belloc's lead, some carrying his ideas even farther. The Russian Dmitri Merezhkovski's *Romance of Leonardo da Vinci*, while more clearly fictional than Belloc's works, was a fictionized biography rather than a biographical novel. This book had some influence on Freud's treatment of Leonardo. In 1902 Gertrude Atherton published *The Conqueror*, a fictionized life of Alexander Hamilton. Mrs. Atherton was not afraid of scholarly research. She pored over hundreds of books and pamphlets. To locate information on Hamilton's early life she visited the West Indies, where she braved "cockroaches three inches long" and lived in a hotel where the guests had bad table manners, the servants were "lazy and impudent," and the bath was "a hole in the ground in a pitch dark room." She waded through piles of dusty, unindexed manuscripts, peered at countless tombstones, and in the end made important contributions to historical knowledge. But she treated her laboriously collected facts "with the methods of fiction." She did this, according to her own account, "so . . . that any reader might delude his lazy mind with the belief that he was reading a novel."

The contribution of the fictionizers of biography was indirect. By and large their books had little permanent value. In many cases their contemptuous view of the reading public's intelligence and their careless use of facts reduced their outpourings to utter worthlessness. Few were better than third-rate, whether considered as biographers or as novelists. Yet they helped to revive biography. They stressed the human element, the lively detail, the vivid action. They tried to be entertaining. Often they were sensational rather than sound, lurid rather than learned, but they were also widely read. They contributed vastly to the great popularity of all types of biography that followed World War I. Their sprightliness, along with the objectivity of the new science and the frankness of the Freudian psychologists, dealt a mortal blow to the dull, pompous, and partisan Victorian "Life and Times" and set the stage for Lytton Strachey and a new age of experiment and growth in biography.

CHAPTER VI

The "New" Biography and the Modern Synthesis

ONE DAY in 1918 a British jailer was disturbed in his rounds by raucous laughter coming from one of the cells he was guarding. Seeking the cause of the trouble, he found the culprit reading a book. Nonplused, he reminded his charge that prisoners were not supposed to enjoy themselves. Prisons were places of punishment. The prisoner was the distinguished pacifist, Bertrand Russell, the book *Eminent Victorians* by Lytton Strachey.

About the same time a bored British soldier awaiting transportation home from Baghdad received a copy of a new book. He was so fascinated by it that he read it through three times in quick succession. It "made me conscious of my destiny," he later recalled. Before the war he had been an actor; upon his return he became one of the most prolific biographers of his generation. The soldier was Hesketh Pearson, the book *Eminent Victorians*.

Few books have had the immediate and powerful impact on public taste, critical thinking, and contemporary writing that these short sketches of four Victorian respectables produced. Strachey, an urbane and witty authority on French literature, had caught the sentiments of the postwar generation perfectly, appealing to its resentment over the mess its forebears had made of civilization and to its cynical contempt for the virtues the Victorians had prized. He demolished his subjects not by denouncing them, but by exposing their hypocrisies.

Strachey introduced what came to be known as the "new" biography, but in many ways *Eminent Victorians* was only a culmination of the trends of the previous twenty years. Strachey resembled Gosse not only in his use of the funeral metaphor in describing Victorian biography, but also in his praise of brevity, his insistence that biography was a unique form of literature requiring special training and skills, and his condemnation of "polite" biography. He was also influenced by the new psychology (although it was not until ten years later, in *Elizabeth and Essex*, that his work reflected the ideas of Freud). Like the fictional biographers, he broke away from documentation and the rigid bonds of fact. In a book review done before the war, he had written: "When Livy said he would have made Pompey win the battle of Pharsalia if the turn of the sentence required it, he was not talking utter nonsense, but simply expressing an important truth in a highly paradoxical way—that the first duty of a historian is to be an artist." "History," he was to write later, "is not the accumulation of facts, but the relation of them." By "relation" he meant not the telling of a story but the construction of an artistic entity; like

VI. The "New" Biography and the Modern Synthesis

Hilaire Belloc, he was more concerned with form than with substance.

But Strachey added new elements to biography as well. Chiefly they were entirely personal and therefore unique—his devilish wit, his mastery of irony and innuendo, his epigrammatic style. He had a genius for damning his subjects by reproducing their own words without comment (and often, alas, out of proper context). These were qualities perhaps better suited to a writer of fiction than to a biographer. Indeed, according to Virginia Woolf, a close friend, Strachey would have preferred to be a poet or a playwright, but felt that he lacked the necessary creative power to do first-rate work of that type. Actually he produced a good deal of verse, and one of his plays, *The Son of Heaven*, enjoyed a brief London run. His reputation, however, came from his biographies, and it was considerable. From 1918 until his death in 1932 he was without question the most influential biographer in the world. His books were few; after *Eminent Victorians* he wrote only *Queen Victoria*, *Elizabeth and Essex*, and some brief critical articles. But his technique was widely imitated, and most of the popular biographers of his era acknowledged his influence on their work.

The recognition afforded Strachey was thoroughly deserved. His great talent was for portraying character, and this he exploited to the full. Although he did not pretend to add significantly to the general knowledge of his subjects' careers, his lives were based on wide reading and deep study. He could have been a twentieth-century Samuel Johnson—as a matter of fact, Johnson was his model. But he lacked one vital element: respect for truth. Livy only *said* he would have altered the outcome of Pharsalia to turn a phrase. Strachey really did bypass the truth to suit his own purposes. He distorted Cook's account of Florence Nightingale even though he admitted the excellence of Cook's biography. To make a fool of General Gordon, he used sources known to be fraudulent. He suppressed pertinent evidence in order to damn Cardinal Manning, and he invented material to shade his image of Queen Elizabeth. As a result his lives, while entertaining, did not contribute directly to the improvement of biography. His contribution was in his theory, not in his practice. He brought together diverse trends and gave them new vitality. He fathered a school that (whatever its faults) made biography interesting and readable. He stimulated the reading of lives and convinced the public that hero-worship was not only stupid, but—far worse—dull. He ushered in a movement that corrupted the biographer's love of truth, but, in time, good sense reasserted itself. Then, purged of deceits, his method and his point of view were put to proper use.

Eminent Victorians appeared at a propitious moment. Surveying biographical trends in 1916, Waldo H. Dunn noted a rise in the popularity of the form, and quoted a student of the book market as saying: "A good biography has a chance amid the welter of war." The brief interpretative study, after the model of Johnson's *Savage*, and the fictional life, were, according to Dunn, particularly active. Strachey's book, however, accelerated the trend. As early as 1920 the *Saturday Evening Post* commented on the "flood of biographical works" pouring from the presses to the booksellers. In an address delivered at St. Andrews in 1922, James Barrie complained that no one was so obscure

VI. The "New" Biography and the Modern Synthesis [125

"but that he can have a book about him." In 1927 a critic commented on "the present high enthusiasm" for biography; the next year another noted "that the interest of the public has been steadily shifting in the direction of biography"; by the end of the decade a third was claiming that the demand for lives was so great that "anyone with spare time and access to a public library can now publish a biography." James Truslow Adams, writing in 1929, told of a publisher who sent for a well-known author and asked him to write a particular biography. When the author protested that he did not know anything about the man in question he was given a list of books to read and a check for $5,000 and sent on his way. In a matter of months the manuscript was delivered and the book published.[1] In the same year Wyndham Lewis bewailed the "passion for biography" which was in fact only "a system of destruction." "There is no person," Lewis wrote, "who can hold a pen or push a typewriter, however contemptible his powers, but can, without taking out any license, go out and hunt his Dickens, his Marlowe, his Rossetti, his Byron—there is no closed season for that game."

Statistics bear out these impressionistic opinions. In America alone about 4,800 biographies were published between 1916 and 1930. And the rate was rapidly accelerating: in 1929, 667 new ones appeared, more than twice the annual average for the period. In 1932, the figure reached 699. Best-seller lists reinforce this evidence. According to one student of trends, J. C. Long, non-fiction had seldom reached the kind of sales figures achieved by popular novels before World War I. In the twenties, led by Papini's

[1] It is a pity, but Adams did not identify the publisher, or the author, or the book.

Life of Christ, Strachey's *Queen Victoria*, André Maurois's lives of Shelley and Disraeli, and Emil Ludwig's *Napoleon*, biographies crowded the best-seller ratings, and many lives sold upwards of 50,000 copies.

The advance flattened out in the thirties, but biography remained very popular until late in the decade. "The present passion for biography is remarkable," an English observer noted quizzically in 1933. "It appears that biography is the one domain in which a publisher can safely speculate. . . . There seem to be readers for any kind of book about anyone, living or dead, who made any kind of a name. . . . Old diaries and letters are, as merchants say, very firm." And as late as 1937 Harold Nicolson complained: "As a biographer myself I resent this flooding of what was once a leisurely market."

The popular biographies of the post-war years were not notable for their scholarship. With a few exceptions they contributed little to historical knowledge. The general trend was toward interpretative analyses of character based on easily available sources, and these superficially tapped. The biographical writing of the whole Western world felt the force of this trend. The Frenchman André Maurois, the German Emil Ludwig, the Austrian Stefan Zweig, the Italian Giovanni Papini, together with Americans like Gamaliel Bradford and Francis Hackett, and Englishmen like Hesketh Pearson and Philip Guedalla were all primarily concerned with portraying personality. But the works of these men and countless others took many different forms.

Some of them ventured daringly beyond the sources; they invented dialogue, described minute actions that *might* have occurred, and presumed to record the thoughts as well as the words and deeds of their subjects. Of course this practice was as old as biography itself—Xenophon could never have remembered Socrates' conversations in the detail with which he recorded them in the *Memorabilia*. Plutarch was a master of this technique as of most others, and even the conscientious Boswell was not above elaborating upon his notes. But after the rise of the scientific method it took a boldness verging on iconoclasm to pass off this kind of work as biography. Many writers hedged by calling their books biographical novels, but the line between the novel and biography was not clearly drawn.

In some respects conditions resembled the early eighteenth century. Somerset Maugham's *The Moon and Sixpence* (1919) was clearly based on the life of Paul Gauguin, yet it was just as clearly a novel (and a very good one), for even the hero's name was changed. Irving Stone's *Lust for Life* (1933) was also unquestionably fiction, but a shade closer to biography, since Van Gogh and other historical persons were the chief characters and the story conformed superficially to fact. The many outpourings of Howard Fast approached still closer to biography, not because Fast was more accurate, but because he subordinated literary and imaginative qualities still farther to his efforts to describe the careers of Tom Paine, John Peter Altgeld, and his other subjects.

In *Glorious Apollo* (1925) Lily Adams Beck explained that in her treatment of Lord Byron she was attempting "to touch biography with imagination and to present the essential truth as I see it, clothing the historical record with speech and action." By her own admission "clothing the historical record" included dressing up the facts with manufactured evidence and abandoning "exactitude" in dates. Francis Steegmuller claimed that his *O Rare Ben Jonson*

(1928) was "a poetically true conception" (he quoted Aristotle to prove that "poetry is a more philosophical and a more serious thing than history"), but he spattered his book with fanciful details and made-up conversations. At one point he described with meticulous specificity a scene in the Mermaid Tavern in which Jonson, Shakespeare, Donne, Beaumont, and Fletcher engaged in a spirited debate on the theater and life in general.

Exactly where, in these examples, the line between fiction and biography is crossed would be hard to say. Perhaps a question of intent is involved: does the writer see himself fashioning a story or elaborating upon truth in order to make it more interesting?

Some fictionizers frankly confessed that it was easier to invent evidence than to dig it out, and offered no more elaborate defense of their methods. Francis Gribble, a twentieth-century Defoe without Defoe's mastery of English prose style, admitted that he wrote only what "could be quickly finished and immediately disposed of," and he freely manufactured anecdotes and other material. But others propounded elaborate theoretical justifications. Hesketh Pearson emphasized the point that much of the so-called "evidence" to which scientific biographers limited themselves was itself highly subjective. He felt that it was just as reasonable for a biographer to rely on his own imagination as to depend upon the faulty memories and unfathomable motives of others. There was nothing wrong, he argued, in making up stories that illustrated typical traits of character; if the over-all impression was accurate, the details did not matter. "The path of art," he wrote in 1930, "is strewn with unimportant error."

VI. The "New" Biography and the Modern Synthesis

I myself believe so thoroughly in the truth-to-life of my "Herbert Tree" that if I were put to oath as to the absolute accuracy of its details, I should find it practically impossible to state where precisely my imagination parted from my memory. This much, however, I can say—Tree was alive with me the whole time I was writing about him, and as I jotted sentences down I could hear his nasal purr in their very pronunciation.

Lewis Mumford, writing in the mid-thirties, argued that the biographer should not confine himself to those historical "facts" which a capricious fate has preserved. Instead, being essentially an "anatomist of character," he should fill in the gaps out of his imagination. "He must be able to restore the missing nose in plaster, even if he does not find the original marble." Every biographer *selects* certain facts from among the total available, Mumford reasoned; why not, therefore, go a step farther and make up evidence if doing so helps to provide a more convincing interpretation? A number of writers adopted this reasoning.

The fictionizer invented "evidence" that fitted a conception of his subject drawn presumably from a reading of the actual evidence. He made intuitive judgments of what his man was like and then created "typical" scenes based on these judgments. Whether he realized it or not, his imaginings sprang from some simplified view of his hero's personality. Many biographers who balked at the deliberate manufacture of material and insisted upon remaining at least within shouting distance of some source, accepted the same implicit philosophy and wrote "intuitive" biography. The basic idea behind the intuitive school was that every personality is essentially simple once the "key to character" can be located. It may sometimes require long study, but when the key is found there comes a flash of insight, after which all the subject's actions fall into a pattern.

Intuitive biography was not unknown before the post-war boom. The nineteenth-century French critic, Sainte-Beuve, for example, achieved his often brilliant word pictures by intuition. Shutting himself up with the works of the person he sought to describe, he would read and meditate until suddenly the revealing trait would appear to him. At this point, Sainte-Beuve recorded, "the portrait . . . speaks and lives; I have found the man!" Another pre-war exponent of intuition was Gamaliel Bradford. As early as 1895, in *Types of American Character*, a Theophrastian study of such generalized individuals as "the philanthropist" and "the man of letters," he began to develop what he called "psychography." Thereafter, in a long series of books, he presented portraits of *Damaged Souls, Saints and Sinners, The Quick and the Dead*, and many others. These were specific sketches of actual persons, but always interpreted in the light of some special insight. "It is a perpetual revelation," Bradford once wrote, "to find how nature herself, as it were, takes a hand, and seems to dictate the structure and composition of the psychograph."

Bradford usually found his "key to character" only after intensive study, and many of his interpretations were very convincing. Most of the post-war intuitive writers were more easily inspired. Emil Ludwig, for example, always had a simple theme to unify his immensely popular lives. In *Goethe* it was the struggle between the poet's genius and his "daemon," in *Bismarck* the conflict between pride and ambition. Kaiser William could be explained by his withered arm, which gave him a feeling of inferiority that he disguised behind a façade of vanity and bluster. But Ludwig established these themes before he opened a single book. His usual method was to study pictures of his subjects. "All my biographies," he explained in 1931, "I began with the portrait I had known for years, before I so much as looked at the other documents; and if the painter lied there were others that could be used for comparison, best of all a photograph." If prolonged brooding over a picture did not bring its reward, Ludwig resorted to other devices. He got the necessary flash that enabled him to "understand" Lincoln from listening to Beethoven! The biographer, Ludwig said, "begins with a concept of character and searches in the archives for what is at bottom corroboration of an intuition."

The underlying motif discovered through the sudden insight was also characteristic of the early work of André Maurois. In his life of Shelley the theme was water, in his *Disraeli* there were two themes—rain and peacocks. These themes disclosed "the well-hidden harmony" of his heroes' careers. "Critical reasoning alone will not make a man understand," Maurois claimed. To comprehend Lord Byron, for example, the writer "must cultivate reactions similar to Byron's, and then, all at once, his character will be illumined by a bright light from within because for one instant, however short, he has coincided with the man himself." "We get our understanding," Maurois explained, "by a *coup d'état*." Stefan Zweig adhered to the same general approach: "When research firmly bound to visual experience ends, the free and winged art of psychological vision begins. . . . Intuition knows more of a man than all the documents in the world."

Other biographers, mistrustful of their intuitions, or at

least seeking a scientific basis for them, turned to psychology for inspiration. The greatest writers who have dealt with man, be they biographers or novelists or poets, have always credited the complexity of the human mind. When Queen Gertrude, in the great bedroom scene, suggests that Hamlet is mad, Shakespeare has Hamlet retort:

> . . . *Mother, for love of grace,*
> *Lay not that flattering unction to your soul,*
> *That not your trespass but my madness speaks;*
> *It will but skin and film the ulcerous place,*
> *Whiles rank corruption, mining all within,*
> *Infects unseen* . . .

thus demonstrating a sound understanding of the processes of rationalization and repression. In his sketch of Thoreau, to select another illustration, James Russell Lowell wrote:

> He condemns a world, the hollowness of whose satisfactions he had never had the means of testing. . . . His whole life was a search for the doctor . . .

and

> Those who have most loudly advertised their passion for seclusion and their intimacy with nature . . . have been . . . solacing an uneasy suspicion of themselves by professing contempt for their kind . . .

statements which may not do full justice to Thoreau, but which show keen understanding of psychological processes.

The intuitive biographers were all psychologically directed. Sainte-Beuve, according to one student, "oriented his critical procedures in a manner significantly psychological." He was aware that personality developed over time, and he stressed the importance of early environment in

VI. *The "New" Biography and the Modern Synthesis* [133

molding character. His writings were full of shrewd insights, such as: "Nothing so much resembles a hill as a hollow."

But after 1910 psychoanalytical thinking began to leave its mark on biography. Freud, despite his daring interpretation, had been cautious to the point of humility in psychoanalyzing Leonardo, confessing frankly that he could not demonstrate his case beyond argument. His many disciples lacked his restraint. In the shadow of his pioneering work, psychoanalysts, particularly in Germany, produced a rash of interpretative articles "explaining" historical figures from Amenhotep IV to Richard Wagner in Freudian terms and with dogmatic certainty. In America the technique was seized upon by some of the "new" historians, such as James Harvey Robinson and Harry Elmer Barnes, for it fitted well with their belief that history should broaden both its fields of interest and its methodology. Even so conservative a biographer as Preserved Smith, the great historian of the Reformation, wrote a Freudian evaluation of Martin Luther, explaining the Reformer's career in terms of the Oedipus complex. "Nowadays," Smith wrote in 1913, "men are turning less than formerly to dramatic incident, and more to psychological struggle; less to the outward phenomenon and more to the inward cause."

The influence of psychoanalysis expanded still farther after the First World War. The experience of doctors dealing with thousands of cases of war neuroses that were obviously not the conventional "shell shock" did much to strengthen Freudian theories. The appearance in English of Freud's *General Introduction to Psychoanalysis*, in 1920, and of many popularizations of psychoanalytic theory, spread the doctrine into non-professional areas. Suddenly biographers began to see the possibilities—the insights into hidden motives, the escape from the limits of "factual" biography, the sensationalism inherent in an approach that emphasized sex, with its healthy effect on sales. Freudian studies like Katharine Anthony's *Margaret Fuller* (1920) and Joseph Wood Krutch's life of Poe (1926) along with lives based on the work of Freud's critics within the psychoanalytical world, such as Ralph Volney Harlow's *Samuel Adams* (1923) and Leon Pierce Clark's *Lincoln: A psychobiography* (1933) appeared by the dozens.

Most of these works, despite an air of professional certitude, consisted of little more than crude exercises in the new jargon. Harry Elmer Barnes was particularly glib. In a series of articles he suggested that all biography must be rewritten in terms of the new theories. Washington, Barnes opined, suffered from a "Jehovah complex," Jefferson from an "inferiority and anti-authority" complex. Hamilton was a victim of "authoritarianism," William Jennings Bryan an example of something called the "psychosis of sanctimony," and Woodrow Wilson displayed a "narcissistic pattern." Many psychoanalytical biographers showed no real understanding of the terms and ideas they used to interpret their subjects. R. V. Harlow claimed, for example, that Sam Adams's shaky hands were caused by an "inferiority complex," while Preserved Smith contended that Martin Luther "inherited a taste for drink," and that his drinking was responsible for his son's physical weaknesses.

Friends of psychoanalytical biography defended the method staunchly. Dr. Clark, the biographer of Lincoln, himself a practicing psychiatrist, argued that the ordinary writer of a life "has not fully exhausted the possibilities of his subject, because of inadequate psychological training," and cited "such competent historical authorities" as Barnes, Preserved Smith, and James Harvey Robinson, to prove that some historians recognized the value of psychoanalysis. And the Marxian-oriented historian Matthew Josephson wrote:

> The dialectics of subconscious motive underlying the conscious proved to be as fruitful in measuring the individual life within a milieu as the dialectics of interest versus idea in the interpretation of collective society.

The psychoanalysts, always handicapped by a scarcity of evidence concerning the inner workings of their subjects' minds, tended to place great stress upon the close connection between a writer and his literary productions. They defended wholeheartedly their use of imaginative writings as clues to an author's personality. Discussing Edgar Allan Poe, Joseph Wood Krutch declared: "The forces which wrecked his life were those which wrote his books." The man and his works, Krutch said, were "nearly identical." Clement Wood, himself a poet, wrote in his life of Amy Lowell: "A poet's work must be studied in the light of the new psychology, with the certainty that . . . we will secure from the poetry a portrait of the author."

Lewis Mumford, in his psychological biography of Herman Melville, made heavy use of Melville's novel *Redburn* in his treatment of the novelist's early life. Mumford stated that a biographer who failed to take into account his subject's unconscious mind was guilty of either "ignorance or childish cowardice." While admitting that the method might involve surmises based on very little evidence, he believed that "it is better to make mistakes in interpreting the inner life than to make the infinitely greater mistake of ignoring its existence and its import."

Another type of biography that rose to popularity in the post-war years was the "debunking" life. Ever since Aristoxenus, angered by Aristotle's preference for Theophrastus, had written his disparaging biographies of Socrates and Plato, lives inspired by hatred or resentment had been common. But unless they possessed a personal animus, most writers who exposed the faults and weaknesses of their subjects did so for the sake of truth or from a desire to paint a realistic portrait. Even during the late-nineteenth-century revolt against Victorianism there were few deliberately unfriendly biographies. Ford's *True George Washington*, it will be recalled, attempted to make Washington more human, not to destroy his reputation.

The debunkers, however, set out deliberately to undermine the fame of history's heroes, or inversely, to build up the reputations of her villains. They substituted an easy familiarity for the respectful awe of the Victorian writers, referring to their subjects, for example, by their first names. They tried to make the intelligent seem stupid, the dignified foolish, the earnest hypocritical, and the humble vain. They dwelt upon petty idiosyncrasies, physical ailments, inconsistent or erratic behavior, and so on, not to illustrate character in the manner of Plutarch, but to prove that great men were neither better than, nor even different from, the common run of mankind.

The author of *Eminent Victorians* was their mentor. Strictly speaking, Strachey himself was not a debunker, but his cynicism, his subtle but unmistakable malice, his contempt for hero-worship, and his obvious relish in disemboweling overstuffed reputations qualified him as the grandfather if not the actual progenitor of the type. Other factors were also responsible for the new form. One was the general cynicism and pessimism of the twenties, reflecting the disillusions of a generation that had fought for a new world order and seen its hopes frustrated. Another was the spread of sensational journalism, which provided the new form with its racy and vulgar style and sharpened the public's appetite for observing the great in undress. The new psychology played a part too, by helping, as Professor Frank Klement has put it, "to undermine the traditional belief in man's intrinsic dignity and importance."

The word "debunker" was coined by William E. Woodward, who first used it in the novel *Bunk* in 1923. Woodward invented a character named Michael Webb, who studied the family of an automobile tycoon in order to "take the bunk out of that family by showing it up in its true relations." Many years later Woodward explained that he had thought of the term while reading about the delousing stations that had been set up in France during World War I:

> All of a sudden the proper description of Michael Webb's profession flashed through my mind. He was to be a "debunker," taking the bunk out of people . . . just as lice were removed at the delousing stations. At that moment the word "debunk" was created.

Woodward went on to remove the "bunk" (and a good deal else) from George Washington and U. S. Grant. Soon a veritable army was in the field, demolishing the conventional images of the great. Businessmen like Andrew Carnegie and John D. Rockefeller, politicians like William Jennings Bryan and William E. Gladstone, poets like Longfellow, and preachers like Henry Ward Beecher all fell before the debunkers' bludgeons. No one—not even the sainted Lincoln—was safe. "The time is coming," Edmund

Pearson warned in 1927, "when the biographers ain't going to the records, but to the neighbors."

Nearly all the debunking lives were designed only to amuse or to scandalize the reader, but some of the honest ones, like Rupert Hughes's study of Washington, were reasonably successful in their portraiture. Hughes once outlined the debunkers' position in a speech to a group of professional historians: "Pedestals are for statues, not for men," he said. But while he argued that Washington's hot temper, bad language, enjoyment of horse racing, and love life were necessary parts of any picture of the whole man, he also paid proper attention to Washington's "sublime achievements" in politics and war. Too many other debunkers were purely destructive critics, more interested in large sales than in truth; even Hughes had some of the debunkers' typical flippancy in his work, as when he said that the moral to be drawn from Washington's life:

> . . . is that one should dress as magnificently as possible and indulge in every luxury available, including the dance, the theatre, the ballroom, hunting, fishing, racing, drinking, and gambling, observing in all of them temperance, justice, honesty and pride, while avoiding excess and loss of dignity.

All of these new methods of biographical writing added to the great popularity of the form in the twenties and thirties. But in the long run they contributed to its decline. In their search for fat royalty checks and vivid characterization, the fictionizers, the Freudians, the intuitive writers, and the debunkers forgot that biographies were supposed to describe what a man *did* as well as what he was like personally, and that, essentially, biography was a form of non-fiction, subject to the restraints imposed by fact and reliable records. As one critic noted in the forties, the experimenters "became so absorbed in writing 'biographies that read like novels' that after a while they began to put in much more fiction than biography. . . . The reading public, being composed of people, could not be fooled all the time."

By the early forties a noticeable slump had set in. In 1941 Norman Cousins was remarking on "last year's depression in American biography," and five years later another observer complained that biography had "fallen into the doldrums." More and more the radical methods of the twenties and thirties came into disrepute. In 1953, commenting on British trends, V. S. Pritchett noted a decline in the use of Stracheyan irony and of imaginary dialogue. Biographers were ignoring psychoanalysis, and were displaying, he said, "a refusal to guess at the burned documents or the missing scene." The debunkers were themselves being debunked. Pritchett's generalizations were not entirely accurate, for the "new" types had not disappeared. But the trend was in the direction of more conservative techniques.

The public reaction against the "new" biography was in part the result of a counteroffensive mounted by conservative biographers and historians. Since the time of Samuel Johnson, "conservative" biography had been under attack, usually for good reasons, since so much of it had been dull, verbose, clumsy, uncritical, and devoid of insight into personality. Neither Strachey nor even Gosse had offered ideas that had not been advanced many times before. Early in the nineteenth century the English critic John Foster had complained of the poor literary quality and chaotic organization of most lives, whose authors, he said, seemed to believe that their pages should be cluttered with every meaningless detail obtainable, "even down to the fate of a wig or a gold-headed cane." In the 1830's Carlyle wrote of one long and cumbersome biography:

> A mass of materials is collected, and the building proceeds apace. Stone is laid on top of stone, just as it comes to hand; a trowel or two of biographic mortar, if perfectly convenient, being spread in here and there . . . and so the strangest pile suddenly arises, amorphous, pointing every way but to the zenith. . . . You leave it standing to posterity, like some miniature Stonehenge, a perfect architectural enigma.

Sir Leslie Stephen, editor of the *Dictionary of National Biography*, fretted constantly about "the verbosity and blindness" of contributors. In 1892 George Saintsbury railed at biographers who collected a mass of diverse and poorly related material, strung it together in chronological order, began by writing: "John-a-Nokes was born on the —th of ———. Of his earliest years we find . . ." and then inserted an occasional connecting narrative to fill in gaps in the raw data, calling the result biography.

Little had been said by the defense because not much could be said. But when the radicals of the 1920's and 1930's pushed imagination, interpretation, and sprightliness to extremes, the conservatives, who had by and large cast off the worst vices of nineteenth-century biography, rose up indignantly. Bernard DeVoto, whose own forthright style would have startled earlier conservatives, was in the forefront of the counterattack. "Biography is different from imaginative literature in that readers come to it primarily in search of information," he wrote in 1933. Since they are by nature interested in creating an illusion, "literary people should not be permitted to write biography."

vi. *The "New" Biography and the Modern Synthesis* [141

Allan Nevins, whose many biographies were models of sound scholarship interestingly presented, flailed both the fictionizers and the intuitive biographers, who, he said, were "substituting cleverness for profundity." In his manual, *The Gateway to History* (1938), Nevins, using conventional historical tools, caught the popularizers contradicting not only the facts, but also themselves. A Canadian historian, Lionel M. Gelber, denounced the oversimplifications by which the intuitive school reduced "the many-sidedness of a famous human being" to "flat planes and straight lines." Other critics deplored the glibness, presumption, and carelessness of the popularizers, and attacked their emphasis on "the man" as being a cheap means of disguising their ignorance of history.

Although most of the debunkers utilized traditional methods of research, they too were subject to attack, and from many sides. The descendants of William E. Gladstone tried to sue one Captain Peter Wright, a biographer who had made uncomplimentary statements about Gladstone's morals, and failing this, avenged themselves by having the culprit expelled from the fashionable Bath Club.[2] Rupert Hughes was denounced from the floor of Congress as a

[2] The Peter Wright case (1926–7) shows that neither Victorian morality nor the Victorians themselves gave up the ghost easily. In a book entitled *Portraits and Criticisms* Wright had said that Gladstone's practice was "in public to speak in language of the highest and strictest principle and in private to pursue and possess every sort of woman." The seventy-three-year-old Lord Gladstone, the statesman's son, thereupon denounced Wright as "a liar, coward, and fool." Wright professed not to be disturbed, saying that Lord Gladstone's reaction was perfectly understandable, but when Lord Gladstone had him expelled from the Bath Club, he sued both Gladstone and the Club. He won £125 damages from the Bath Club, but after a sensational trial, in which the late Prime Minister's relations with a number of women including the actress Lily Langtry and a mysterious Russian female agent named Olga were thoroughly explored, Lord Gladstone was acquitted of libel and his father's name "cleared."

"literary cormorant"; another politician called him "a cur that enters a graveyard and wantonly digs up bones." Conservative scholars, less shocked perhaps than certain relatives and Congressmen, nonetheless joined the attack. The debunker, one critic claimed, wished not to "reveal" his subject, but to "demonstrate what a clever iconoclast the biographer was." Claude M. Fuess charged a debunker of Abraham Lincoln with knocking the Great Emancipator off his pedestal and then smashing his broken image into fragments. "Every great man nowadays has his disciples," Fuess wrote in 1932, "and it is always Judas who writes the biography." And Allan Nevins castigated John K. Winkler for his "frankly cynical and hostile" approach to Andrew Carnegie. Howard Mumford Jones accused the debunkers generally of falsely undermining the heroes of American history, and thus weakening patriotic feeling at a time when the rise of fascism and communism posed grave national dangers.

But the biggest guns of the conservative critics were trained (unfortunately but understandably) on the psychoanalytical biographers. Some attacked them for the wrong reasons. "The worst foe of biography that has yet appeared," Charles Whibley wrote in 1924, "is the disciple of Freud, who crawls like a snail over all that is comely in life and Art." And the American historian Wilbur C. Abbott, inveterate foe of all historiographical radicalism, denounced the psychoanalyzers for "all their sex nonsense and their ridiculous reconstruction of their characters' psychology." Others, however, struck at the methodology of the psychoanalytical biographers without necessarily questioning psychoanalysis itself. Historian Jacques Barzun, for example, argued that the typical Freudian biography did

VI. The "New" Biography and the Modern Synthesis [143

not really explain its subject; it merely substituted a new jargon for old expressions. Philip Guedalla spoke of "the familiar cake iced thinly with a little mental slang imported from Vienna," and claimed that psychoanalytical lives were constructed of "one half of something we all knew before, and . . . the other half of something which is not so." Howard Mumford Jones, himself a biographer as well as a shrewd critic of all forms of the "new" biography, denounced the glib manner in which the psychoanalytical writers made use of the Freudian theories of sublimation and reaction formation. "So long as any symbol can be translated into any other symbol from the subject's past, so long the psychoanalyst may roam at will," Jones complained.

Writers of fiction and even some of the "new" biographers joined in attacking the psychoanalytical biographers. In 1926 Stephen Vincent Benét directed a blast at all types of biography. He compared the heavy-handed methods of the debunkers to the firing of "a biographical elephant gun." The old-style conservative biography, he said, was like a "three story gingerbread monument to a defunct reputation (written by the neediest member of the family and published at about seventeen pounds dead weight)." But his keenest shaft was directed at the literary psychoanalyzers:

> And as for the poor devil's really loving his wife—well I know that every authentic utterance of his on the subject says he did, and there are those dedications of his books, that sound fairly sincere. But honestly, he simply hated her all the time. . . . Don't you realize that his unconscious portrait of her as the degenerate scrubwoman with leprosy in chapter four of "Wedded and Wooed" represents his real feelings toward her?

André Maurois, despite his talk of insights and of penetrating to the inner soul of a subject, considered psychoanalysis useless in biography. "Who is keeping a record of Bertrand Russell's dreams, so that the Freudian biographers may interpret them at a later date?" he asked in *Aspects of Biography*, a series of lectures on his craft delivered in the twenties. Emil Ludwig, though he claimed to have discovered the Oedipus complex, wrote a book about Freud in which he reviewed a good deal of the psycho-biographical literature and found it uniformly worthless.

But the conservative biographers struck the most numerous and the heaviest blows. Psychology, wrote James Truslow Adams, "is about as useful in the hands of an ordinary biographer as a stick of dynamite." DeVoto, who considered Freud's own moderate and cautiously phrased *Leonardo da Vinci* "absolute bilge uncontaminated by the slightest possible filtrate of reality," summed up the general reaction of conservatives. "Psycho-analysis has no value whatever as a method of arriving at facts in biography," he said. "No psycho-analytical biography yet written can be taken seriously—as fact."

Although no one could measure the effect on public taste of all these attacks, conservative criticism probably speeded the decline of the "new" biography. After about 1940, most of the radical forms were distinctly out of fashion. However, one new school then developed which attempted to synthesize the many radical methods and to combine with them extensive research in primary sources after the model of the best scholars. For some reason, nearly all of the synthesizers were women, the most successful of whom were Catherine Drinker Bowen, Louise Hall Tharp, and Madeleine B. Stern.

VI. The "New" Biography and the Modern Synthesis [145

Mrs. Bowen called this approach the "narrative" method, Madeleine B. Stern, the "chronological" or "biography-in-present-tense" technique. The method was fictional in that it permitted the use of manufactured quotations and imagined details. It was also intuitive; in writing *John Adams and the American Revolution*, Mrs. Bowen surrounded herself with pictures of her hero for inspirational purposes and consciously sought a "plot" around which to develop her story. Books of this type were also pervaded by psychology—the subject's thoughts and inner feelings received great stress—though they were usually not Freudian in orientation. Finally, they placed much emphasis upon minute description of the scene, with almost incredible labor often expended in the presentation of the pettiest details. Thus Mrs. Tharp pictured Horace Mann emerging from the Exchange Coffee House in Boston on January 7, 1829, and buttoning his greatcoat before climbing Beacon Hill to attend his first meeting of the state legislature. An elaborate footnote, based on a study of Mann's financial records, "proved" that he was probably wearing his greatcoat because, of his two overcoats, the greatcoat was the newer, and therefore more suitable for this important occasion.

The opening lines of Miss Stern's *The Life of Margaret Fuller* illustrate most of the techniques of this school in capsule form:

> Timothy Fuller tucked the *Columbian Centinel* under the arm of his greatcoat and glanced at the date [sic] to be sure the news was the most recent: May 23, 1810. Suddenly it seemed to him as if it might be a memorable day.

Similarly, Katharine Anthony's life of Dolly Madison begins with an elaborate description of Dolly walking to school. Birds flutter from branch to branch, the child's dress is carefully pictured, and so are her thoughts as they pass through her nine-year-old cortex.

Yet writers of this type considered themselves highly scientific. Made-up quotations were "used sparingly," and were "always based on fact." The difference between this and fiction, according to Miss Stern, was that "the fictional biographer writes the thoughts or conversation he would have had if he had been the subject. The chronological biographer writes the thoughts and conversation he knows the subject did have from evidence in the latter's journals and letters." Or, as Mrs. Bowen explained: "Our method is no deception. The reader knows we are not God, knows we cannot actually be inside John's mind—and knows also . . . that behind our narrative is historical source and historical evidence. . . ."

John Adams's thoughts might be "paraphrased into dialogue," and imaginary scenes (such as having a character rehearse a speech in a stagecoach in order to avoid lengthy quotations) might be created so long as each tale was based on fact. When Mrs. Bowen wrote: "On a morning of early autumn, 1746, over the rim of a tossing, wild Atlantic Ocean, the sun rose, a round red disk," she was, by her standards, being scientific, for surely the conditions she described must have occurred sometime that autumn in that location. The purpose of it all was "a portrait." "I have found instruments with which to measure and then I have gone ahead and painted. In brief, I studied the available evidence and, on the basis of it, built pictures which to me are consistent with the evidence." How "consistent with the evidence" her "pictures" actually were may be judged by this comparison of one bit of source material and her use of

VI. The "New" Biography and the Modern Synthesis

it, as noted by a careful reviewer. In his autobiography, Adams once wrote:

> Colonel Chandler had sent so many expresses that he found it difficult to get persons to undertake the journeys. Complaining of this embarrassment one evening, in company, I told him I had so long led a sedentary life that my health began to fail me, and that I had an inclination to take a journey on horseback.

Mrs. Bowen made of this:

> Colonel Chandler . . . ran out of post riders. . . . John heard about it from Dr. Willard, whom he met on the main street, riding out to see a patient. Willard pulled up his horse, leaned down, asked John gravely if he knew anyone who would volunteer as messenger to Providence. John looked up quickly, caught his breath. "Do you mean me, Dr. Willard?" he asked. . . . "Why not?" Willard asked. He grasped John's hand, shook it heartily and rode on. In a state of high excitement, John turned, walked straight to Colonel Chandler's, knocked at the door and offered his services.

Whatever the weaknesses of the "narrative" biography, it was not hastily thrown together or merely clever. It might be based on an oversimplified interpretation of the hero's character, it might slight or ignore the complexities of his career and the historical significance of his activities, but great effort went into its construction. Its popularity reflected the growing demand of the public for real meat in biography, rather than for the skimpy fare which, as Allan Nevins once said in discussing Maurois, was hardly more nourishing than ginger ale.

This changing public taste affected the older biographers who had first achieved popularity during the twenties.

Maurois, while still dependent upon the one insight that "will suddenly illuminate a character," was, by the fifties, convinced of the value of thorough scholarship, and even of footnotes. His later biographies, such as his studies of George Sand and Victor Hugo, were far more substantial than anything he had produced in the twenties. Hesketh Pearson, continuingly prolific, came by 1946 to think of himself as a leader in "the reaction against fictional biography."

As the radicals became more conservative, the conservatives became more radical. The excesses of the "age of Strachey" were a reaction against the extreme objectivity of the scientific historians and the pomposity and restraint of the Victorians. While scholarly biographers could never accept the sloppy research and cynical sensationalism of the "new" biographers, they learned from them the value of liveliness, concern for character,[3] frankly confessed interpretation, and artistic organization. Many scholars who had disparaged biography early in the century and who were contemptuous of the methods of the popularizers, eventually altered their views about biography and then borrowed from the techniques that the popularizers had invented.

Several factors contributed to the scholars' revived interest in biography. One was a "normal" swing of the pendulum away from scientific and deterministic interpretations of history. In the English-speaking world at least, the threat of communism and fascism to the democratic belief in the importance of the individual caused many scholars to reconsider and then modify their opinions about the role

[3] "The spotlight must ever be on the central character," Marquis James wrote in his life of Andrew Jackson. "This is the salient contribution that 'moderns,' for all their general lack of scholarship . . . have brought to this branch of letters."

vi. The "New" Biography and the Modern Synthesis [149

of the single person in history. For many American academicians, the publication of the great *Dictionary of American Biography*, completed in 1936, served both as an introduction to the writing of biography and (through its amassing of so many lives) as a demonstration of the usefulness of biography in the study of history.

Scholars were further influenced by the small minority in their ranks who *did* write biography in the early postwar years. Drawing upon American illustrations exclusively, one could point to Claude Bowers's *Jefferson and Hamilton*, which demonstrated the value of a frankly subjective interpretation when combined with careful research and vivid writing, Henry F. Pringle's *Theodore Roosevelt*, which proved that sprightly Stracheyan irony need not be dishonest, Allan Nevins's *Grover Cleveland*, which proved that a biography could be long and "conservative" without being dull, and Marquis James's *Andrew Jackson*, a fine example of good writing combined with footnotes and the other paraphernalia of scholarship.

Scholars were also attracted to biography by the monetary rewards that awaited the writer of a successful life during the boom. Few actually achieved large sales, for they did not enter the field in large numbers until the boom was over, but in a period of more moderate public interest they were able to compete successfully with the popularizers.

The present generation of biographers seems to have approached what Frederick B. Tolles has called "a new conception of biography, combining the research and scholarly integrity" of conservative scholars "with the imaginative, artistic qualities and readability" of the popular writer of the twenties. Tolles, a scholar of impeccable reputation, himself illustrated the new tendencies in a book on George

Logan, an early proponent of "scientific agriculture" and a United States senator in Jefferson's day. Faced with a shortage of conventional sources relating to Logan's childhood, he produced an imaginative reconstruction based on such evidence as visits to Logan's home, knowledge of the Quaker environment in which Logan grew up, known facts about the personalities of Logan's father and of his teachers, and even an understanding of child psychology derived from observing his own seven-year-old son. "Twenty-five, fifty years ago," Tolles confessed, "no scholar would have accepted that chapter; probably no one who called himself a scholar would have written it. . . . I venture to suggest that our ideas about biography have changed over the last half-century."

Tolles was correct, at least in saying that biography had changed. Change has been a continuing characteristic in the history of biography. There is a vast difference between Egyptian tomb inscriptions and any modern life history. Yet certain constant factors, certain continuing problems, remain. Complete re-creation of a life is still only an ideal. The panegyrical and commemorative motives still perform their work of distorting truth. There is little essential difference between a medieval saint's life and a contemporary movie biography, where vice is always punished, virtue has its quittance, and the individual is subordinated to a formula. A *New Yorker* profile differs from a sketch by Plutarch mainly in that its purpose is less exalted and its hero perhaps less worthy of commemoration. Apologists flourish now as in the days of the Roman emperors, and sex and scandal are as popular and usually as clumsily described as in the time of Suetonius. Scholarship is often as dull and undirected as in the age of John Leland and Anthony Wood,

VI. The "New" Biography and the Modern Synthesis

and sometimes as bereft of critical insight as when Conyers Middleton wrote of Cicero. The millennium has not arrived for the biographer.

But centuries of effort have left their mark. Not even in the eighteenth century were lives being written, read, and criticized in such numbers, and on so many levels of appreciation as at present. Seldom has the general level of biographical writing been higher. Biography, having passed through a period of growing pains after World War I, and having then endured a consequent slump, seems to be achieving a new degree of maturity. Perhaps, even now, another Boswell is reaching for his pen.

METHOD

❖❖❖❖❖❖❖❖❖❖

"BIOGRAPHY," Allan Nevins once said, "is indeed a house of many mansions, not to be pent up by rigid prescriptions, but left free to make its own terms to suit its special audiences and subjects. . . . The really outstanding biographer will always be big enough to make his own rules." How true this is! Yet, alas, how true also that there are not very many "really outstanding" biographers. And even the occasional genius cannot be harmed by a summary of the techniques of his art. It may be possible to write a good biography in many ways, but there are sound principles that all should adopt. What follows are not "rules," but general suggestions based on some personal experience, considerable observation of the practices of others, and a thorough study of what has been written about the technical problems of biography.

CHAPTER VII

Choosing a Subject

It may seem unnecessary, on first thought, to give any extended consideration to the question of how biographers select their subjects. Common sense would seem to indicate that the result rather than the cause is important. But the result is obviously the outcome of the cause. A successful biography (like any other first-rate literary achievement) is the product of a harmonious mixture of writer, subject, and surrounding circumstance. This mixture is not easily compounded. "To have a talent for biography," according to Cecil Woodham-Smith, "is not like possessing an electric motor whose force can be applied to make any machine work. The relation between the biographer and his subject is strange and mysterious."

Too many biographers drift to their subjects haphazardly, depending upon chance alone for a happy combination. They have not weighed their interests and capabilities against the requirements of their selected tasks. Therefore, the reasons why lives are written and the factors that must govern the rational selection of a subject deserve study.

FREQUENTLY, the subject chooses the biographer. A son writes the life of his famous father, as Winston Churchill did of Lord Randolph Churchill; the life of a recently departed poet is recorded by his widow; the student edits the papers of his former professor, with a biographical introduction.

Books of this type run to extremes; they tend to be either very good or very poor indeed. Intimate knowledge is a priceless asset; close personal ties are a threat to objectivity. As Lord Asquith once said, the "enormous advantage to the biographer of personal intimacy" must be balanced against "the bias of kinship." Where else but in Romola Nijinsky's life of her famous husband would one be likely to learn that the dancer's incredible agility was in part the result of the peculiar shape of his feet? Yet her book is poor biography because of its unwavering justification of Nijinsky's every action, its strong prejudice against Diaghilev, and its generally uncritical approach.

Many writers have warned against biographies by relatives, but none more colorfully than Edmund Gosse. "The Widow is the worst of all the diseases of biography," Gosse proclaimed. "She is the triumph of the unfittest. . . . She paints her husband quite smooth and plump, with a high light on his forehead and a sanctimonius droop of his eyelid." The difficulty usually is not that the widow tries to evade telling the truth, but rather that her "truth" is not the objective reality the world is interested in. Editor Josephus Daniels of the Raleigh *News and Observer* learned from long experience that when he asked the wife of a

VII. Choosing a Subject

candidate for political office to supply a photograph of her husband for publication he was likely to get a picture taken many years earlier, when the husband had been young and handsome. "I recall," Daniels wrote, "that when I wired to the wife of a candidate for Judge in North Carolina for a photograph, she sent one taken on their bridal tour when his hair was abundant and he was clean shaven. At the time of his candidacy he was so bald that his head looked like a billiard ball and he had a flowing gray mustache. If I had printed the picture sent by the wife, the voters would not have recognized him." Love is not necessarily blind, but it tends to be astigmatic.

The pen of the relative can distort even when it is confined to editing. John C. Hamilton's edition of the papers of his father, Alexander, has been found by later students to be very unreliable, full of unindicated omissions, doctored passages, and careless errors. Anna Robeson Burr, after studying hundreds of autobiographies, wrote: "The honest toiler's heart sinks within him at the mere sight of those words on the title-page 'edited by his son'. . . . The editor is apt to fear to wound the feelings of some extant third cousin. . . . Bare, garbled, bereft, the document lies before us shorn of the rich minutiae which might have given material to the psychologist, suggestions to the sociologist, or aid to the imagination in forming a picture of the past."

On the other hand, there have been many first-rate biographies by relatives and friends, including most of the really outstanding studies of all time. Even widows have occasionally managed to overcome their natural partisanship. Dorothy Caruso's touching sketch of her life with the great tenor, while admittedly not a work of the first importance, was as honest and objective as anyone could desire. She discussed Caruso's illegitimate children and described his bluntness and his petty foibles as thoroughly as his warmheartedness, his devotion to his art, and his many other fine qualities. The relative who writes a biography must strive to avoid reticence in telling what he *knows*, and at the same time curb with tight rein the expression of his *prejudices*, or better, check these carefully against those of others less friendly to the subject. The difficulties involved were well stated as long ago as 1856 by James W. Alexander. Alexander's father, the founder of Princeton Theological Seminary, had expressed a death-bed wish that James prepare his biography:

> I girded myself for it under all the disadvantages of a conviction long since formed, that in many respects a son is not the proper biographer of a father. Though his knowledge of facts and character may be supposed to be intimate, he is in danger either of writing a panegyric, or of falling below the truth in attempting to avoid it. In almost every page I confess myself to have been haunted by the apprehension of overstating, overcolouring, and giving undue importance to domestic traits.

Actually, because he was aware of the problems, his *Life of Archibald Alexander* was a fine biography.

But most biographers write of men and women they have never known; more often than not of persons of an earlier time. How do they select their subjects?

André Maurois once explained his choice of the hero of his earliest biography as follows:

> At first sight it may seem strange that a Frenchman, with no particular training in English studies, should conceive the idea of writing a Life of Shelley. . . . Can he really have felt an over-mastering need of writing the Life? And,

VII. *Choosing a Subject* [159

if so, what were the secret springs which were at the bottom of this desire?
When I read a short Life of Shelley for the first time, I experienced a keen emotion. I will tell you why. I had just left the *lycée* and was full of philosophical and political ideas which, *mutatis mutandis,* represented just those ideas which possessed Shelley and his friend Hogg at the time of their arrival in London. Then, as circumstances rather brusquely forced me into action, I found my ideas in conflict with my experience. . . . I was at once irritated by my past youthfulness and indulgent towards it, since I knew that it could not have been otherwise. I longed to expose it, and explain it at the same time. Well, Shelley had experienced such checks as seemed to me to be somewhat of the same nature as my own. . . . I felt that to tell the story of his life would be in some measure a deliverance for myself.

Maurois selected his topic "as a means of expression" of his own personality. But if he thought his approach was original, he was deceiving himself. Plutarch had done much the same thing, and Freud had explained the psychology behind such actions. In 1920 William Bayard Hale had argued that every biographer projects "his own prepossessions and desires into his conception of the career of his hero." A writer of fictional biography, William E. Wilson, once confessed to identifying himself so closely with his subjects that he dreaded writing about their illnesses—he always acquired the symptoms of their diseases himself! Maurois was merely more clear-sighted and franker than most in understanding what was going on and admitting it.

Many biographies are the result of mutual interest. A specialist in some field, whose work has made him aware of the contribution of one of his predecessors, decides to expand his knowledge and ends in writing a biography.

Dr. Harvey Cushing's life of Sir William Osler is an illustration of this, as are such works as Ernest Newman's four volumes on Wagner, Senator Henry Cabot Lodge's life of Daniel Webster, and Ernest Jones's *Sigmund Freud*. Similarly, professonial historians who begin by specializing in a particular period of history often end writing the biography of a central figure of that time. James G. Randall's biography of Lincoln, the outgrowth of a lifetime of research in the Civil War period, is a good example of this tendency. By the same token, intense historical study frequently results in the "discovery" of an obscure but significant individual, leading the scholar to bring the "new" figure before the eyes of the world through a biography.[1]

Other biographies are written frankly for a market. It is a standing joke among publishers that a book with the name "Lincoln" in its title is an assured success, a fact that has lead to such titles as *Abraham Lincoln and the Fifth Column, Lincoln's Fifth Wheel, Lincoln and the Blue Grass, Lincoln's Choice,* and *Lincoln Finds a General.* While it would be wrong to say that Lincoln as a subject has been exhausted, it is nonetheless true that there are many more books about Lincoln than the circumstances warrant. The same would apply to other historical and literary personages: Napoleon, Marie Antoinette, Byron, and (already) Franklin Roosevelt, to name only a few. People whose lives have been marked by scandal, sensation, sexual abnormality or excess, are particularly likely to fall into this category,

[1] In 1921 Broadus Mitchell wrote *The Rise of Cotton Mills in the South,* the thesis of which was that since the Civil War the future of the South has depended upon the spread of industrialization. An early proponent of this idea had been William Gregg, whose writings Mitchell utilized in his book. Several years later Mitchell published *William Gregg: Factory Master of the Old South,* an obvious outgrowth of his earlier book.

for there are always writers ready to cater to a low taste, even to the extent of embellishing the record with the effervescences of their own imaginations. In *Elizabeth and Essex*, Lytton Strachey made the Virgin Queen into a vaguely described kind of pervert, victim of "profound psychological disturbances of her childhood" which made normal sexual intercourse impossible for her. Strachey even invented an early traumatic experience for Elizabeth, in which "Manhood—the fascinating, detestable entity" is first discovered by her "concealed in yellow magnificence in her father's lap."

This sort of thing produces a truly vicious circle, for the spate of such works itself makes it easier for the unscrupulous or lazy writer to produce a "new" life by combining several already in existence. As in the era of the saints' lives, the invention of last year's "student" becomes the "source" of next year's. The difference between plagiarism and research, some wit once remarked, is that research consists of copying from more than one book.

Some biographies are produced to order. The family may hire a writer of established reputation to turn out an "official" life. The weakness of most of these works is their less than candid approach to controversial matters, often the result of the close control placed upon the project by the family. The distortions in Burton J. Hendrick's *Andrew Carnegie*, for example, are more easily understood when it is remembered that he was writing an "official" life. If, in such circumstances, the hired writer maintains his integrity, and in so doing offends the family's sensibilities, he runs the risk of having his work completely suppressed, or of being denied the right to publish vital materials. Any reader having access to one of the really great American libraries will find there a biography of a certain oil baron who flourished around the turn of the century. Only seventy-five copies of this book were printed, though it was issued by one of the world's largest and most respected publishers, and a market exists for thousands. Even these few copies would not be available but for the determined pressure (backed by a threat of recourse to the courts) of the author, who needed them to meet the requirements of a doctoral dissertation. He had been paid to write the book by members of the oilman's family but had presented the story as he saw it—and they and the oilman's company had been displeased. Control over the papers on which the work was based enabled them, for all practical purposes, to suppress it.

Occasionally a man's descendants, out of rare objectivity or supreme confidence in the untarnishability of their forebear's reputation, turn an "official" biographer loose without restrictions. Then the result is usually more objective, the book more interesting, and the reputation of the subject far better served than otherwise. Such was the case, for instance, with Harold Nicolson's life of George V. The only real difference between an "official life" and one which is merely subsidized lies in the freedom of the author to write and print anything he pleases from his subject's papers, save for restrictions based on the laws of libel. If this freedom is granted, no critic may legitimately complain about the subsidization in itself.

Another variety of the "to order" biography is the product of the graduate schools. Students seeking topics for their doctoral dissertations often turn to biography. This is a relatively new development. Dumas Malone, speaking of academic circles in the early twenties, once recalled:

VII. *Choosing a Subject* [163

"The candidate for the doctorate who presented a biographical subject had considerable professional obstacles to overcome. If he attempted such a subject, the chances are that he was expected to deal with it in an impersonal way; he was supposed to show an actor upon the stage, not to describe the whole of a human life." This was a result of the professional stress on "scientific" history and of the reaction against Carlyle's "great man" theory of history. But professors now frequently assign biographical subjects, and a host of minor characters has been "immortalized" in this manner. In most such works the cause of history is better served than the cause of biography, for few show much interest in the basic problems of describing personality.

WHATEVER the motives impelling one toward the selection of a hero, many factors should be considered before definitely making a choice and settling upon the approach best suited to it. It would be belaboring the obvious to stress the importance of interest in the subject. Since writing of any kind is usually a voluntary occupation, it is rare for a biographer to consider a subject that bores him. A subsidized biography may be an exception, but if the financial appeal is powerful, even a dull subject may have its own peculiar interest. So, too, a doctoral candidate may undertake a life in which his sponsoring professor has the primary interest, though here the only real excuse is lack of imagination on the student's part. Certainly, with the wealth of existing possibilities, there is no reason for undertaking a biography unless the writer finds the subject truly engrossing.

This fact leads to a related point: the writer's *attitude*

toward the subject. The "scientific" school of biography would insist upon cold impartiality, but aside from its impossibility, such an approach is unwise. Most first-rate biographies have been written by persons sympathetic to their subjects. This does not mean apology or eulogy; it means that the chief goal has been *understanding*. The sympathetic biographer does not hide the hero's faults, he does not pass over discreditable episodes or stifle the comments of unfriendly witnesses. He subscribes to Cromwell's advice to the artist: "Paint me as I am, warts and all," believing, as Cromwell obviously did, that the truth will do the subject more credit than the shiniest gloss. A few excellent biographies have been produced by authors who have disliked, even hated, their subjects; yet by its very nature biography seeks to show a man as he lived, and few men have been wholly evil. The man who hates the person he describes usually finds it hard to show how the subject saw himself, how he justified his own existence. The sympathetic biographer is more likely to present both sides. "A good biography is like a marriage," Allan Nevins once wrote. "It requires a sympathetic union of writer and topic, and biography-by-attack is as certain to fail as marriage-by-bickering." In short, impartiality should be the *ultimate* goal. It has more frequently been achieved by sympathetic than by unfriendly biographers.

A third consideration should be the importance of the subject. The insatiably curious eighteenth century gave rise to the theory (the words are Samuel Johnson's) that "there has rarely passed a life of which a judicious and faithful narrative would not be useful." Since then many writers have expressed similar ideas. Phillips Brooks said in 1886: "The intrinsic life of any human being is so interesting

VII. *Choosing a Subject* [165

that if it can be simply and sympathetically put into words it will be legitimately interesting to other men." Given the infinite variability and complexity of man, this reasoning seems sound enough. Certainly novelists have created fascinating characters who are not "great" in the ordinary sense of the term. Why cannot biographers do likewise with actual persons? Since the worth of any biography arises from the skill with which it is written, as well as from the inherent significance of the subject, will not any man's life story merit description if it is well enough told? "An old woman paring her nails may achieve immortality if she chances to be painted by a Rembrandt." This is as true of word pictures as of those done in oils. Certainly there have been biographical gems devoted to rather unimportant people—Carlyle's *John Sterling* and John Gunther's touching memoir of his young son, *Death Be Not Proud*, come to mind.

But many ponderous tomes devoted to the careers of obscure mediocrities are gathering dust on the shelves. Fame is not necessarily the crux of the question. Far better to write of a forgotten person of some significance than to add to the mass of works on a relatively small number of constantly rehashed "names." But unless one is so talented as to be able to produce a work of artistic merit *sui generis*, one ought to steer clear of the *deservedly* forgotten figures of history. Perhaps the criterion of interest applies here. If a topic interests the writer deeply, there is probably justification for some kind of biography—if not an extended study at least a sketch. Marchette Chute, one of the best of the popular modern biographers, has emphasized the necessity of having faith in the importance of one's chosen subject:

It takes a long time to write a book. There is a wide gap, sometimes of years, between the day when a book is first conceived and the day when it is finally finished, and the writer is going to be tempted over and over again to think he made a mistake in starting the thing at all. The conviction that it will turn out all right in the end is essential equipment for a writer—as essential as for a mother who is bringing up a child.

The biographer's personal interest is at the source of such faith as this.

Besides considering the basic question of *whom* he will write about, the biographer must decide what *kind* of life he is interested in producing. His decision will depend upon his own tastes, but also upon the subject. Obviously the biography of a poet requires a different orientation than the life of a second baseman. In the one case the primary interest is intellectual, in the other, physical. Yet one poet may be interesting only in his works (William Blake is a good illustration), while another, like Shelley or Byron, may have led an exciting and varied life, full of incident and sensation. Essentially the biographer must decide whether to emphasize career or character, never forgetting that in every instance *both* are necessary if the true task of biography is to be accomplished.

In settling upon his approach, he ought to show proper regard for the other books already written about the subject. If there are none, the prospective writer, provided he believes the person worth studying and can find adequate source materials, has a clear field and is free to tackle the job from whatever angle seems best. But more likely, books are already available. Their type and number will inevitably affect the new student. Certainly a neophyte

VII. Choosing a Subject

should avoid a person who has been already much written about. Lincoln, for example, is not for beginners. When the basic research has already been done, mere diligence is not enough. Even the talented Carl Sandburg, though his biography of Honest Abe has become a classic, committed grave errors of judgment and interpretation in his earlier volumes because he lacked experience in evaluating complex historical problems. Leave Lincoln to a man like Benjamin P. Thomas, who, after long years of research was able to synthesize the tremendous Lincoln literature and condense it into a single volume authoritatively and with sound balance. The inexperienced biographer interested in Lincoln can follow the example of David Donald, who, as a graduate student, wrote a fine life of Lincoln's friend "Billy" Herndon. This task prepared him for more ambitious expeditions into Lincolniana.

But the inexperienced biographer probably will not find his subject to have been a Lincoln. There are very few Lincolns. Suppose, to cite a hypothetical case, one is considering a life of Senator X, a politician prominent in the years just after the Civil War. Senator X wrote his own memoirs in two thick volumes. After his death in the eighties, his wife published a biography full of eulogy and quotations from the *Congressional Record*. Around the turn of the century, a prominent journalist published a collection of character sketches of men he had known, including one of some thirty pages on the Senator. Recently a grandson has died, leaving X's papers, in a chaotic but complete condition, to a state historical society. Here, assuming X to have been a man of some significance in his day, is an ideal set-up for a full-length scholarly biography which should not overpower the intelligent beginner and which should teach him a great deal about history and human nature.

Or take another example. Y was an American painter of the "ash can" school of the early twentieth century. When he died in 1924 one of his friends wrote a long biography, supplemented by two volumes of letters, full of everyday detail, describing all his major works, quoting from reviews of his one-man shows, and recording the opinions of many contemporaries on Y as a man and as an artist. What is needed here is an interpretative study taking advantage of the perspective gained from the passage of time and of the memoirs of fellow artists published since his death, together with other new materials. A short volume defining Y's importance to his times and attempting to explain his influence upon later painters, a book making heavy (and legitimate) use of the earlier biography, but adding new insights and judgments,[2] would be far more valuable than one that attempted to deal comprehensively with every incident in the artist's life.

Other possibilities can easily be imagined. The point is that the author should consider early just what kind of book is needed, for this will greatly influence the nature of his research and organization.

Another question to consider is: How much technical knowledge does a biographer need of his subject's specialty? Usually biographies deal with *professionals*, be they

[2] The advice of Godfrey Davies is pertinent in this connection. Davies warned against overemphasizing "new" material, and the natural tendency of the writer to stress evidence which *he* has discovered, forgetting that a biography should be a unit in itself, which tells the story of a man's life with proper proportion and balance. "The magnification of the unprinted and the depreciation of the printed are errors of judgment that a good biographer must avoid."

VII. *Choosing a Subject* [169

politicians, writers, scientists, or artists. Can a man uneducated in art write the life of our imaginary Mr. Y? Could anyone but a physicist deal adequately with Albert Einstein? Could a Western European Christian produce a satisfactory biography of Gandhi? In 1716 Joseph Addison argued that satisfactory biographies of statesmen could be written only by persons who "have themselves been versed in public business, and thereby acquired a thorough knowledge of men and things." In our own day, Cecil Woodham-Smith has contended that "few people . . . are qualified to write about any period but the period of which they have made a lifelong study." On the other hand, Plutarch dealt successfully with the whole range of the ancient world, John Morley mastered with equal competence subjects as diverse in time and occupation as Cromwell, Voltaire, Cobden, and Gladstone, and other biographers have been equally versatile. Lincoln Barnett, whose writings span a vast concourse of time and knowledge, once claimed that the key to such facility lies in knowing how to ask the right questions (of libraries as well as people). "*Any*thing can be explained provided the reporter has enough curiosity to want to understand it himself." But the question remains.

The answer, of course, is that one must comprehend the activities of one's subject in order to tell others about them. Though it is possible to learn what one does not know to begin with, enormous amounts of time and effort can be saved if the writer of a life of Einstein, for example, is also a physicist, rather than a man who has never heard of the formula: $E = mc^2$. The greatest difficulty arises in the study of those rare, gifted individuals whose careers cut across many fields of specialization. The politician who was also a great lawyer with a busy practice in some complex field, the scientist who made important contributions in philosophy—these are instances in which the biographer may find himself wallowing beyond his depth in a sea of unfamiliar concepts.

Consider the challenge faced by any biographer of John Maynard Keynes, who, besides being the outstanding economist of his generation, was also a politician, a biographer, a director of important corporations, a speculator in foreign currencies, a professor and university administrator, a balletomane, and a shrewd collector of modern painting! Under the circumstances R. F. Harrod's life of Keynes, despite some deficiencies and an archaic structure, was a remarkable achievement, for it managed to describe all these varied activities clearly and succinctly.

Still another problem that the biographer must face is the *availability* of materials. Perhaps he is interested in a well-known statesman whose life story has never been told. But the man's papers are jealously "protected" by an aged niece. Or perhaps he wishes to write about the founder of a large corporation whose business papers are sealed by the present management. Great labor might result in the location of enough evidence in scattered depositories to make these projects possible, but it would be better to put them aside and wait for the demise of the niece or for a change in the management of the corporation, thus saving a great expense of time and effort. There is the additional reason that when a man's papers do become available, works produced without them are sure to be superseded.

A more delicate situation often arises when descendants, while not withholding essential papers, attach "strings" to their use. A young historian, Walter Johnson, was once working through the papers of the Sage of Emporia, William Allen White, who had generously opened his files to him. One evening White came into the room where Johnson was working and said: "Young man, do you know the first rule for any biographer?" Johnson asked what it was. "Kill the widow!" White replied, advice which many biographers have surely been tempted to follow.[3]

But the murder of elderly ladies (moral questions aside) would not always provide a solution, for the control of anyone's literary remains may be passed on indefinitely. Robert T. Lincoln conducted a long running battle with a series of biographers who wanted to use his father's papers. As early as April 1865, he rebuffed the advances of Charles Eliot Norton, and sixty years later he refused the appeals of Senator Beveridge. In between he denied the papers to Ward Hill Lamon, Ida M. Tarbell, Lord Charnwood, William E. Barton, and many others. He made a single exception in the case of his father's trusted secretaries, John Hay and John G. Nicolay, but then he exercised what Hay called "plenary blue pencil powers" over their work, altering sections that displeased him even when they were not in the remotest way based on the Lincoln papers. Thus, when Nicolay and Hay wrote of Lincoln's father:

> . . . Thomas, to whom were reserved the honors of an illustrious paternity, *appears never to have done anything else especially deserving of mention. He was an idle, roving, inefficient, good natured man, as the son of a widow is apt to be according to the Spanish proverb. He had no vices so far as we can learn but he also had no virtues to speak of. He* learned the trade of a carpenter *but accomplished little of it.* He was an easy going person . . .

[3] When White had been collecting materials for his lives of Woodrow Wilson and Calvin Coolidge, both Mrs. Wilson and Mrs. Coolidge had urged people not to give him any information.

it was at Robert T. Lincoln's behest that all the italicized portions were removed before publication. For some reason he took an especially strong dislike to Albert J. Beveridge. (Perhaps it was Beveridge's threat to resort to "dynamite, or chloroform, soothing syrup, or quinine, cocaine, or T.N.T." to get into the papers.) When he finally agreed to deposit the Lincoln manuscripts at the Library of Congress, he is supposed on good authority to have consulted actuaries as to Beveridge's life expectancy, and then to have attached a condition closing the papers for twenty-one years after his own death. Not until 1947 were they finally made available to Lincoln students.

The case of Robert T. Lincoln is, alas, in no way exceptional. There exist in the United States today manuscript papers of long-dead notables over which now-remote descendants still stand guard. Only within the course of the present decade, for example, have the descendants of John Adams, second President of the United States, who departed this earth on July 4, 1826, allowed properly qualified persons to see and use the Adams papers.

The biographer who "runs into a widow" should conduct himself with tact, and should recognize also the genuine and quite reasonable feelings of individuals who wish to see full justice done to loved ones and who desire to protect the privacy of persons still living. Robert T. Lincoln's attitude becomes more understandable when it is remembered that (on very flimsy evidence) his father's law partner had given currency in print to the theory that the Great Emancipator was a bastard. On the other hand, once those who control papers realize that an author is only after the truth and has no malicious intent, they should allow him full freedom to use the papers as he sees fit. If

VII. *Choosing a Subject* [173

only our "widows" would consult the record, they would see that their own interests are served by openhandedness in these matters. The release of the Adams papers has already produced a biography greatly enhancing the reputation of John Quincy Adams—and incidentally has won for its author, Samuel Flagg Bemis, a Pulitzer prize. When Henry F. Pringle was working on his *Theodore Roosevelt*, he was denied access to Roosevelt's papers for the important period after the Presidency. When he wrote his life of William Howard Taft, he worked without restriction. It is no mere coincidence that the *Taft* is both sounder historically and better balanced and more sympathetic as a portrait than the *Roosevelt*.

Thomas Jefferson's family understood the value of turning a biographer loose without any impediments. When Jefferson's grandchildren were approached by Henry S. Randall they adopted, in Randall's words, the "profoundly sensible idea that their grandfather would 'pass muster' with posterity *exactly as he was;* that exaggeration would both injure and discredit the whole picture." This despite the fact that Randall was a man of fierce integrity, determined to throw "all milk and water noncommittalism to the winds!" in his search for truth. "I would rather be a dog and bay the moon," Randall wrote a friend, "than write in that sickly, silly, adulatory, mutual-admiration-society, mutual scratch-back, tickle-me-Billy-&-I'll-tickle-you-Billy spirit in which most of our American biographies have been written." Randall's biography stood for nearly a century as the "definitive" account of Jefferson chiefly because he had the unrestricted use of the papers.

The attitude of the Borden Company illustrates the biographer's ideal of the perfect executor. When Joe B. Frantz wrote his life of Gail Borden, founder of the corporation, he was given access to all the pertinent information in the company's files. After finishing his book, he suggested that a Borden official might want to check the manuscript for errors. "Dear Joe," the official replied: "It's your reputation and we know you'll do your best to avoid mistakes. Besides, if someone charges you with being influenced by the Company in what you have written, I want to be able to say that no one in the Company saw a word of it until it was in type, and could not possibly have dictated to you."

When free access to the sources cannot be obtained, the biographer must arrive at a clear understanding (in writing if possible) as to what kind of restrictions are to be imposed. Protection of an estate against the publication of libelous material, for instance, is perfectly reasonable. A stricture against quoting material embarrassing to persons still living may also be acceptable, provided there is agreement as to the meaning of "embarrassing." If still tighter clamps are applied, the biographer must balance the advantages of obtaining new material against the dangers inherent in publishing only part of any record. In all cases he ought to make clear in his finished work exactly what restrictions he operated under. It should be kept in mind, however, that material which cannot be quoted may often be paraphrased with impunity, and that once a fact is discovered in an unreproducible manuscript it can often be located elsewhere in an unrestricted source.

The practical question of the great cost of research also demands considerable thought. A century ago, James Parton, the first American who tried to make a living by writing biographies, complained of this problem: "To make a real and vivid biography . . . require[s] an amount and minuteness of investigation which could never be repaid in money, nor done without money." He also said: "An industrious writer, by the legitimate exercise of his calling—that is, never writing advertisements or trash for the sake of pay—can just exist, no more. . . . The best way is to make a fortune first and write afterwards." Parton's way out, in an age when source materials were hard to come by and widely scattered, was to expend a large proportion of his energies producing potboilers and articles of ephemeral interest, buying time with this dull and exhausting work for the writing of his still-useful lives of Jackson, Jefferson, Franklin, Aaron Burr, and Voltaire, books that were "best-sellers" in their day.

Nowadays, although the development of great depositories like the Library of Congress and the perfection of photoduplication devices have eliminated much of the need for extensive traveling, the cost of writing biography is still very great compared with the return that can reasonably be expected from royalties. Some biographers solve the problem by attaching themselves to colleges or universities, and foundations have been liberal in supplying funds for worth-while projects,[4] but the problem still remains for many. Some of the most important biographical studies cannot be expected to pay their own ways, which in part accounts for the deluge of works about popular heroes and villains.

All these matters should be considered by the prospective writer before he becomes deeply involved in any char-

[4] The monumental biographies of Washington and Jefferson by, respectively, Douglas Southall Freeman and Dumas Malone, for example, were made possible by grants from the Carnegie and Rockefeller foundations. In a typical year (1953), the Guggenheim Foundation supplied funds for more than a dozen biographical projects.

acter. For only if he has a subject that interests him, that will be a useful contribution to knowledge, that is within his powers—only if he knows what he is trying to do, what obstacles he must overcome, what resources he must command—can he produce a result that will represent his best ability.

CHAPTER VIII

The Materials of Biography

Once a writer has chosen his subject, he should locate the sources of information he is to tap. In their broadest scope the materials of a biography include any information relating to the life of the subject or to the environment in which he lived. But of more practical import is the question: What are the *particular* sources most useful to the biographer as distinct from the historian?

Most valuable are the subject's own writings, for of course no one else can know as much about him as he himself knew. Yet personal documents must be used with care and subjected to special tests, for they vary greatly both in candor and in biographical worthiness.

The types of personal documents are as follows: 1) *Autobiographies.* Obviously, if the hero has told his own story, he has done later writers a great service, for he has interpreted himself. 2) *Journals and diaries.* A day-by-day record of a man's life, whether merely perfunctory and concerned with externals or profoundly introspective, is invaluable. 3) *Letters.* Many subjects do not write their own histories, either formally in an autobiography or indirectly in a diary. All men, however, write letters, and remarkably large numbers of these are preserved. Here again, the material varies tremendously from person to person. What a difference between Theodore Roosevelt's impetuous volubility and Calvin Coolidge's restrained taciturnity! A few days after the assassination of McKinley had elevated Roosevelt to the Presidency, he wrote his close friend Henry Cabot Lodge: "I must just send you a line . . . for naturally you have been in my thoughts almost every hour of the last fortnight. It is a dreadful thing to come into the Presidency this way; but it would be a far worse thing to be morbid about it. Here is the task, and I have got to do it to the best of my ability." When Harding's sudden death elevated Coolidge to the Presidency, "Silent Cal" wrote one of his friends: "Dear George—I know you are thinking of me. I am all right." But in every case a man's letters tell a great deal about his life—either directly or indirectly. 4) *Published works, creative and otherwise.* Most persons important enough to be immortalized in a biography have left published records of one kind or another. Literary figures, for instance, cannot be considered aside from their works, and conversely, these works tell the biographer a great deal about the men who wielded the pen. Political leaders at least make speeches if they do not write books, and even the most non-literary subjects have usually given interviews to newspapers or found their ways into print in some other manner. In addition, this class of material should include other artistic productions—the composer's

VIII. *The Materials of Biography* [179

music, the artist's paintings, the buildings designed by the architect. 5) *Other personal remains.* Here there is room for infinite variety. Scrapbooks, collections of all kinds, portraits and photographs, old clothing—anything which the subject owned or used or influenced has a potential value for his biographer.

Personal material of this kind must be handled with understanding and insight. A nineteenth-century cynic once said that a biographer wishes instinctively to conceal his ignorance, whereas a man who writes about himself has a "secret desire" to "conceal his knowledge." Perhaps the cynic exaggerated, but no matter how honest the writer, complete candor is rare in personal documents. W. Somerset Maugham, whose own autobiography, *The Summing Up*, is surely one of the most objective self-evaluations in English, has issued this warning:

> No one can tell the whole truth about himself. It is not only vanity that has prevented those who have tried to reveal themselves to the whole world from telling the truth; it is direction of interest; their disappointment with themselves, their surprise that they can do things that seem to them abnormal, make them place too great an emphasis on occurrences that are more common than they suppose. Rousseau in the course of his "Confessions" narrates incidents that have profoundly shocked the sensibility of mankind. By describing them so frankly he falsified his values and gave them in his book a greater importance than they had in his life. There were events among a multitude of others, virtuous or at least neutral, that he omitted because they were too ordinary to seem worth recording.

Others have made the same point. The autobiographer, according to Herbert Spencer, "is obliged to omit from his narrative the commonplace of daily life and to limit himself almost exclusively to salient events, actions and traits. . . . But by leaving out the humdrum part of the life, forming that immensely larger part which it has in common with other lives, and by setting forth only the striking things, he produces the impression that it differed from other lives more than it really did. This defect is inevitable." If the best-intentioned writers of personal documents leave distorted or incomplete records, those who wish to use these materials must ask many searching questions as they work.

Why was this autobiography written? To whom was this letter addressed? How introspective is this novel? A few general warnings about personal material may be offered before examining the specific problems of each type. First the biographer must beware of purposeful deception. Just as the forged document is a constant danger to the historian, so the deliberately misleading personal document, though it may be "authentic" in the sense that it meets the normal standards set by historians, can throw the biographer off the track in his search for truth. The letter-writer who was a liar, the diarist consciously writing for posterity—such are the forms this danger takes.

Still greater is the threat of the *unconsciously* deceptive personal document. Everyone is familiar with the nature of rationalization and other forms of self-delusion. Theodore Roosevelt's numerous "posterity letters" written after various important incidents in his career to specific persons but really for history, are seemingly frank and factual accounts, and they probably were conceived with honest intent, but they are filled with distortions of the truth. When Roosevelt wrote, after the death of John Hay, that Hay "was not a great Secretary of State . . . his usefulness to me was almost exclusively the usefulness of a fine figurehead," it was

VIII. The Materials of Biography

easy enough for Hay's biographer to disprove his statement by reference to a host of generally known facts. But on another occasion, when T.R. was embroiled in a controversy with railroadman E. H. Harriman, he released a "posterity letter" which, by telling less than the entire story, created a false impression that could only be straightened out by a study of his private papers many years later. Psychologists have made progress in clarifying the forms of self-deception, and suspicious statements can be checked against other sources, but the danger is constant.

A similar problem arises from the fact that much of the value of personal evidence lies in its subjective nature. We learn from an autobiography something of a person's feelings, whom he liked and disliked, and why. But the best of us are pitifully inadequate at introspection; how little we really understand of why we act as we do! The diarist who "explains" his actions may be far from the truth. But how can the biographer check up on him?

The same difficulty results from the weakness of human memory. Memory, as the existentialist philosopher Nikolai Berdyaev once said, is a dynamic process. "Remembrance of the past," he wrote in *Dream and Reality*, "can never be a passive attitude; it cannot be a mere objective record of past events. . . . Memory needs be active: it is characterized by individual emphasis, partiality and, therefore, prejudice. Memory is selective. . . ." In his life of Goethe, George Henry Lewes noted that the famous *Dichtung und Wahrheit* was often a most misleading source, not so much because of its factual errors as because of its "inaccuracy of tone." In reporting on his early life, Goethe unconsciously distorted the truth. "The pictures of youthful follies and youthful passions come softened through the distant avenue of years," Lewes wrote. "The turbulence of a youth of genius is not indeed quite forgotten, but it is hinted with stately reserve. Jupiter serenely enthroned upon Olympus forgets that he was once a rebel with the Titans." Letters and other contemporary evidence enabled Lewes to correct the distortions of *Dichtung und Wahrheit,* but sometimes the corrective evidence does not exist.

The autobiographer writes of his childhood. Material of this type is usually beyond verification because there are seldom contemporary written records. Yet how many of anyone's childhood recollections are accurate? In the very area where the biographer is most dependent upon personal documents for facts, these documents tend to be weakest. However, memories of childhood are often very frank. As psychologist Edwin G. Boring once wrote: "You can be proud of your childhood or sorry for yourself as a child; in either case you are free to say what you think without ego-involvement because childhood is separated off from manhood. But when you get to your twenties, then the responsibility for the mature continuous individual comes in and you are constrained."

Finally, the biographer must be on guard against certain subsidiary factors. The mood of the letter-writer may influence what he says. The autobiographer, particularly if he is an experienced writer, may be affected by the sound of his own words and permit aesthetic considerations to distort his recollections. The biographer must be especially wary of aesthetic distortions when he attempts to draw autobiographical conclusions from novels. For years Melville's *Redburn* was used as a major source on the novelist's young manhood, for the superficial resemblances between the story and the known elements of his career were great.

VIII. *The Materials of Biography* [183

But the discovery of new evidence by W. H. Gilman destroyed the validity of what had seemed a plausible approach.

THE biographer, then, must tread with caution when he enters the potentially rich storehouse of personal materials. Each type of evidence, indeed each separate document, presents its special problems. Let us begin with *autobiography*.

The first question to ask is: Why did the subject compose this story of his life? Did he write like the pain-racked Ulysses S. Grant, grim, determined, dying of cancer, chiefly to provide for his family? Or was he, like Lincoln in 1860, writing to provide ammunition for a political biographer in a Presidential campaign? Was the autobiography written in bitter old age to explain away failure, or, as in the case of Andrew Carnegie, at the peak of a career to serve as a guide for ambitious youths? Was it produced for a propagandistic end, either worthy, like Clifford Beer's *A Mind That Found Itself*, or evil, like Hitler's notorious *Mein Kampf*? Or was it a venture in happy reminiscence of a time long past, like Carl Sandburg's *Always the Young Strangers*? Most autobiographies have been composed with publication in mind, but some, like Martin Van Buren's engagingly frank account of his career, written in retirement while "at peace with all the world," have been designed only for family eyes, and not brought to light until long after the writer's death. Others, though always intended for publication, have been, like Henry Adams's *Education*, deliberately concealed from the public until after the author's death. All such variations in motive ought to be kept in mind in using an autobiography.

Once the question of motive has been settled, autobiographies should be tested for reliability. A general reading will tell a great deal. Does the story hang together? Is the use of detail precise and assured or vague and doubtful? Is the author plainly attempting to justify himself, or is he at least trying to be fair and candid? Does he tend to magnify his own exploits and deprecate his foes, or is he plagued by a false modesty that gives too much credit to others and seems in effect to say: "See how generous, how magnanimous am I!" It is, as the poet Abraham Cowley noted, "a hard and nice subject for a man to write of himself; it grates on his own heart to say anything of disparagement, and the reader's ears to hear anything of praise from him." The perceptive reader can learn a great deal from the way an autobiographer treats this "hard and nice" problem.

On a less intuitive level there are other questions to ask. Does the writer supply evidence other than his own memory (such as letters, and references to books, records, newspapers, and other documents) to buttress his statements? Is he frank to admit that there are some things he can no longer remember, is uncertain about, or does not feel free to discuss? The book which seems truthful by such general standards is likely to be trustworthy in detail as well.

Whenever possible, the biographer should check autobiographical material against other sources, as Lewes did when studying Goethe. Much of the most interesting evidence will be beyond verification, but if the things he can check are accurate, the chances are good that the other material is also accurate. If investigation discloses the writer to have been careless, forgetful, misleading, or self-deceiving, all unverifiable material must be viewed with the greatest suspicion.

Even in the most conscientiously "truthful" autobiography, the biographer must distinguish between different types of statements. This problem was carefully thought out by Douglas Southall Freeman. In writing his life of Lee, Freeman had to deal with many supposed quotations of the General's conversations which he found in the autobiographical writings of contemporaries. The temptation to use these quotations freely was great; they would give his book "an atmosphere of reality." But they also presented "possibilities of misinterpretation," for how was one to test their accuracy? The principles Freeman applied in deciding when a quotation could be presumed accurate were these: (1) The shorter the elapsed time between the event and the writing, the more reliable the quotation was likely to be. (2) The less frequently the writer had talked to Lee, the better the chance that he would remember Lee's words as they were actually spoken. (3) Conversations dealing with matters of small import (if reported upon at all) would be reported correctly more often than those which concerned moments of great "historic" significance. (4) The recollections of professional lecturers and story-tellers must be viewed with special suspicion.

These special rules devised for a special situation can be applied with modifications to the evaluation of most autobiographical writings. More generally, one might add: When the writer speaks out of his own experience he is more to be trusted than when he describes what he has learned at second hand. Yet when he deals with matters closest to his heart he may lose the objectivity with which he views less personal matters.

Many of these points can be illustrated by considering a particular autobiography, Henry Cabot Lodge's *Early Memories*. Why was this book written? Lodge himself gives a simple explanation. All of us autobiographers, he says, "whatever ingenious phrases we may employ," write for our own satisfaction. "I do it because it gives me pleasure." A little investigation indicates that this was probably the truth, for no more complicated motive is apparent. Monetary considerations cannot be completely discarded, for this story was serialized in a popular magazine and it sold well in book form, but since Lodge was a wealthy man to begin with, the financial motive can be minimized. In the same way, although Lodge was a politician and an intense partisan, there can be no question of political motivation, because he kept nearly all mention of his career and of politics out of his pages. He could not have benefited (or been harmed) by the autobiography except in the very remote sense that readers of his reminiscences might be more inclined to remember his name in future visits to the polls.

The book, then, passes its first test fairly well: no ulterior motive for publication can be discovered. It also seems reasonably accurate as to facts. Lodge's account of his family history checks well with genealogical information; he cites reputable sources for many of his statements about New England affairs and for the characters of many of the persons he describes; he quotes occasionally from family letters, and in dealing with later events, from his own journal. He even writes: "I was born in Boston, *as I have been credibly informed,* on May 12 . . . 1850."

But in many places, critical appraisal leads to doubts. In relating his experiences as an undergraduate at Harvard he deplores the great change wrought in the college by

VIII. *The Materials of Biography* [187

the introduction of the elective system under President Charles W. Eliot in 1869. Superficially his statements seem to make sense. He was an eyewitness, for he was at Harvard for two years before Eliot and for two more under the new regime. The elective system *did* produce profound changes at Harvard.

But Lodge's criticism (chiefly that it made it easy for a lazy boy, such as he claimed to have been himself, to avoid difficult courses and graduate "with as little effort as possible") must be approached with caution. First of all, at the time that he wrote *Early Memories* he and Eliot were on bad terms, estranged by a long series of political differences. Secondly, the passage of time itself indicates a possible blurring of memory. Finally, a little investigation brings out the fact that the elective system was introduced by Eliot only gradually, and was not really in effect until several years after Lodge's graduation. The courses Lodge took were pretty generally those he would have taken under the old system had Eliot never appeared.

Lodge read back into his college days later developments of which he disapproved, a common phenomenon. His autobiographical account of this period is to this extent invalid. On the other hand, when he describes a particular college ceremony in which he played an important part, or when he says that he made a great hit in a certain student theatrical production, other evidence can be located which proves him correct. Even if there were no corroboratory sources, the general rule applies that the more specific the incident recalled, the more detailed the memory, the greater the likelihood of accuracy.

Even ideas and matters of opinion mentioned by an autobiographer can often be checked. At one point Lodge describes his adventures in Europe with a college friend named Simpson. He claims that Simpson had a profound effect upon his development, making him realize that "a life of unoccupied leisure" was not a worthy goal for a young man of wealth. Simpson convinced him that "the more fortunate a man was in his circumstances and conditions the heavier the responsibility which rested upon him," and, according to Lodge, that the well-to-do should devote at least part of their time to politics. Simpson proposed to work for "what he believed to be right and in behalf of the Republican party . . . in the principles of which he had entire faith."

Since all of this account is based upon Lodge's memory of unrecorded conversations, it may seem beyond verification, but this is not entirely so. That the two men were in Europe together is easily demonstrated. That Lodge did undergo a profound change in his general outlook toward life at just this time is also clear both from letters he wrote to his mother and from his subsequent actions. His later career and much of his writing indicate the depth of his belief in "service" as a duty of the rich. His stalwart Republicanism was certainly of the type which he attributed to his friend's influence. But in this case there is also conflicting evidence. When Lodge returned from Europe he plunged into work—but it was academic and literary work, not political. And when he did begin to dabble in public affairs it was as an Independent, a violent foe of the political regularity which he later espoused and which he implies he absorbed from Simpson. Thus, part of his account of the influence of Simpson is almost certainly accurate, and part is in error.

A recent biographer of Franklin D. Roosevelt has un-

VIII. *The Materials of Biography* [189

covered another good example of this type of problem. In the first volume of his autobiographical history of World War II, Winston Churchill mentions his first meeting with Franklin D. Roosevelt in London during the summer of 1918, claiming that he was "struck by [Roosevelt's] magnificent presence in all his youth and strength." This seems reliable enough, for it is easy to prove that the event did take place at that time. But further investigation discloses that in 1941 Churchill did not remember the meeting at all, and that Roosevelt had been quite irritated by that fact. Obviously, in his history of the war, Churchill was (belatedly) making amends for his lapse of memory.

Experience soon helps the writer to identify the autobiographical statements most likely to be incorrect or distorted. On the other hand it is true, as Anna Robeson Burr pointed out many years ago in her monumental study, *The Autobiography*, that minor factual errors do not reduce the value of a good autobiography as a picture of the writer's *personality*. "Contemplating human nature in an introspective mood, one must be prepared to find in self-study a certain looseness as to exterior matters," she warned. "The eye cannot look both in and out at the same time."

In some ways *diaries and journals* are more reliable than autobiographies. They are usually written much closer to the events they describe (though not always on the same day, as they are supposed to be), and are therefore much less likely to suffer from the evils of faulty recollection. They more often reflect a person's true reasons for his actions, being written without the perspective of time—without a knowledge of the "right" solution or attitude. Autobiographers are seldom candid about their mistakes, their foolish opinions, or their unsuccessful ventures, but diarists commit themselves to paper before they know they have erred. Although diaries occasionally are altered by their authors in later years, and usually lack the integration which any writer gives to his autobiography, although they often consist of little more than the externals of life, and frequently contain much that is dull and repetitious, they always reveal a great deal about their authors. Every close student of the form has reached this conclusion. "Diarists cannot help explaining themselves," says Sir Arthur Ponsonby, and William Matthews, editor of the comprehensive *British Diaries: An Annotated Bibliography*, has pointed out that even what a diarist omits can help to explain "the dominant views he has of himself." Furthermore, no matter how reserved he may be in recording his thoughts, the diarist is bound to reveal his standards of judgment in his comments on other people. Diaries also tell a great deal about the times of their authors. Bernard Berenson was hardly exaggerating when he wrote: "When I read Greville . . . I feel the same sensation of being in it, of touching history in the making, as when looking through a batch of morning papers." Much can be learned from the barest record, such as a "desk diary" outlining an executive's day-to-day appointments.

Diaries take different forms. Most of them contribute to both the historical and the psychological sides of life-writing. A self-revealing diary like Marie Bashkirtsev's *Journal of a Young Artist* still has a great deal to say about the externals of the author's life, while Washington's, "as devoid of introspection as a furniture catalog," discloses much of the man himself in the process of recording a host of routine facts. Or consider the anonymous *Diary of a Public Man*. Ever since its publication in 1879, historians

VIII. *The Materials of Biography* [191

have been scrutinizing this Civil War journal in an effort to determine who composed it. One student was able to list "eighteen points of personality" indicated in the diary which he proceeded to check off against possible authors. The problem has been complicated by the suggestion that the document is a hoax, and despite a number of ingenious hypotheses it has never been solved to the universal satisfaction of historians, but it illustrates the way in which a journal can be a key to its author's personality.

While it seems psychologically sound to say that every diary is kept with the idea that *someone* will eventually read it over, more often than not this "someone" is not defined in the diarist's mind. The biographer should try to determine, if he can, the intended audience for the journal he is using. Some journals are specifically directed at the edification of the writer's descendants or at posterity in general. But most are probably kept for self-reference later in life, or for an undetermined future reader, with a practical immediate objective (such as clarifying one's thoughts) serving as the actual incentive for composition.

The material in a diary should be checked against other evidence, but unless there is reason to suspect a deliberate hoax,[1] statements of fact need seldom be questioned. For instance, if Lodge had kept a diary as an undergraduate and recorded: "Today I registered for the fall semester's classes. Hooray! Thanks to the new system I have dropped Greek, Latin, and Mathematics and am taking only easy courses, for my one interest is to get through college with a minimum of effort," his unsupported word could hardly be challenged.

[1] Ponsonby describes the diary of a murderer who attempted to cover his tracks by writing of his horror and shock upon learning of the deaths of his victims!

On the other hand, the biographer must guard against even "factual" statements if the diarist is recording information second hand. Rebecca West, for example, was once told a fantastic story about Henry James by an English writer who had known him. James, according to his friend, was subject to periodic attacks of religious mania. During these attacks he was constantly attended by a faithful nurse, who protected him from situations in which his distressing condition might have been noticed. Since her informant—in her account Miss West did not mention his name—had been a trusted friend of James's, there seemed no reason to doubt his word. She therefore wrote out a detailed account of the incident in her diary, adding 'a solemn note to the effect that these pages were not to be published until it was perfectly certain that no persons whom they might offend still survived." Later, purely by accident, she again mentioned the subject to James's friend, who categorically denied both the story and the fact that he had told it to her! But for this chance second conversation, the story would have remained in the diary, and might someday have been accepted as fact by biographers of James.

Questions of feeling must always be handled cautiously, for self-deception is as easy for the keeper of a journal as for a man who writes an autobiography. "Don't start a diary," a friend warned George Creel when Creel became chairman of the Committee on Public Information during World War I. "When you sit down at night to record the events of the day, in spite of honest resolves you'll soon be giving yourself the best of it in every conversation and every incident, and before you know it you'll have a hell of a case of big head. When you feel the craving, my boy, yell for friends and have them tie your hands behind you." For

VIII. *The Materials of Biography* [193

certain temperaments this danger is very great. The diaries of Harold Ickes, for example, show Ickes in a very unfortunate light because he could not resist giving himself "the best of it." Some diarists who appear reticent or unimaginative may in fact merely be humbly conscious of the danger of self-deception. "I do not enter on interior matters," Gladstone recorded in his journal. "It is so easy to write, but to write honestly nearly impossible."

Diarists also tend to pass over routine matters and concentrate upon the high points of life, and, as Virginia Woolf once pointed out, a diarist easily falls into the habit of recording certain types of feelings and neglecting others, perhaps equally common, therefore leaving a record that is essentially unbalanced.

Unlike autobiographies, few diaries are ever published, and those which are have usually been severely pruned by an editor. Unless there is no alternative, the biographer ought never to be satisfied with an edited version, for, to quote again from the outstanding English authority, Sir Arthur Ponsonby: "No editor can be trusted not to spoil a diary." The small details which might bore a general audience in undiluted form, the large spaces devoted to "insignificant" matters, the material of "no historical importance" which a "good" editor will remove, are vital to the biographer. Leonard Woolf's edition of his wife's diary may well provide a clearer and more concise summary of her ideas as a writer than would be available in an unexpurgated edition, but there is a chance (in the words of one reviewer) "that the picture may be lopsided, or that the editor's sense of what made for continuity may have been over-arbitrary, or that pain-saving excisions sacrificed too much else to the interests of a pacific caution." Woolf, however, was well aware of the pitfalls of his path. Excisions, he said, tend to "produce spiritually what an Academy picture does materially, smoothing out the wrinkles, warts, frowns, and asperities." Many editors are less aware of the perils, or are simply determined to alter or delete passages for one reason or another. In writing his memoir on his years of service in Wilson's Cabinet, for example, Josephus Daniels inserted frequent "quotations" from his diary. Actually, Daniels's diary consists of nothing but occasional sketchy notes jotted down as aids to memory. In his memoir he expanded these, often at great length. That the result is hardly reliable is shown by the following absurdity: After describing a momentous Cabinet meeting at which the question of declaring war on Germany had been discussed, Daniels added: "I wrote in my Diary that night: 'If the American people possessed television and a dictaphone and could have seen and heard the President . . . they would have felt a confidence in him and an admiration which nothing else could have imparted.'" This, Daniels would have the reader believe, was written in 1917!

In this case the "editor" cannot be accused of an unworthy motive, and his alteration was so obvious that it could hardly escape notice. Most distortions are more serious. "Few editors and still fewer families," according to Howard K. Beale, "have the sense of historical values, the public spirit, and the confidence in their hero's fundamental soundness to resist the temptation to protect him or others by censoring passages." [2]

The biographer should not use a diary only for details,

[2] One of the "few" who have been able to resist these temptations is Professor Beale himself, whose *Diary of Edward Bates* is as close to perfect editing as is likely to be attained. His preface (pp. v–ix) is an admirable exposition of the problems of editing diaries.

VIII. *The Materials of Biography* [195

anecdotes, and other small bits of information. Exactly because it is written from day to day, piece by piece, without knowledge of the future, a diary forms an incomparable record of the *development* of a personality. This growth, however, is so gradual that it is often hard to see except in the long view. The biographer should seek the over-all picture at the same time that he delves into the details for specific information.

One weakness of both autobiographies and diaries is that they result from a person's self-conscious efforts to record his actions or thoughts for future use of some kind. This is much less true of *letters*, which, in the words of Thomas Jefferson, usually "form the only full and genuine journal" of a man's life.[3] Letters generally have the aim of transmitting information from one person to another for some *immediate* purpose. The letter-writer looks outward rather than inward, and is therefore less likely to traffic in rationalizations. This, of course, does not mean that letters tend to be written with greater frankness than more personal records. It means only that the letter-writer is not often (there are exceptions like Theodore Roosevelt) history-minded as he writes. He is concerned with the present even more than the diarist, and much more than the autobiographer. Letters show a man in one form of interaction with his contemporaries, and thus offer insights into his personality that more self-centered personal documents do not.

The evaluation of evidence found in letters is a complicated process involving knowledge of the recipient as well as of the writer. Naturally the letter a man writes to his wife differs from one he sends a business acquaintance, and

[3] According to Lord Morley, "the most satisfactory form of biography is a well edited correspondence."

a letter to his grandmother contrasts with one dispatched to a college friend. In general, the more familiar the relationship between author and recipient, the more useful the letter, but even this common-sense rule does not always hold. An English critic, Sir Robert Rait, has raised an interesting caveat in this connection: "A man, writing to an intimate friend, says things that he would not say in print, and these are not necessarily his real or secret thoughts; they are more often the whimsies of the moment." That this is *usually* true (as the writer states) may be doubted, but his point highlights the complexities involved in analyzing letters. The biographer must always stop to ask himself: "What exactly was the relationship between my subject and the person here addressed?"

The answer to this question has a double value. First, it helps the biographer to interpret the significance of the letter itself. This is its historical value. Secondly, it enlarges his understanding of the personality of the writer. This is its psychological value. The intricacies and rewards of the careful analysis of letters are well brought out in the correspondence between Oliver Wendell Holmes, Jr., and Harold Laski. Laski in particular revealed himself (how unintentionally!) in his letters to his aged friend. The flagrant flattery, the boastfulness, as well as the wit and intelligence of the writer are easily noticed. But as Fred Rodell discovered by a "careful cumulative reading," some of the traits of Laski's character exhibit themselves more subtly. Laski reported his "discovery" of one interesting book three separate times under entirely different circumstances, and his supposed purchase of the same rare edition of an obscure work in political science six times over a period of twelve years, together with many fictitious accounts of

VIII. *The Materials of Biography* [197

meetings with famous people. These letters rank Laski, in Rodell's words, "as no less than the Baron Munchausen of the twentieth century."

In his life of Freud, Ernest Jones provides another illustration of the way in which letters can be used by a thoughtful biographer. He discusses Freud's letters to himself, Karl Abraham, and Sandor Ferenczi. "Freud conducted a regular and extensive correspondence for many years with those of us who were not in Vienna," Jones writes. "On reading it all through (several times!) one is struck by several features. One is that Freud did not often mention the other friends in his letters; it is as if each relationship was distinct and personal. . . . The contents of the letters also differ much more than one might have expected. Even the scientific points he would discuss read differently in the various sets." Jones goes on to compare these letters with Freud's correspondence in an earlier period of his life, and notes that there is a great difference. The earlier letters indicate that Freud wrote them primarily to relieve his own "inner tensions," whereas the later cnes show clearly that "he was primarily thinking . . . of how he could best help his friends." Insights like these do not often come easily, but they are worth searching for.

The biographer who has large masses of correspondence to examine will soon learn that certain kinds of letters are more valuable than others. In this modern age a handwritten letter is usually more significant than a typed one, at least as a source of personal material. And as the Holmes-Laski correspondence shows, a series of letters to one person is generally more useful than an equal number to scattered recipients. Many letters are merely routine and can be put aside with a casual glance, but others are worthy of line-by-line perusal and extensive quotation. It is also true that the biographical significance of a subject's correspondence varies with the individual. Some persons are frank and open in expounding their feelings and ideas. Thomas Jefferson is a good example of this type. Woodrow Wilson, on the other hand, is an example of a letter-writer who, except when writing to his closest friends, remains reserved and impersonal. His letters, in contrast to his public speeches, are generally rather dull.

Letters, like other personal documents, can be misleading. They are especially dangerous when used individually or in small numbers. Letter-writers are subject to changes of mood, which will be reflected in their correspondence. A morose statement, if taken by itself, may create an incorrect impression, for it may reflect only a temporary feeling of despair. André Maurois offered a good example of this point in his *Aspects of Biography*. He quoted two letters written by Alfred de Musset. The first, to his paramour, George Sand, runs: "Posterity will recall our names as those of such immortal lovers as have nothing in the world but each other, such lovers as Romeo and Juliet, or Héloïse and Abélard." The second, written at about the same time to a friend, says: "While I was composing my poems, she was scribbling over reams of paper. . . . This tête-à-tête every day with a woman older than myself, a face growing always more and more serious in front of me—all this revolted the spirit of youth within me and filled me with a bitter regret for my former liberty." As Maurois remarked: "In the volatile personality of a Byron or a Musset, such impressions are, no doubt, perfectly sincere and illustrate the varying moods of the men themselves." This illustrates one reason

VIII. *The Materials of Biography* [199

why a *series* of letters written over a considerable span of time is of special importance to a biographer.

However, too many letters can be as bad as too few. Indeed in our own day the general significance of letters to the biographer is on the decline—the victim of overproduction. The biographer who has dealt with people whose lives span the late nineteenth century hails the perfection of the typewriter as a great blessing. Somewhere in the nineties, the great change appears. Away with the illegible script, the cramped and blotted handwriting of earlier periods! Welcome to the trim printed page—margins neat and even! But technology has depersonalized letter writing along with everything else. It has imposed a third person between the writer and the reader, for no matter how "confidential" a secretary may be, the situation is no longer the same as when the writer took pen in hand and scratched out his intimate thoughts, sure that they would be read by the intended reader alone. The typed letter is seldom really personal, however boldly PERSONAL may be printed across its face, and the busy politician, writer, or businessman has become a slave to his stenographer and his Dictaphone.

Aside from the restrictions imposed by the presence of a third person, the typed letter is usually subjected to reexamination between the time it is dictated and the time it is signed. Statements made impetuously can be reconsidered, then modified or amended, if not destroyed. Furthermore, the typewriter has increased the volume of mail tremendously. A busy executive can dictate letters many times as rapidly as he could pen them himself. He therefore "writes" more, and conversely he receives more letters requiring replies. Soon he becomes bogged down in a morass of unanswered mail. His solutions are the form letter, the mimeographed reply, and the "ghostwritten" letter prepared by a secretary and perhaps glanced over quickly by the "writer" as he splashes his signature across the bottom. When one considers that during one session of Congress, Senator Lehman of New York received some 127,000 letters in a period of six months and dispatched at least that many himself, it becomes clear that the chances of the venerable Senator's having had very much to do with any particular letter are infinitesimal. Things have reached the point where a busy Congressman cannot be approached *directly* by mail. No letter reaches his eye until it has been read by someone else.

The fantastic bulk of the papers of recent Presidents, increasing from Theodore Roosevelt, who left some 100,000 of his own letters, plus an uncounted number of other documents, to Franklin Roosevelt, whose papers *weigh* about forty *tons*, makes the biographer's traditional methods of perusing letters increasingly futile. When the excitable Mr. Truman occasionally seized a pen and dashed off a note to a Congressman, the item immediately assumed a greater importance for his future biographers than hundreds of typed dispatches in the Truman papers. This problem of bulk reaches an extreme in the case of politicians, but is only somewhat less serious for biographers of businessmen, authors, and other famous men.[4]

Another technological reason for the declining importance of letters in biography has been the general speed-up in transportation and communication. The trend in this direction was noticed as early as 1892 by George Saints-

[4] As Leon Edel has said "The contemporary biographer is forced, by the mere dead weight of paper, by the mountains of letters and journals and newspapers, to melt his materials or be smothered by them."

VIII. *The Materials of Biography* [201

bury, who wrote: "It is quite possible that the materials for biography are not so promising as they used to be. . . . There are great temptations not to write letters. Telegrams, post-cards, correspondence-cards, letter-cards—all of these things the truly good and wise detest and execrate; it is not so certain that they abstain from them." In 1913 G. R. Agassiz remarked in editing his father Alexander Agassiz's letters that "no longer . . . do we write the leisurely and carefully penned epistles of our forefathers."

Nowadays, the telephone is the bane of the biographer. In the past, when a busy man wished to communicate with someone about an important matter, a letter was his only practical means, even if the object of his thoughts lived only a few miles away. Now the spin of a dial instantly connects any two points on the globe. "The telephone," one commentator notes, "is proving the death of good political biography. Where the statesmen of a lifetime ago wrote notes to each other, which were carried round by messenger and preserved by the recipient, there is no record of a telephone call." Furthermore the airplane has made it possible for persons residing far apart to engage in face-to-face conversation with relative ease. Thus, the limited means of expression offered by the letter, together with its lack of privacy in the age of the secretary and the inevitable delays that it involves, have largely reduced letter-writing to the mechanical exchange of unimportant information, usually between people who are strangers to each other.

Some history-minded individuals, like former Secretary of the Treasury Morgenthau, aware of the declining importance of the letter, have had their telephone conversations recorded and included in vast "diaries." From the biographical viewpoint, this is a great help, but it is expensive, and few important people have been willing to face the sacrifice of privacy which it entails.[5]

Yet for what is still the major part of human history, the letter remains a most vital source. Many biographers, however, see only one side of the picture; they are interested in their hero's letters, but pay little heed to the replies these evoke. As Ernest Newman has said in criticizing the many biographers of Richard Wagner: "A man's letters . . . are at best only the equivalent of our listening to one end of a telephone conversation. The rule that no man is to be accepted as judge of his own cause, and, indeed, not always as the advocate in it, is blandly forgotten by . . . musical biographers."

Actually the "in" letters are almost as important to the biographer as the "out." One learns a great deal about a person from the way others handle him, and the way he responds to different approaches. Do flattery and subservience produce a favorable reaction in the subject? Do threats influence him more than reasoned argument? The character of each writer will affect his replies, but from a large group of letters certain generalizations can usually be made.

The importance to the biographer of any man's published works is self-evident. Of course the biographer must read the statesman's speeches, the novels or short stories of the writer of fiction, the essayist's criticism. Essentially these

[5] Frank Freidel, whose work on Franklin Roosevelt has brought him in contact with all the problems of contemporary biography, argues that technological improvements in communication rather than the increase in the volume of correspondence have been his chief stumbling block. "The enemies of the person working on fairly recent history are the telephone and the conference at which no minutes were kept. I don't think bulk should give anyone much cause to be balked."

VIII. *The Materials of Biography* [203

works are the *raison d'être* of the biography, the cause of the subject's present-day significance. While it is true that M. Maurois managed to write Ariel without paying much attention to Shelley's poetry, the conventional biographer would never consider such an approach.

But there is an additional importance to the works of the subject. Careful study of this evidence can often provide a great deal of personal material. The swallowing whole of so-called "autobiographical" novels is, as has been said, extremely dangerous, for novelists, being creative individuals, have a way of subtly altering the past in such works without destroying the appearance of reality. Fine theories can be worked up from such evidence, but they are often false. "Why are people not more careful in deducing biographical and semi-biographical facts from an author's books?" Thomas Hardy once asked a visitor. "Mr. Hedgcock is continually drawing on the novels for descriptions of my character. His dissection would not be in good taste while I am alive, even if it were true. But it is based chiefly on characters and incidents in the novels that are pure invention."

Yet who would deny the importance of *Look Homeward, Angel* to the biographers of Thomas Wolfe? Only a bold critic would quarrel with Bernard DeVoto's analysis of the autobiographical importance of the later writings of Mark Twain. It is true, as Chateaubriand once said, that great writers "put their history into their work," and "paint nothing so well as their own hearts." That this "history" is often subtly disguised does not mean that it is not worth searching for.

Non-fictional writings can be an even better source of personal information. The subject may have made speeches containing reminiscent remarks ("When I was a boy . . ."). The kind of examples he uses to illustrate his points may aid in understanding his background. An individual's other personal remains, together with the records of his physical appearance, can also tell a great deal about his life. His hobbies, his taste in clothes, furniture, and books, his scrapbooks, and his "doodlings" often provide helpful insights. As to appearance, one need not go so far as Emil Ludwig, who based his entire conception of Napoleon upon a study of one of the Emperor's portraits, but photographs and paintings can certainly be of some use in interpreting personality. "The physical traits of man," writes Somerset Maugham, "influence his character and contrariwise his character is expressed, at least in the rough, in his appearance. You cannot make a tall man short and otherwise keep him the same. A man's height gives him a different outlook on his environment and so changes his character." As Gordon Allport has said, these "many-sided expressions of the single personality" can be "made to contribute to a fully rounded study of the individual." Psychologists have scarcely begun to control this kind of observation to a point at which it can be employed as an objective measure, but as an intuitive guide its usefulness is great.

Frequently the biographer also profits from visiting the haunts of his subject. Military men have long followed the practice of walking over the ground where great battles were fought, observing the configuration of the terrain first hand, weighing the decisions of past generals against their own hindsight *on the spot*, and thus gaining an understanding that no photograph or topographical map can provide. By retracing his man's steps through life a biographer can

VIII. *The Materials of Biography* [205

accomplish the same result. Perhaps the most successful venture of this type was Samuel E. Morison's Caribbean wanderings in the ancient wake of Christopher Columbus, which added so much to his brilliant descriptions in *Admiral of the Ocean Sea*.

Logically, after the personal material of the subject, the records left by other members of his family ought to be of greatest importance to the biographer. Whether they are or not depends upon many factors. The most common record of this type is the memoir written by a member of the family about a recently departed loved one. As has already been pointed out, with a few exceptions these works are extremely partisan, prone to outrageous sentiment, and therefore most untrustworthy.[6] Yet they always contain some useful material. Personal details, anecdotes, characterizations of contemporaries, and similar information can be syphoned off from the mass of eulogy. What the perceptive biographer objects to most in these works is not their biases, which though annoying are obvious enough, but what they could say and do not.

Rarer but more rewarding are the autobiographies of family members. Few are as fine or as frank as Eleanor Roosevelt's two volumes or contain as much material on one's subject as these books do on F.D.R. More usual are books like Mrs. William Howard Taft's *Recollections of a Full Life* and Edith Bolling Wilson's *My Memoir*. In any case, since the wife of a famous man is more concerned with herself than with her dear husband, present or de-

---

[6] One should not ignore, however, those biographical curiosities in which a wife or other close relative writes an unfriendly life of the hero. Mrs. Bernarr Macfadden's life of her vegetarian, physical-culture-faddist husband is a good example of the type.

parted, she is more likely to present a balanced picture of him in her own life story than is usual in a memoir about him.

Still more useful is a diary kept by a wife or other close relative. Husband-and-wife letters are not very common, for the average family spends most of its time together. The letters of John and Abigail Adams are perhaps the best-known collection,[7] though those of military men away at the wars (the letters between General "Ben" Butler and his wife during the Civil War for example) are more typical. A wife's correspondence with other individuals may also be valuable—for the details of the family's goings and comings if for nothing else.

In addition to making full use of all family personal documents, the biographer should seek out the opinions of other contemporaries. Except for biographies of persons recently dead (where interviewing is possible), this involves the use of autobiographies, memoirs, recollections, published letters, newspaper and magazine files, and other printed sources. Besides the general rules for judging historical evidence, one should also pay special attention to the relationship between the writer and the subject, for it will inevitably influence the opinion expressed.

The character and philosophy of the writer are also important. Many nineteenth-century reminiscences, for example, are marred by an overenthusiastic adherence to the principle: *de mortuis nil nisi bonum.* "In the presence of the great reconciler, Death," wrote George Frisbie Hoar in a typical autobiography of this period, "ordinary human

---

[7] These letters, edited by Charles Francis Adams, must be used with great caution, for his "glacial discretion" led him to eliminate anything that might offend "even the descendants of the contemporaries of John Adams."

VIII. *The Materials of Biography* [207

contentions and angers should be hushed." It was this sort of attitude which Voltaire was spoofing when he wrote: "I have just been informed that Monsieur Blank is dead. He was a sturdy patriot, a gifted writer, a loyal friend, and an affectionate husband and father—provided he is dead." On the other hand, spiteful comments by a man's enemies have been common in all periods of history.

The assessment which a biographer makes of contemporary opinions about his subject is a good test of his own integrity and judgment, for few men of any historical importance have failed to evoke a whole range of characterizations from saintliness to devilishness. "Wait till you lose by death some eminent friend," Van Wyck Brooks once wrote, "and then go about in circles he frequented and try to piece together the legend of his life. You will find that he survives . . . both as a sentimentalist and a cynic, a crimson revolutionist and a sky-high tory, a simpleton, a snob and a bourgeois, a man of bold ideas and a teacher's pet."

Was Henry Cabot Lodge "a skillful boss, a compromiser on moral questions, and a promoter of suspicion and distrust between the United States and Great Britain," as President Eliot of Harvard pictured him? Or was he "the most admirable public man . . . in our national Senate," which was the view of Professor Barrett Wendell of the same institution? The biographer ought to evaluate these opinions in the light of the facts that Eliot was a lifelong antagonist of the Senator from Massachusetts, Wendell a close friend. Yet he should also make use of *both* statements, for each man knew Lodge well, and their views add to the total picture.

The more controversial or unusual the subject, the more

likely that the biographer will discover all kinds of conflicting statements about him. Consider the difficulties of a recent biographer of William Beckford, an eccentric English writer who produced a number of interesting novels and travel books while dissipating an income of £100,000 a year. Beckford's biographer had to deal with such diverse opinions as these:

> "A courteous gentleman . . ."
> "One of the vilest men of his time . . ."
> ". . . vraiment un sujet pour un moraliste. Des extravagances tenant plus au don quichottisme qu'à la dépravation, l'ont perdu sans retour. . . ."
> "The man of the greatest taste."

Add to these Beckford's own comment: "Not an animal comprehends me," and one can appreciate the biographer's problem.

Reminiscences are also suspect for the temptations they offer in the form of anecdotes and directly quoted dialogue. Few biographers, even the most conservative, have been able to resist these temptations entirely. Writers who would never for a moment make up a story or put words into their subjects' mouths have blithely copied (naturally with the proper citation of sources) statements which almost certainly are "reconstructions" made by memoirists with very weak scruples. In the same manner, newspaper accounts (and everyone knows how garbled a newspaper story can be) are often taken for more than they are really worth, purely in the interest of a good story or a lively quotation.

The same applies to personal interviews. The biographer who can talk to persons who knew his subject taps a valuable source, but one easily misused. Too often biographers publish statements purported to be direct quotations from the lips of their subjects which actually consist of the writer's memory of what a person who knew his subject told him that his subject had said twenty years before.

Catherine Drinker Bowen, who made wide use of interviews in gathering material for her life of Oliver Wendell Holmes, Jr., once said that it is poor policy to take notes during an interview. "Private persons are scared by it and even veterans of public life sometimes retreat at the sight." After discussing Holmes with Justice Brandeis in his Washington apartment, Mrs. Bowen rushed to Union Station and wrote up her notes in the waiting-room before boarding her train, and she trusted her memory enough to include in quotation marks what was said. That the *sense* of her conversation could be preserved in this manner is possible, but it is less than likely that the words which appear in quotation marks on the printed page were actually the ones spoken by Brandeis, and it is highly doubtful that the quotations attributed to Holmes were accurate. Frank Freidel, a more restrained biographer than Mrs. Bowen, explains his interviewing procedure as follows:

> I try to follow a common sense criterion. . . . If the statement is at all elaborate, either not present it as [the subject's] words, or say that it is someone else's recollection years later. But if it is something like, "Do it at once," as often as not I leave it in quotes, since it is probably an approximation of what was said, even though not the exact words. . . . As long as the meaning is not in question, I do not think one has to be [a] purist.

Freidel adds that he is not at all sure that his policy is justifiable. It is really a most difficult question to generalize about. But it would seem that the distinction between the generally accepted practice of quoting interviews directly and the highly radical practice of "converting" letters and journals into dialogue is slight.

Boswell's success in creating at least an illusion of reality in his records of Johnson's conversations has subjected every later biographer to a powerful temptation. But Boswell's was a special case. He knew Johnson intimately and spent a great deal of time in his company. Further, his single-minded devotion over the years to the task of studying the living Johnson has no parallel in history. Fanny Burney's account of his incredible persistence and concentration illustrates the point: "Of everything else, when in that presence, he was unobservant, if not contemptuous," she recalled. "The moment that voice burst forth, the attention which it excited in Mr. Boswell amounted almost to pain. His eyes goggled with eagerness; he leant his ear almost on the shoulder of the Doctor; and his mouth dropped open to catch every syllable that might be uttered." Boswell was also a gifted and practiced diarist, who did not permit his recollections to grow stale before he put them on paper. "I found, from experience," he wrote in his life of Johnson, "that to collect my friend's conversation so as to exhibit it with any degree of its original flavor, IT WAS NECESSARY TO WRITE IT DOWN WITHOUT DELAY." Otherwise, he said, the result was comparable to "preserving or pickling long kept or faded fruits." To excell Boswell in reproducing oral sources would seem beyond human ability; even so, Boswell's records were not entirely accurate, and his use of them in the biography was not always faithful to his notes.

Because of the hazards involved, many biographers have eschewed oral records. Froude, for example, despite an op-

VIII. *The Materials of Biography* [211

portunity almost equal to Boswell's to observe his subject, would not quote Carlyle's conversations as direct discourse. "To report correctly the language of conversations, especially when extended over a wide period, is almost an impossibility," he wrote. "The listener, in spite of himself, adds something of his own in colour, form, or substance."

The whole problem of the oral source calls for further study. Certainly the Oral History Project inaugurated at Columbia University by Allan Nevins, in which recordings are made of the recollections of persons connected with important events while they are still alive, is an excellent idea. But it touches on only part of the interviewing problem— the accuracy of the recollector's quotations of past conversations remains in doubt. In judging this kind of material, one should keep in mind the warning of Lincoln's biographer, John Hay: "When Nicolay and I came to Washington we thought we should have a great advantage in personal conversation with Lincoln's contemporaries in regard to the important events of his time, but we ascertained after a very short experience that no confidence whatever could be placed in the memories of even the most intelligent and most honorable men when it came to narrating their relations with Lincoln." [8]

Particularly useful to the biographer are the letters and journals of persons who knew his subject, containing excerpts written about him but not *to* him. Here are the really candid opinions; here are often the "choice" stories and anecdotes; here is the many-sided nature of the man as his

[8] For an important study of the effect of verbal transfer of factual evidence upon accuracy, see G. W. Allport and L. Postman, *The Psychology of Rumor* (New York: 1947), pp. 65–74. Another problem faced by Columbia's Project is the difficulty of getting individuals to recall and record what is historically important. Skilled interviewers are often necessary and not always available.

varied contemporaries really saw it, free from overtones of flattery and fear alike. The locating of such material is slow work, but rewarding. Some discrimination is still necessary, to be sure; statements in a letter to the subject's mother, for example, are hardly likely to be completely objective. But ordinarily this sort of evidence is excellent.

Most of the materials not yet mentioned in this survey are purely "historical" in nature, and it is not my purpose to discuss the larger question of the judging of historical evidence as such. There is, however, one other special problem involving the sources of *biography*: How does one use earlier biographies of one's subject?

Some authors believe that these biographies should not even be read by the later writer—that their interpretations may influence his, and, in any case, that he should verify all evidence by reference to primary sources. Marchette Chute, for instance, claims that in her life of Shakespeare, she only used sources which appeared within nineteen years of her hero's death. While it is certainly wise to trace all facts to their ultimate origins, there is no reason why a fair-minded author cannot read secondary accounts and take advantage of the information and insights that they may offer. Earlier works frequently contain valuable evidence not obtainable elsewhere, even though they may be poor biographies. The author, for example, may have known the subject himself, in which case his book will probably be full of firsthand accounts of great potential importance. Such material may be suspect, and should be checked, but it ought not to be ignored. If the writer did not know the subject, he may have talked to persons who did. Or he may have had access to letters and other documents since lost. In writing a life of Silas Wright, for example, I found that there were three biographies of Wright written by men of his own day. None was an adequate study by modern standards, but all contained letters and personal reminiscences which made them important to me. The many works of James Parton are outstanding illustrations of the value of "old" lives, for Parton always collected contemporary information and, living in an age when men still remembered Franklin, Jefferson, Burr, and other figures, Parton drew together materials that might well have been lost forever.

Older biographies can also supply the modern biographer with a feeling for the times. The phases of the subject's life emphasized by earlier writers may be different from those which seem significant today, and may help the writer to achieve a truer balance.

Less dated biographies of one's subject can also be put to profitable use. They will usually be full of bibliographical hints. Their very inadequacies may suggest ideas and materials to be examined. If biographers A and B have concentrated upon the subject's professional life and neglected his personal side, the present student may feel that his own book must reverse the process. A study of the already existing lives will point the way to the kind of biography needed. An analysis of the biases displayed by previous writers may lead to a more nearly impartial approach. To ignore other works is to deny the whole purpose of writing and the co-operative nature of all scholarship. In other words, earlier studies should be mined for information, and should serve as a guide to what should and should not be done.

A final point may be raised concerning the problem of background material. Some is essential; much may be desirable. How should the biographer obtain this information? Deep investigation of the surroundings of every incident in the subject's life could lead the author far astray. In general, there can be no objection to the use of sound secondary sources for background. By the same token, published works (if they are accurate and detailed enough) may be substituted for the examination of manuscript collections in the case of persons who play only minor roles in the hero's career. A biographer of Woodrow Wilson ought certainly to examine the E. M. House papers in the Yale library, but a biographer of, say, Theodore Roosevelt might safely confine himself to Charles Seymour's four volumes of *The Intimate Papers of Colonel House*. Unless one wishes to devote a lifetime to a single monumental study, this kind of short cut is essential. Judgment is very important in deciding where laborious original research is called for and where it is not. If one's subject kept elaborate scrapbooks of clippings, a great deal of aimless digging in newspaper files may be unnecessary. If his papers contain carbon copies of his own letters as well as his incoming mail, the papers of his less important correspondents may be bypassed without danger. And while it is always *possible* that a new piece of evidence, discovered in some long-ignored depository, may radically alter the picture, the more research one has done on a man's life, the smaller the chance of such a revolutionary find becomes. All biographers sooner or later discover that the search for material can be endless; it becomes part of each writer's task to decide when he should stop collecting evidence and begin writing.

CHAPTER IX

The Problem of Personality

THE variegated attempts of biographers to portray character indicate that there is no formula for presenting personality in biography any more than there is a formula for the creation of a convincing character in fiction. Thorough analysis of all the sources is a primary necessity, of course. But long study alone will not lead to an understanding of personality. A man's character is always so complex and variable that it can be understood only imperfectly, and that with great effort. "What the historically-minded biographer tries to do," according to Dumas Malone, "is to live with his subject in spirit long enough and intimately enough to form definite impressions of his character and personality." Another modern biographer, Eleanor Ruggles, has claimed that it requires at least two years of close study before any subject "becomes alive."

Traditionally, the biographer has used several kinds of

evidence in trying to understand the personality of his subject. First, there are the subject's own introspective observations. Even so reserved a man as Woodrow Wilson, for example, often explained himself quite frankly:

> When I am with anyone in whom I am specially and sincerely interested, the hardest subject for me to broach is just that which is nearest my heart. An unfortunate disposition indeed! I hope to overcome it in time. I can at least speak plainly in writing.
>
> It isn't pleasant or convenient to have strong passions. . . . I have an uncomfortable feeling that I am carrying a volcano about with me. My salvation is in being loved.
>
> It would be a sheer impossibility for me to confide anything concerning myself—especially any secret of my intellect—to anyone of whose sympathy I could not be absolutely sure beforehand.

A second source of information of this type consists of the comments of contemporaries, samples of which have been offered in Chapter VIII. Another, equally direct, approach is by way of the subject's specific actions. "Actions speak louder than words." In many ways this adage is true. At least the overt, superficial aspects of personality can be directly observed. The historian seldom needs special tools to determine, for example, whether or not a man was selfish, honest, or unprincipled. Occasionally a biographer will even make legitimate use of folklore in building up his hero's portrait. The hundreds of tales and stories that make up the Lincoln legend, for example, are mostly either beyond historical verification or patently false. Yet the total picture they create has an unquestionable basis in fact. Perhaps they tell the student more about the times in which Lincoln lived than about the man himself, but they tell

ix. The Problem of Personality

something of the man too. The legends clustered about Lincoln's great rival Stephen A. Douglas, for instance, are quite different.

These "traditional" methods of studying historical personalities, sound enough so far as they go, leave much to be desired. An individual's own insights never provide a complete picture of his nature. There are some things he does not know, other things he will not tell. He cannot penetrate what Tennyson called "the abysmal depths of personality." The comments of others are also unsatisfactory or at least incomplete tools for understanding personality. There is seldom general agreement about the character of any outstanding figure even among those who knew him best. Consider again the case of Woodrow Wilson. Here are two comments by members of his cabinet:

> *Secretary of the Navy Josephus Daniels:* It has been so rare for a public man to be utterly frank and genuine, to mean wholly what he says, and to carry out his public pledges regardless of all obstacles. . . . He never learned that in public business the longest way round is the nearest way through.
>
> *Secretary of War Lindley M. Garrison:* I once heard a description which as nearly fits the case of President Wilson as any other I know. In describing someone it was said, 'He was a man of high ideals but no principles.'

Or compare these comments by two friends:

> *Josephus Daniels:* Those near Wilson never had the least trouble in understanding him perfectly.
>
> *David Lawrence:* Woodrow Wilson died as he lived—unexplained and unrevealed. None—not even his intimates—ever knew the mental processes which crystallized his decisions. . . .

In addition to the contradictory nature of such evidence, nearly all of it is superficial. It is also in part haphazard. The opinions of intimates are not always preserved—any attempt to give numerical weight to comments by contemporaries would be thwarted by the impossibility of obtaining a sound sample.

In short, traditional methods of studying historical personalities are wholly satisfactory only in so far as they relate to facts and specific actions. Where motives and the internal dynamics of personality are concerned, they can provide only impressionistic answers to the student's questions. Other techniques are urgently needed.

There is no reason why many of the "unsound" approaches used by some biographers cannot be adopted safely—if they are properly handled. Who will complain about this paragraph from Benjamin Thomas's *Abraham Lincoln*?

> Frequently he must rise before dawn and ride all day in order to reach the next court on time. The blustery winds that swept the open prairie in early spring and late autumn, sometimes bringing sleet or snow flurries, caused the young lawyer to hunch his shoulders, lower his head, and pull his heavy shawl closer about him as his horse plodded on against the blast. Sticking his long legs out of the covers in a farmhouse bedroom where he had put up for the night, and clambering out of bed in his short, homemade, yellow flannel nightshirt, he might find the water pitcher filled with ice. Heavy showers overtook him on the prairie far from shelter; he might ride all day in drizzling rain. When floods swept away the bridges, he had to swim his horse across the swollen streams.

Thomas defends this passage, saying: "My treatment has a factual base leavened with imagination. But I have

ix. *The Problem of Personality* [219

never used imagination without what appeared to me a valid reason for doing so. . . . I strove consciously to put myself in Lincoln's place, strove to feel as he must have felt . . . and then tried to convey that feeling to the reader." The difference between this and the fatuous attempts of the fictional biographers "to touch biography with imagination" is subtle but profound.¹

In the same way, there is no need to cast aside *completely* the methods of the "intuitive" biographers. Emil Ludwig's use of photographs was foolish. But this is not to say that pictures have no function in understanding personality. The point is that intuitive judgments ought to *follow*, not *precede*, a thorough examination of the sources. After criticizing André Maurois's intuitive use of the "water motif" in *Ariel*, another biographer of Shelley, Newman I. White, wrote: "undoubtedly the biographer should be alert to any pattern that might become recognizable, but his adoption of it should be late rather than early."

Even the psychoanalytical approach, despite the legitimate arguments raised against it, can often be useful. Occasionally, where evidence is plentiful and the conditions clear, psychoanalysis can certainly be employed with justice. In the case of George III, who was insane, and whose madness was thoroughly examined by contemporaries, the records are adequate, and a study such as M. S. Guttmacher's *America's Last King* is perfectly acceptable to the most conservative historians. On the other hand, it may be argued that where the ordinary evidence is extremely skimpy, as in the case of Leonardo, a psychoanalytic interpretation like Freud's may also be justified. When conventional evidence is missing, the biographer must guess, in

¹ See above, p. 127.

any case, and an intelligent guess based on psychoanalysis, provided it is clearly labeled a guess (as Freud's was) can surely be defended.

In the vast majority of biographies, which fall between the two extremes, no one should object to the use of Freudian techniques if they are explicitly described as speculations, and if known facts are not twisted or ignored in order to bring the subject into a preconceived pattern. We cannot get our Luthers, Wagners, and Napoleons on the couch, but we know some of the things they could have revealed there and no harm can come from considering the available facts in the light of Freud's insights. Much of the criticism that has been aimed at psychoanalytical biography has arisen from the dogmatic way in which the authors of such works have stated their cases. As Bernard DeVoto once said: "*Must* is the mechanism of psychoanalytical biography. . . . Biography proper is not concerned with the *must* but only the *did*." If the psychoanalytical writers would confess to the speculative nature of their conclusions, their critics would be less bitter.

With a measure of tolerance and co-operation, historians and biographers could learn a great deal from the psychologists, but they have seldom been willing to try. When the Social Science Research Council conducted an inquiry into the use of personal documents in psychology, history, anthropology, and sociology, its historian, Louis Gottschalk, begged the question by presenting a paper which confined itself almost wholly to an analysis of general historical technology. "For the historian the method of dealing with human documents is all of *historical method*," he wrote, ignoring even such an outstanding study of ideas adaptable to historical research as G. W. Allport's *The Use of Personal*

IX. The Problem of Personality [221

Documents in Psychological Science, published in 1942, three years before Gottschalk's monograph appeared.

Studies like Allport's are especially important to biography, which depends so largely on personal documents. And as Allport clearly proved, personal documents reflect the writer's psychological make-up in nearly every case.

Perhaps modern psychologists have not done much more than to demonstrate what perceptive students have intuitively understood to be true. Still, it is often difficult to extract the meaning concealed in personal documents which may be evasive and ambiguous. "Sometimes," André Maurois has confided, "*one* sentence cut out of an apparently unimportant entry in a diary will suddenly illuminate a character." Illuminate it for Maurois perhaps, but how can the soundness of his insight be proved? As the editor of the *Dial* noted, back in 1898, we need "a finer method of analysis than critics have been wont to apply," if we are to "disclose personal elements in the most impersonal of utterances."

Many techniques being used by psychologists in their studies of living persons could be borrowed by biographers for a more revealing dissection of personal documents. For one thing, the biographer might make use of psychological studies of handwriting. Long neglected by American psychologists, and thus consigned to the quacks and the Sunday-supplement writers, graphology has recently been developed as an important field of personality research. While it would be dangerous to interpret a historical figure in terms of his handwriting alone, it cannot be denied that a person's writing is a form of expressive movement, that it is really "brainwriting."

Early experiments, such as those of Alfred Binet half a

century ago, made it clear that certain gifted "professional" graphologists could interpret character from handwriting with an accuracy far exceeding chance. Yet these professionals differed among themselves as to how they operated, and untrained individuals who applied the methods which the graphologists claimed they were using could not duplicate their results. However, more recent experimenters have developed measuring devices that are reasonably objective, and that have high correlations with other measurements of personality. One graphologist, G. R. Pascal, devised a long list of handwriting "variables" and classified the script of a number of individuals according to the prevalence of each one. He then compared these results with personality judgments of the subjects made by a group of psychologists. Many of the "variables" proved useless, but at least six could be related significantly to the psychologists' conclusions. Pascal made only modest claims for his experiment, but obviously, a study of these "variables" in the handwriting of a historical character might provide a biographer with a number of insights into his subject's personality.

The best modern students, analyzing such things as the form, size, and slant of writing, the upper and lower projections of letters like "t," "p," and "f," the pressure applied by the pen, the relative size of margins, and the way all of these complex factors are combined, have made a useful contribution to psychology—and one that historians, especially biographers, might apply to their own specialties.

The psychological study of handwriting is still not really objective. There are, for example, national styles of handwriting which make it impossible to set up universal standards for measuring this personality variable. Further, these styles change over the years, so that to judge any sample, one must know the nationality of the author and the approximate date of the writing. The writing of a nineteenth-century German and of a present-day Englishman cannot be analyzed by the same criteria. In addition, the differences of opinion among handwriting "authorities" are almost as numerous as the agreements. Assessment can only go so far—style, for example, can be described, but not measured. The techniques are perhaps too esoteric and complicated for today's biographer to apply himself. He might profit, however, from the opinions of one or more of the graphologists, and consider their views in relation to his other evidence.

Another psychological aid that could be enlightening to the biographer is the mechanical analysis of the elements and ideas used in a subject's writings. In *The Story of a Style*, written in 1920, William Bayard Hale attempted to study the personality of Woodrow Wilson through the mechanical analysis of his writings. Hale's approach was completely unscientific, for while he dealt with supposedly objective facts about the kind and number of words that Wilson used, his methods of classification and selection were entirely capricious. His personal view of Wilson was violently prejudiced as well, for he hated the President and was determined to expose him as a hollow fraud. But even so, Hale threw a great deal of light on Wilson simply by noticing certain facts about Wilson's writing, such as his fondness for adjectives and for repeating certain pet words and phrases. Since Hale's day, psychologists have developed theoretical explanations of the kind of phenomena that Hale observed, and they have, it may be hoped, developed a more objective approach to their subjects than his. The psychologists argue that individuals have highly specialized ways of using words (ways which are more basic than the vague thing we call "style"), that must, within limits, reflect personality. A German psychologist, A. Busemann, devised an action quotient (Aq) by dividing the number of active (verbal) ideas in a given passage by the number of qualitative (adjectival) ones. He postulated that an increase in qualitative words was an indication of emotional instability, and found that there was a good correlation between his findings and the results of Rorschach ink-blot tests applied to the same subjects. Busemann's work was further developed by an American, David P. Boder, who studied selected legal documents, fiction, scientific papers, advertisements, and private letters, and arrived at "standards" concerning the ratio of adjectives to verbs in each type. A complicated scientific treatise striving for exactitude will naturally have more adjectives in it than an informal letter, but having standardized the ratios for different types of writing, Boder found it possible to judge emotional instability with some accuracy. Some of his experiments are extremely suggestive for biographers. He took, for example, 132 samples from Emerson's Journals over a fifty-year period [2] and discovered wide variations in the ratio of adjectives to verbs, though over the years the percentages compared closely to the "standard" for that type of writing.

Boder did not attempt to correlate his data with the known facts of Emerson's life, but such a comparison would obviously be of interest to a biographer of the man. What is the significance of these figures indicating the number of

[2] For each month of the year 1820, and for every fifth year thereafter, he selected a passage of approximately 350 words.

ix. *The Problem of Personality* [225

adjectives per 100 verbs, based on the journals for 1845? July—21, August—107, September—43. Can some event calculated to have stirred Emerson deeply be located in August 1845? Perhaps the cause of such a disturbance will be obvious, but if it is not, a study of adjective-verb ratios could well lead to its discovery. If a high degree of consistency should be found between Emerson's use of adjectives in his journals and his emotional ups and downs, one could assume that Boder's device would prove extremely valuable for obtaining insights into the personality of Emerson or any other subject who has kept a journal, or written letters, or done any kind of sustained writing over a period of years.

Another of Boder's suggestive studies dealt with the letters of William James. Having determined the number of adjectives per 100 verbs for a series of letters dating from 1882 to 1910, he compared his figures for letters written to men with those written to women at different times in James's life. He found that between the ages of forty and fifty James's letters to women contained many more adjectives than did the ones he addressed to men, but that in letters written after sixty the opposite was true. Here are the figures:

Adjectives per 100 verbs in letters

	TO MEN	TO WOMEN	AVERAGE
Age 40–50	43.2	62.7	52.9
Age 60–65	61.5	42.2	51.8

The meaning of these statistics may be subject to debate, but it is surely worth debating.

The number of similar studies that might be adapted to the purposes of biographers is considerable. Semanticists like Alfred Korzybski argue that bad semantic habits are a sign of a cranky, jumpy, even paranoid personality. A psychologist, F. H. Sanford, surveyed the whole field in 1942 and concluded: "There is . . . a reasonable argument, reinforced by some experimental evidence, that quantitative analysis of written expression can discover individuality." Later research has reinforced this view.

There are other tools which might assist the biographer in digging out the subtleties of his subject's personality. John Dollard and O. H. Mowrer have developed a means of measuring tension as expressed in personal documents. Dollard and Mowrer studied the verbatim reports of social workers who had interviewed people with various emotional problems. Their purpose was to discover whether or not the social workers were actually helping their clients. By counting the number of words in the reports which expressed some form of discomfort or tension (D), and those which reflected relief or reward (R), they arrived at a Discomfort-Relief Quotient, expressed in the equation $DRQ = \frac{D}{D + R}$. Working out a separate DRQ for each page of an interview, they found that the results, when plotted on a graph, correlated highly with the apparent state of mind of the client at any particular time.

Although Dollard and Mowrer employed recorded interviews in their experiments, biographers might try their method with any kind of personal document. It would be interesting, for example, to figure out DRQ's for a series of letters written by a subject over a considerable span of time. One could then relate the fluctuations noted to the known facts of the writer's life at the time each letter was written. Or a biographer might be interested in knowing whether or not his subject's DRQ fluctuated according to

IX. *The Problem of Personality* [227

the age, sex, or social position of the persons he corresponded with. The possibilities of this device are almost unlimited. What was Thomas Jefferson's DRQ when he wrote the Declaration of Independence? Was it different when he penned his first inaugural address? Was Franklin D. Roosevelt more disturbed emotionally when he asked Congress to declare war on Japan than when he assured the depression-racked nation that it had nothing to fear but fear itself?

Since autobiographies are so important to biographers, any device that enabled them to extract additional meaning from an autobiography would naturally be useful. Possibly "value-analysis," a method by which autobiographical and other personal data "can be described with a maximum of objectivity and at the same time with a maximum of relevance to the underlying emotional dynamics," is such a tool. This technique, developed by Ralph K. White, was first applied to a study of Richard Wright's autobiography, *Black Boy*.

In order to test the usefulness of the method, White first read *Black Boy* carefully and wrote out his impressions of Richard Wright on the basis of his reading. This is the way in which any conventional biographer would use the book as a source on Wright's personality. But then White went over *Black Boy* again, noting in the margins every value-judgment and goal expressed by the author. He developed a set of shorthand symbols to represent these goals and standards of judgment, and counted the number of times each appeared. Finally he wrote another analysis of Wright based on the emphasis Wright had given to the various values he had expressed.

Naturally (since White was a competent psychologist to

begin with) the conclusions reached in his preliminary appraisal were duplicated in the counting procedure. The things about Wright that struck the *reader* were the things he mentioned a great deal in his autobiography. The obvious fact that Wright had had an extremely unhappy childhood, for example, was borne out in the counting—the book contained 1,205 examples of frustration and only 349 representing positive satisfactions. White's observance of the author's aggression and disapproval of others were also verified, for aggression was the second most prevalent characteristic noted in his book, and 89 percent of his comments on persons mentioned were unfavorable. Wright's hatred of his father (every mention of him in the book was unfavorable), his ambivalent attitude toward his mother, his relative absence of interest in sex, and his concern with knowledge and truthfulness were similarly "proved" by the statistical analysis.

But several aspects of Wright's personality, often expressed subtly and possibly unconsciously, did not stand out until they had been enumerated. By far the most important of these was his emphasis on physical safety. In his preliminary, subjective appraisal, White had not noticed this at all, yet it was by a large margin the most frequently mentioned goal in the autobiography, accounting for eighteen percent of all Wright's judgments! The counting also disclosed Wright's lack of interest in social goals, his failure to identify himself with other Negroes, and his tendency to record *complete* disapproval (as in the case of his father) of persons he disliked.

All of these characteristics might well have been noticed by a different reader. But such a reader might in turn have missed many of the traits that White discovered in his pre-

ix. The Problem of Personality

liminary appraisal. "Value-analysis" can at least act as a check on intuitive judgment. As White pointed out, the method is useless without the ordinary subjective study which preceded it, and it assumes its full importance only when another subjective analysis of the material is made on the basis of the new ideas brought to light by the counting. The "discovery" of Wright's concern with physical safety, for instance, did not explain its meaning. White weighed the possibility that it might indicate Wright's aggression—"*to accuse others of attacking is itself an effective form of attack.*" Or it might mean that his aggression was part of his search for safety, that it was fundamentally defensive, based on the principle that the best defense is a good offense. Actually, the statistical evaluation even helped to discriminate between these two hypotheses. In 122 cases, Wright connected some aggressive thought or action with the goal of safety; instances in which he was aggressive for some other reason, such as to gain acceptance by the "gang" in a new school, were relatively rare.

Whatever the conclusion, however, the value of the statistical analysis seems clear. The final interpretation of *Black Boy*, in White's words, was "both broader and sounder because of the inclusion of much critically interpreted statistical material."

One great virtue of this method for the average biographer is its relative simplicity. While the actual scoring of a long autobiography would take a great deal of time, it would not call for any particular psychological training. The mechanics could even be performed by an assistant—indeed, having two people score an autobiography separately would be an admirable check upon the reliability of the results. Actually, reliability is not likely to be a problem, for, as White pointed out, observers will agree as to the facts even if they differ as to the meaning of the facts. Of course, the final judgment of the biographer must always come into play. He cannot be a slave to the figures. All that counting can do is offer him ideas that may not have occurred to him in the course of an ordinary reading of the material.

A similar, though slightly more complicated technique has been developed by the psychologist A. L. Baldwin. He performed a minute content analysis on a group of letters written by "Jenny," an old woman, to "Glenn" and "Isabel," a young married couple. Jenny's life story, in rough outline as it might appear in the mind of a biographer, was as follows: She was born in Ireland, but had been taken to Canada at an early age. As a young girl, she was burdened with the support of her brothers and sisters. Later she married, but the death of her husband left her with a month-old son to care for. For this child, "Ross," she developed an extremely close attachment, skimping and depriving herself in order to give him luxuries incommensurate with her income. Their relationship was close and happy until Ross grew up and began to live his own life. Then Jenny became very jealous of his girl friends. When he married, she ordered him from her sight forever, but she was not able to adjust to the separation, and after Ross and his wife were divorced she re-established contact with him. They became friends once more, but continued to quarrel over Ross's interest in various women. Later Ross contracted a mastoid infection and died quite suddenly. Jenny then tried a number of different jobs without finding happiness, and finally entered an old ladies' home. At first she seemed satisfied,

ix. The Problem of Personality

but soon began to quarrel with the authorities and other inmates. The last years of her life were bitterly unhappy.

This information was pieced together by Baldwin from a series of letters which Jenny wrote to Ross's college roommate and his wife. Baldwin used them, first, to arrive at a subjective analysis of Jenny's personality. His analysis, as he pointed out, rested upon four types of evidence. He made use of the *frequency* of certain ideas and attitudes expressed in the letters, the *insights* into her own personality which Jenny herself offered, the *contiguity* of various facts and feelings mentioned, and, finally, his own past experience with other cases. Any biographer would use these methods in studying Jenny's personality, and the validity of his conclusions would depend upon his intelligence and his diligence.

But how can the biographer (or his public) be sure that his interpretation is correct? It is this flaw inherent in even the most brilliant subjective analysis, which Baldwin's second evaluation, "a personal structure analysis," was designed to mend. By *counting* frequencies and contiguities [3] in Jenny's letters, perhaps he could reinforce his subjective analysis of her personality.

Of course, the content analysis was in itself partly subjective. Baldwin had to classify Jenny's statements under various headings. Some were not classified at all; others were lumped together into general categories. He had a category, "men," and another, "women," but he placed Ross in a separate category, and considered Glenn and

---

[3] Jenny's insights into herself are actually examples of contiguity. Thus, when she says she feels sorry for a child in an institution where she is working because he reminds her of her son, Ross, her sympathy and her memory are contiguous, and they are also an example of self-insight.

Isabel as a unit in themselves. Each decision was based upon the understanding of Jenny which he had obtained through subjective study. In all he selected fifteen headings,[4] each broken down into the different attitudes that Jenny expressed in connection with them. Under "Ross," for instance, all references were classified as favorable, unfavorable, or neutral, and then further defined under such headings as attacked, selfish, lazy, and dishonest, and their opposites. In this way judgments based on *frequency* could be mechanically checked.

To test the soundness of conclusions based on *contiguity*, Baldwin subdivided the letters into general periods covering broad sections of Jenny's life, and then into incidents, "small temporal segment[s] of the letters during which Jenny is writing about one general topic." These decisions, too, were entirely subjective. All of the categories referred to in a given incident were judged to be contiguous. In other words, when the categories "Ross-unfavorable" and "Money-saved" appeared together with a frequency exceeding chance, Baldwin assumed that these two concepts had some relationship in Jenny's mind.

When all the "incidents" in the letters had been categorized and the information transferred to punch cards, an IBM machine made it possible to determine quickly the number of times that any person, goal, or idea was mentioned, the ratio of each kind of reference (such as favorable or unfavorable) to the total references, and the interrelationships of ideas and persons in the mind of the writer. Once significant frequencies and relationships were estab-

---

[4] Ross, Women, Men, Her Family, Herself, Money, Death, Health, Jobs, Religion, Nature and Art, Gifts and Purchases, Children, Homes, and The Past.

ix. The Problem of Personality

lished, many valuable insights came to light. The frequency with which Jenny associated favorable references to her son with references to "The Past-relived," for example, pointed up her wish to return to the happy days when Ross was growing up and completely dependent upon her.

Baldwin found that certain groups of categories tended to relate themselves in clusters which he could describe schematically. Here is one of his clusters, together with his interpretation of it:

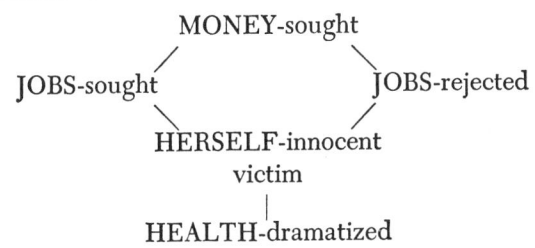

```
              MONEY-sought
            /              \
   JOBS-sought              JOBS-rejected
            \              /
           HERSELF-innocent
                victim
                  |
           HEALTH-dramatized
```

This cluster, Baldwin wrote:

> contains the categories with the highest frequencies. The large frequencies suggest that the search for a job was the most important problem in Jenny's life during period one [covering her life up to the time of her reconciliation with Ross]. . . . The presence of two opposite attitudes in the same cluster suggests an ambivalence. There is not sufficient information . . . to determine the reason why she needed a job (although *money-sought* certainly gives a clue), nor why she rejected them. From the fact that *herself-innocent victim* is related to both attitudes toward jobs, it is clear that Jenny externalized the source of her difficulty and felt that she was not at fault in requiring work and at the same time being unable to work. It also appears in this cluster that Jenny's health was bad. At least she considered her health to be part of her unfortunate condition.

Another cluster illustrates both the strength and the weakness of the method:

```
            DEATH-planned for
           /                \
MONEY-scrupulously ─────── MONEY suspiciously
    regarded                    guarded
```

This suggested to Baldwin that Jenny expected to die, and therefore guarded her money with great care, but he could not explain her *suspicious* guarding. Neither was the connection between *death* and her scrupulous regard for money apparent. But the fact that a statistically significant correspondence existed between these seeming unrelated attitudes led him to re-examine the letters themselves in search of more details about Jenny's attitude toward death. He then noticed things he had previously passed over as insignificant—her emphasis on making sure that her money fell into hands of friends when she passed on (she even sewed money into her corset lest some stranger steal her purse in the event she should drop dead in the street), and her fear of dying with unpaid debts on her hands, which led her before leaving on a trip to send some cash to Glenn to cover the expense of burying her in case she should die while away. While Baldwin had noted Jenny's scrupulous regard for money and her careful protection of her assets, and had therefore included these categories in his analysis, he had missed their relationship to her attitude toward death. As a result of the counting process "a mysterious pattern of correspondences" produced "the insight which was previously missing."

Baldwin further established the effectiveness of personal structure analysis by comparing his own evaluation of Jenny's personality with those of five other psychologists who studied the letters but did not use his statistical analysis. Only one of these experts extracted as much information

IX. The Problem of Personality   [235

from the letters as the experimenter, and all agreed that the conclusions reached by the statistical study seemed sound. In addition, Baldwin had still another psychologist perform a "blind analysis" by studying the statistical results *without* reading the letters, and then writing a description of Jenny. His characterization agreed substantially with Baldwin's and with those of all the others. Indeed, only two of the subjective analyses contained any information that he had missed.

As in the case of value-analysis, Baldwin's "Personal Structure Analysis" requires a considerable mass of material if its conclusions are to be statistically reliable, and much tedious effort in scoring the record. And it will not in itself explain personality. Significant relationships having been uncovered, the analyst still faces the task of understanding and interpreting them.

In summary, it seems clear that content analysis can render valuable assistance to biographers. It can provide a means of *measuring* personality, a scientific check on intuitive, subjective judgments. It can help in the resolution of conflicting interpretations either by settling doubtful questions or by illustrating ambivalences in the subject. On the other hand, at least as far as the above methods are concerned, it does not eliminate the subjective element. Prejudices and preconceptions may influence the investigator's conclusions. The very decision as to what to count must also affect the outcome. The value of the results is completely dependent upon the setting up of proper categories, and upon the accurate coding of the material. The reliability of the coding process, of course, can be checked, but the validity of the conclusions depends upon the soundness of basic subjective decisions.

Another factor (in the more complicated forms of analysis) that seems purely subjective and relatively unscientific involves the weighing of certain statements more heavily than others. In value-analysis, for example, R. K. White assigned five emphasis units to each strongly expressed value. The principle seems sound enough, but why five, rather than three, say, or ten? White also urged experimenters to be constantly on the lookout for subtleties and for over-all meanings, which again involve highly subjective factors.

Finally, there are certain difficulties involved in the use of content analysis from the historian's point of view. Published personal writings (especially speeches and autobiographies) today are often the product of pens other than the "official" author's. Would a content analysis of President Eisenhower's television speeches (or of his book, *Crusade in Europe*) provide valid conclusions about his personality or about the personalities of his ghostwriters? Then there is the question of reticence. While it is true that the theory of projective techniques postulates that no one can help expressing himself when he writes, degrees of expressiveness vary. Many individuals, held back either by personal inhibitions or by considerations of taste, reveal very little of themselves in their letters and autobiographies. Also, psychologists have not resolved the problem of literary style as an influence on personal writings. "Style," writes F. L. Lucas in his recent volume on the subject, "is personality clothed in words, character embodied in speech." Buffon made the same point in the eighteenth century when he wrote: *"Le style est l'homme même,"* and so did Gibbon and many, many others. But style may detract from the usefulness of any quantitative analysis of personal documents by introducing artistically contrived distortions into the record.

But it seems clear that content analysis offers history and biography a new area of research. In a field where so many conclusions tend to rest on impulse and prejudice, careful, imaginative use of the method ought to reduce the biographer's dependence upon subjective judgments, enable him to resolve doubts rising from conflicting evidence, and, in general, add confidence to his conclusions by reducing them to measurable limits.

In many broader ways psychology can be brought to bear on the problems of the biographer. In an interesting volume on *Power and Personality*, for example, Harold D. Lasswell has applied a knowledge of the dynamics of personality to the study of politicians. He argues that certain types of people find both outlet for ambition and compensation for frustration in political activity. His conclusions are discouraging to anyone who would hope for well-balanced and unselfish political leaders. The "political type," Lasswell says, possesses "an intense and ungratified craving for deference," which he cannot satisfy in his personal life. He turns outward for gratification, seeking office to compensate for his low opinion of himself. Lasswell does not suggest that every statesman conforms to "type." Nor do his conclusions presuppose even the "typical" politician to be necessarily an evil influence upon the polity he rules. In any case, his theories can be tested by any politician's biographer. Sometimes, no doubt, his insights will lead the biographer to a better understanding of the subject. In Alexander and Juliette George's *Woodrow Wilson and Colonel House*, Lasswell's theories form the basis of an interpretation of Wilson and House which is one of the most convincing explanations of these difficult men and their complex friendship yet written.

Cannot other professions be treated the way Lasswell has dealt with politics? As with psychoanalytical tools, the danger is that the biographer using such a method may fall victim to overemphasis and oversimplification. But biographers must be brave, albeit sensibly cautious, in the face of such dangers.

Biography can also draw upon social psychology. The work of social psychologists in the fields of mass movements, hysteria, and crowd psychology can help to explain the influence of the times on a person's behavior. G. M. Gilbert's analysis of the rise of Hitler in his *Psychology of Dictatorship* and Hadley Cantril's studies of the "Father" Divine cult and similar phenomena in his *Psychology of Social Movements* are primarily concerned with the genesis of social groups, but they throw a great deal of light on the way leaders are affected by their environments. Psychological-anthropological investigations of national character, like Margaret Mead's *And Keep Your Powder Dry* and Ruth Benedict's *The Chrysanthemum and the Sword*, which attempt to account for national differences by studying patterns of child-rearing and other cultural norms in different countries, might also be adapted to biographical problems. Such studies have seldom been convincing to historians, and they fail utterly to account for the individual differences among people of the same culture which are so important to the biographer. Methods that work well enough in studying primitive peoples seem to break down when applied to complex modern societies. Still, men are influenced by their environment, and particularly by their early environment. The biographer usually lacks detailed information about his subject's earliest years. Anything that he can learn about the dominant habits of his subject's social group may help him to interpret whatever evidence he does have. Certainty, as I have said before, can only be approximated in the study of personality.

This much, at least, seems clear: Anything that psychology has to say about the motives, actions, and psychological processes of people in general which can be applied to particular persons ought to be listened to attentively by biographers, who are, after all, primarily interested in human beings.

A Shakespeare may master human nature "instinctively," but ordinary writers can surely benefit from general and systematic perusal of the human mind. The biographer who studies man in general may, perhaps, see something in his particular subject that might otherwise escape him.

One of the chief criticisms directed against much of the older biography has been that it oversimplified its subjects. Modern writers talk of the "complexity and mobility of human beings," of the "development" of character, and of the impossibility of reconstructing a three-dimensional personality on the flat surface of a piece of paper. In *Roosevelt: The Lion and the Fox,* for example, James MacGregor Burns writes of the complexity and the "bewildering" contradictions of his subject. He points out Roosevelt's kindness, but notes also "a thin streak of cruelty" in his nature; he portrays him cavalierly disposing of billions of dollars, yet wasting precious minutes cutting a telegram down to ten words; he shows his courage and his caution, his seriousness and his frivolity; in short he argues that Roosevelt was both lion and fox, "a deeply divided man . . . lingering between two worlds," a child of the nineteenth century living in and adapting superbly to the twentieth. No one can quarrel with the modern attitude, but it is wrong to dismiss the problem of presenting personality as insoluble or to overemphasize the complexities of men's characters and make the presentation of their inconsistencies an end in itself. To say that a convincing portrayal of a man must be subjective, that it must depend upon "the artist's approach," based on "his sympathetic understanding of the subject, his experience with previous cases, his seemingly intuitional selection of certain points and neglect of others," is not enough. "As a supplement to his more or less brilliant insight," the student of personality needs, as A. L. Baldwin puts it, "a technique of evaluation and analysis which will have the virtue of objectivity and will also reveal aspects of the material that may have eluded his scrutiny."

The use of psychological techniques by biographers should result in the reconciliation of many seeming contradictions in their subjects' characters, leading not to simplification, but to understanding.

CHAPTER X

The Writing of Biography

ONE way in which modern biographers have differed greatly from their predecessors has been their willingness to describe their methods of writing and research. Prior to the eighteenth century, accounts of methodology were unheard of. Even in that age of rapidly developing techniques and searching criticism very few discourses on method were produced. On occasion a biographer like Conyers Middleton described in a preface the principles he used in digging out and presenting his evidence. Others, Boswell for instance, dropped hints in their pages which reveal a great deal about their methods. But those who, like Johnson, wrote formal essays on the genre usually confined themselves to philosophical questions and to general comments dealing with the advantage of personal acquaintance with one's subject, the usefulness of anecdotes, and so on. It was not until the nineteenth century that writers began to describe their methods and suggest to others how biographies should be put together. Even then, published accounts were rare. Only in very recent times have such descriptions become common.

In 1813 James F. Stanfield published his *Essay on the Study and Composition of Biography*. Stanfield was a critic rather than a writer of biography; he dealt with such subjects as the qualities of a good biographer (he mentioned imagination, fairness, intelligence, and a wide knowledge of every aspect of human affairs) and the difficulties in the way of presenting an accurate story of a man's life. Lacking personal experience, he did not try to answer the question: "How should the author actually write his material?" but he did discuss the organization of biography, and he offered an ideal plan of his own.

According to Stanfield, a biographer should begin with a general review of his subject's times and a character sketch, in effect presenting his conclusions at the start. Then the subject's life should be discussed by stages: parentage, birth and infancy, childhood, adolescence, young manhood, maturity, and old age, with the emphasis in each stage concentrated on those aspects of the life which were most important in forming the mature character. The story should be rounded out with an analysis of the subject's "Professional Biography," that is, his career in his field of specialization, and a general summary, which Stanfield did not clearly distinguish from the opening character sketch.

Stanfield's book does not seem to have had much influence, although an occasional author has adopted his suggestion of beginning with a summary of character. Usually, however, such summaries have been confined to prefaces. Still, it was an interesting attempt at codifying the subject—something that has rarely been attempted on the same scale.

The idea that life can best be studied by dividing it into distinct stages has been developed elaborately by the Austrian psychologist, Charlotte Buehler, who analyzed the life histories of 250 persons in search of "laws" concerning the general sequence of biographical facts. She concluded that life can be broken down into five periods: *Youth*, which actually precedes what she calls life; *Trials*, marked by groping for an approach to the basic tasks of life; *Early Maturity*, in which the person works out his destiny and finds his proper role; *Maturity*, when the subject not only does what is right for him, but does it well and achieves his goals; and *Decline*, an age of retrospect and preparation for death. For example: In the *Trial* stage Queen Victoria attempted to exercise her authority personally and considered Albert merely as her husband. In *Maturity*, she came to appreciate his ability, allowed him to exercise the royal power, and accepted her "proper" role as wife and mother.

Occasionally, in the nineteenth century, the comments of a practicing biographer were recorded outside his preface. An admirer who chanced to meet Washington Irving at a Saratoga hotel at the time he was working on his life of Washington asked him to describe his system of notetaking. "Ah," Irving replied, "don't talk to me of system: I never had any. . . . I have, it is true, my little budget of notes—some tied one way—some another—and which when I need, I think I come upon in my pigeonholes—by a sort of instinct. That is all there is of it." Actually, Irving cribbed vast sections of his five volumes on Washington from the work of Jared Sparks, with no more acknowledgment than a cavalier and condescending reference in his preface to Sparks's "essential accuracy."

One of the first biographers to describe his method carefully was James Parton. Superficially, Parton's biographies look very much like the weighty Victorian monstrosities that Strachey and so many others have denounced. They are long and detailed. But Parton was a popular writer in the best sense, scholarly yet eminently readable. Modern historians have found reason to question many of his judgments, for his ability to discriminate between subtle differences and to balance delicate pieces of evidence was far from perfect. But modern biographers, especially those who have tried to write about some of the men whose lives he undertook, have been almost unanimous in praising him. For Parton had the knack of character portrayal. "The fact remains," Marquis James once wrote, after outlining Parton's faults, "that a *man* walks through the numerous pages of Mr. Parton." For this reason Parton's comments on biography are well worth examination.

Only by chance have Parton's views been preserved, for he expressed them in personal letters that remained unpublished until after his death. Late in life, when his reputation had been established, he was approached for advice by an amateur, Alfred R. Conkling, who wished to write a biography of his politician father, Roscoe. Parton, who was a kindly man and an enthusiast about his profession, responded elaborately. "The great charm of all biography is the truth, told simply, directly, boldly, charitably," he wrote. "But this is the great difficulty. A human life is long. A human character is complicated. It is often inconsistent within itself, and it requires nice judgment to proportion it." He then listed six rules, expanded upon in later letters:

(1) "To know the subject thoroughly myself." Parton always devoured every scrap of evidence he could track down; he spent months following his subjects' trails, interviewing persons who had known them, and picking up local materials. (2) "To index fully all the knowledge in existence relating to it," and (3) "To determine beforehand where I will be brief, where expand, and how much space I can afford to each part." Parton's works show the results of this careful planning. "You can give a sufficiently 'complete account' of an event without giving a long one," he advised Conkling. "The art is, to be short where the interest is small, and long where the interest is great." Further: "A good thing is twice as good when it comes in just where it ought." (4) "To work slowly and finish as I go." (5) "To avoid eulogy and apology and let the facts have their natural weight," and (6) "To hold back nothing which the reader has a right to know." To Parton this meant being honest and candid, but not impartial. His approach to all his own subjects was frankly sympathetic. "I do not believe we can do justice to any human creature unless we love him," he wrote Conkling. "A true love enlightens, but not blinds." On another occasion Parton wrote: "If we ask a public benefactor to sit for his portrait we should not deny him the privilege of brushing his hair and arranging his cravat."

That Parton was no mere apologist, however, is clear to anyone who has read him. When Conkling's biography of his father finally appeared, Parton considered it overly partisan and did not hesitate to tell the author what he thought. "You must not expect the public to remain satisfied with the omissions and suppressions of your book. Sooner or later, somebody will supply them, and you might just as well have told the whole story."

To these rules may be added certain bits of advice which, since they were occasioned by special problems of Conkling's, may not represent general principles subscribed to by Parton. For one thing, he urged Conkling to avoid breaks in continuity; biography, in other words, should be chronological. "The modern reader is very shy, and easily breaks away from you, if you only give him a pretext." Also he said that odds and ends can best be saved for the end and included in the final chapter in which the author "sums up" his man. He also suggested the lavish use of letters and speeches in treating "a man of words" like Roscoe Conkling and a careful description both of the environment into which he was born and of his parents. He urged the inexperienced Conkling to let the subject tell his own story as much as possible. Comments necessary to fill in gaps and set the stage were fine, but "let *him* have the whole floor."

Henry Adams also left an account of his biographical technique which he wrote for reasons very similar to those which motivated Parton. Late in 1903 Sarah Hewitt, daughter of Abram S. Hewitt, the ironmaster and politician, asked Adams for advice on writing her father's life. Probably she was hoping that Adams would volunteer his services, but he fended her off deftly by outlining a method she could follow in doing the job herself.

"The first step," he told her, "is to find out what material you have, and arrange it in chronological order. You would even save labor by making a rough index as you go." This material should be filed in manuscript binders and should be supplemented with "all your notes and memoranda; all your extracts from letters written or received; all speeches, reports, controversial papers on both sides . . . and . . . any comments or suggestions that may occur to you as you go on, for nothing escapes the mind more easily than those occasional remarks." This arrangement would point up any gaps in the evidence requiring further research and would indicate roughly how to apportion space among the "necessary divisions" of Hewitt's life. "Proportion is everything."

"When you come to writing, I can recommend only one rule," Adams went on. "Strike out every superfluous sentence, and, in what is left, strike out relentlessly every superfluous word. An adjective of any sort is commonly superfluous in that branch of literature." Because she should let her father tell his own story with "as little foreign aid as possible," and because it would not be proper to delete anything from the quoted materials, her own prose should be extremely concise. She should not be afraid, for fear of offending her father's contemporaries, to speak plainly. "You can say almost everything if you can keep your own temper. You can positively say everything, if you smile." An introductory "possibly" or "perhaps," or even a "well-bred air of hesitation," would be all that was required in this connection. "No one objects to being called names, if it is done civilly and sympathetically." He also suggested that she have her manuscript set up in type and strike off a few copies "for private circulation and correction," a practice he was himself to adopt a few years later with his *Education*.

More recent accounts of method are very profuse. Some have dealt with the particular problems of individual biographers. One of the most useful of these for understanding the nature of biography comes from Joseph Hergesheimer, who once wrote a life of General Philip H. Sheridan. Approaching biography with the habits, training, and philosophy of the novelist, Hergesheimer was aware of the need for controlling his artistic imagination, but was nonetheless unprepared for the rigorous restrictions the form imposes. His experience shows well the conflict between the scientist and the artist.

He began with a resolution of Spartan self-control. "It was not part of my undertaking to comment upon anything, but only to repeat, as far as it was possible, what actually had occurred." But as a novelist he could not avoid considering Sheridan's life as a story; he was distressed by the anticlimax inherent in the fact that the General lived for long uneventful years after his hours of glory during the Civil War. He decided to ignore his subject's post-war career, "honest but insignificant," and also to compress all of his life before 1861 into a brief foreword. Yet, perhaps unaware that "it is easy to say nothing but the truth about a man and yet give a thoroughly erroneous idea of him," he still believed he was telling the story of Sheridan's life.

When Hergesheimer plunged into the task of research, he again discovered that writing a biography was very different from writing fiction. He settled down in Washington at the Carlton Hotel and began to study in the Library of Congress. But the histories of Civil War battles were dry, partisan, and undependable, the complications of troop movements and topography difficult to untangle. Sheridan's military career, he found, had been practical and plodding rather than heroic. "I wished twenty times a day that I had never heard of General Sheridan," he complained. "Shut up in my room . . . I came to hate him and the biography of him I had so lightly agreed to write."

Seeking a more congenial environment, Hergesheimer traveled to Palm Beach. There he began to put his material together, but the Florida sunshine did not help very

x. The Writing of Biography

much, for he was still confronted with the (for him) rigid restrictions of the biographical form. "My hatred increased," he recalled afterward. "I wrote, when it was humanly possible, three thousand words a day, and often it took an hour to put down a line, a word." In desperation he put the work aside (he was now calling it "the bitch of a biography") and went sailfishing in the Gulf Stream.

Evidently the fishing was good, for when it was over Hergesheimer managed to struggle through the remainder of his task, finding that he could think of the book "at last" with affection, even if it did not seem likely that many people would ever read it. He did not write any more biographies.

Quite different from Hergesheimer's was the experience of Holmes Alexander, author of lives of Martin Van Buren and Aaron Burr. Where Hergesheimer found it difficult to keep his imagination under control, Alexander found it hard to turn his loose. "I became a biographer only because it was the next best thing to being a novelist," he wrote. He had served in the New York State Legislature and wished to write a novel about his experiences. But he could not. Instead, he did a biography of Van Buren, who was the sort of hero he had conceived for his novel.

When Alexander became interested in Burr, he struggled desperately for the proper approach. He thought of himself as a playwright trying to write a part for a great actor. He skimmed through a few books and read some of Burr's writings. But he could not get started. Finally he became desperate.

> Hand outstretched and mumbling a polite greeting, I would cross to my office door and welcome Colonel Aaron Burr. Showing him to a chair, I would bid him talk, being my-

self his mouthpiece. At other times I would pretend to be a lawyer for his defense, a history professor, a political or after-dinner speaker, introducing him to an audience. I wrote letters to the man. I even began the book in the form of Burr's Autobiography.

At last, after reading a book about Nietzsche, he was inspired to treat Burr as a sort of amoral superman. He collected piles of books, settled down in a comfortable armchair with his pipe and plentiful supply of Coca-Cola, and began to read. He took no notes, relying upon the force of "poignant facts" to imprint the important information on his memory. When the main outline of his book was clear, he began browsing in the stacks of a large library for background material. He eschewed card catalogs and bibliographies. Although he realized that his procedure was inefficient, he felt that it was more interesting than a more systematic approach. "Though it is easier to kill a fox with a gun than to chase him all day with hounds, the sport is worth more than the animal's pelt." In all his reading he was deliberately non-objective. "The research," he confessed, "was less a seeking after Truth than a seeking after material which would best fit my needs."

When his book was finally written, almost entirely out of his memory of what he had read, he had to reread all the sources to check his quotations. "When I came to something I remembered using, I thumbed through the manuscript and tacked on the identification." This technique, he admitted, "was not without its imperfections," but "the way of a transgressor is at least his own."

Neither Hergesheimer nor Alexander suggested that other biographers should adopt his methods. Some modern biog-

x. The Writing of Biography [251

raphers, however, have offered general plans based on their own experiences for others to imitate. A few of these representing widely differing points of view, may be briefly summarized:

Harold Nicolson procures a large notebook, numbers the pages, and prepares an index and chronology of the subject's life. Then he reads the "standard work" on the man, outlining it in his notebook, devoting a separate page to each incident. He then reads all other published works on his subject, filling in the pertinent information on the proper pages. Next he examines unpublished evidence in the same manner. All this is indexed as he proceeds. Extra pages are added to the notebook as necessary. After the paper work is completed, he visits the scenes of important events in his subject's life. Then he writes. In the writing process, he stresses literary artistry and selectivity. The chief object, he says, should be the truth, but not necessarily the whole truth, as unorganized masses of details are only confusing and eccentricities and unusual incidents, if emphasized, may leave a distorted picture in the mind of the reader.

Hesketh Pearson's first step is to read all extant biographies of his subject quickly in search of a general impression. He takes no notes at this time. He turns next to the published reminiscences of his hero's friends and enemies, which he considers the most revealing of biographical sources. Then he reads the subject's published works and hunts down anecdotes in other contemporary memoirs. The next step is to interview living persons who knew his man. At this point he rereads the early biographies carefully and fills in background from histories of the period. Then he sorts out his notes re-evaluating the evidence, weighing conflicting evidence, and balancing the probabilities. There follows a "period for gestation," during which he drops the project completely and sits around the house just reading, smoking, and thinking. Finally, he writes.

Catherine Drinker Bowen has described her method in writing her *John Adams*, and the principles seem to typify her technique. First she read generally about Adams and his family. Then she examined all printed and manuscript sources available, copying out every passage of possible importance. Unlike many biographers (Douglas Southall Freeman is an outstanding example) she did not trust any of this work to research assistants. Her material was filed chronologically, although some topical files were developed on subjects like *Boston: streets and buildings* and *George Washington*. After the research, she passed to a saturation period, going over her notes until they were practically memorized. At the same time she read widely in seventeenth- and eighteenth-century works to get the feel of the the language. She also tacked up pictures of Adams on her bedroom wall to keep him ever-present in her mind. In writing, she sacrificed the textual integrity of the sources in the interest of readability. Over her desk she placed a sign asking: "Will the reader turn the page?" Artistic considerations were dominant. Her story had to have a plot stressing conflicts in order to stimulate reader interest, and this dictated the arrangement and the scope of her book.[1]

In writing *Abraham Lincoln: The War Years*, Carl Sand-

[1] Mrs. Bowen was most specific in stressing this careful arrangement of her story when she described her method in a lecture at Scripps College in 1950. However, in an article written in 1953, she contradicted herself, saying: "Having brought my narrative to the year 1776, I found that I had used up all my space, six hundred printed pages, and had to end my book with my hero at a mere forty. . . ."

burg used, besides conventional sources, pictures, cartoons, posters, and other unusual materials. He bought hundreds of books containing Lincolniana and tore them apart, extracting the pages he considered pertinent for his work. These, together with his other notes, he thumbtacked to an upright screen set next to a large cracker box which supported his typewriter. He was assisted by two copyists and by his wife and three daughters, who filed and organized material. He worked in the attic of his home, surrounded by masses of books. In fine weather this paraphernalia was transferred to the yard, where Sandburg, clad only in a green eyeshade, a "loincloth," and sandals, typed away in the midst of his flock of pedigreed goats. When the work was about three-quarters completed, he revised and rewrote what he had done, "in order to feel the scale and proportion better for the final quarter."

Douglas Southall Freeman never recorded an account of his own methods of research and composition, but his friend Dumas Malone has given us an admirable description of Freeman at work in his essay, "The Pen of Douglas Southall Freeman." A prodigious and extremely systematic worker, Freeman was seldom satisfied with secondary sources. He made extensive use of assistants, but primarily in tracking down and copying materials; he always insisted upon examining important documents himself. He took few notes, preferring to work directly from the sources. If he came upon a long and important passage in a book, for instance, he would simply note the location and general nature of the item; when he came to write, he would turn to the book itself.

All his books and papers were kept in perfect order. He

had special weights designed for keeping stiff-backed volumes open at the proper pages, and a place to write standing up when he became cramped from long hours at his desk. He even used a special type of ruled paper which gave him an automatic check on the number of words he had written in each chapter. Yet despite this efficiency, he prepared his first drafts in longhand, having discovered that "his typewriter, by its very speed led him down false trails . . . and into inaccuracies." He rationed his time rigidly and maintained a careful check on how he used it. Each week he had to work a given number of hours—actually, he was nearly always far ahead of his schedule—but he tried to leave at least an hour a day for exercise and additional time for relaxation. He was able to tell exactly how much time went into any given part of his huge life of Washington. Chapter eight of volume one, for example, was written in eighty-four hours, of which twenty-five were spent in preparing an outline, forty-two in composition, and seventeen in revisions. Such precision and concentration enabled Freeman to write as many as 4,800 words a day, and to turn out, despite his heavy schedule as a newspaperman, radio commentator, and lecturer, his massive biographies.

These illustrations show that modern biographers differ among themselves in method as widely as in results. Perhaps it is impossible to standardize biographical technique. Gordon W. Allport once made an effort to lay down a set of rules for writing and evaluating life histories. The result was a model of logic and scientific objectivity tempered with a full awareness of the complexities of the human mind. Allport's rules may be briefly summarized.

(1) The author should determine his purpose. Allport

x. *The Writing of Biography* [255

lists eight purposes ranging from hagiography through literary creativity to the clinical analysis of personality. (2) He should aim at "maximum fidelity to the life" by blending sympathetic understanding with strict critical interpretation of all data. (3) He should indicate all sources used and seek out all possible information. (4) Unless possessed of special training or aptitudes, the writer should stick to subjects with background and training similar to his own. "As a rule, the closer one's mental life swings with that of another, the better are his understanding and interpretation, provided some detachment and distance are maintained." (5) In judging personal documents, "statements about the objective situation by the subject" should, wherever possible, be checked against other sources "to guard against deception and projections," yet even inaccurate information should be utilized as "expressive evidence" of the subject's personality. (6) Form and content must be adapted to the individual case, but the subdivisions of the biography should always parallel the subdivisions of the life depicted. (7) The opening paragraph (chapter) should set the tone for the entire study. Such techniques as a thumbnail sketch, physical description, or the use of a characteristic anecdote are recommended. (8) Proper weight should be assigned to the times in which the subject lived, especially to his own view of this background. (9) Family life, factors of heredity in so far as they can be measured, and sex life must be considered, but the importance of early experiences in each case must be proved, not assumed. (10) More space should be devoted to conflicts than to periods of calm, yet in interpretation, the conflict should not be overemphasized. For example, "there is less to tell about a happy childhood than about an unhappy one," but "the quiet happy years *may* be the more important." (11) Liberal use should be made of the subject's own language in describing his feelings and experiences. (12) In describing personality traits, each trait should be illustrated with concrete examples which particularize it in the individual described. (13) The author should avoid irrelevance, distraction, and repetition; strive for maximum brevity.

But these splendid rules did not work. The case histories written with strict adherence to them were stiff and unlifelike, not as useful to the psychologist as less consciously organized studies that "violated" one or more of the rules. Professor Allport wrote off his "rules" as an unsuccessful experiment.

Thus a search of the records discloses no fully acceptable pattern for the writing of biography, but shows that many contradictory theories and practices have been applied by all sorts of writers. Some of these precepts have been silly, some ambiguous; most have been advanced by their protagonists with a dogmatic assertiveness indicating, to take the most charitable view, that the writers have not troubled to study the history of the biographical form very closely. That biography is by its very nature a subject attractive to individualists may explain its bewildering variety of form and theory. Yet if there is no one way to write a biography, there are still sound principles upon which serious students are in general agreement.

As to mechanics, few would deny that the biographer should read before he writes and (Holmes Alexander notwithstanding) take notes on what he reads. He should utilize whatever bibliographical tools he can lay his hand

x. The Writing of Biography

on, and should exhaust the possibilities of every significant source he finds. It matters not whether he collects his materials in notebooks, on file cards, or, like Sandburg, by snipping them from the pages of books, but he should assimilate their contents thoroughly and organize them in some logical pattern before he puts pen to paper.

As to organization, there is room for more diversity of approach, but people live their lives from birth to death and biographers who seek to trace the paths of men and women ought generally to conform to chronology. Successful writers have sometimes begun in the middle of things, and many have made effective use of flashbacks. At least one biography (Selden Rodman's life of Ben Shahn) has been written backwards. Every effective biographer has had to combine materials topically in order to reduce the complexities of existence to understandable form. But a topical biography is only a collection of essays. The thread of development is vital if reality is to be approximated. *Importance* should be the measure when allocating precious space, not availability of material, or desire to show off obscure knowledge and newly discovered evidence. Interpretation may dictate a particular emphasis, but this merely narrows the scope of the biography—within any framework, length should be proportionate to significance, although significance may be a matter of judgment.

Within these general rules there is room for endless variety as long as the biographer honestly tries to describe his subject's career and character and does not encumber his work with what very long experience has proved to be extraneous and essentially unworthy motives. The difficulties are enormous, and perfection is beyond the biographer's reach. Man's essence is such that no description of him is self-evidently true to every observer. Further, the nature of the biographical form demands an almost impossible act of synthesis—the creation of a comprehensive and unified "portrait" out of numerous seemingly unrelated and specific details. From close, analytical observation the biographer must derive the kind of universal insight that is also sought by the uninhibited artist.

What he must do is easy to describe; how he is to do it in a particular case defies explanation. From the multiplicity of facts he must select what logic and controlled imagination tell him is typical and significant. He must be an impartial judge, remembering always that while judges should be fair, they must make decisions. He should put himself in Lodovico's place, and when his Othello begs:

> *Speak of me as I am; nothing extenuate,*
> *Nor set down aught in malice.*

he should try to master the subtle contradiction between "nothing extenuate" and "nor set down aught in malice." This he can do if his chief objective is to understand—only then can he explain without either apology or condemnation, be sympathetic without lapsing into partisanship.

"Speak of me as I am." The biographer must strive to heed this simple, human plea. It is his best hope if his work is to have lasting value. For the significance of every man's deeds changes as time goes by. Because the effects of events are unending, no account of events can ever be final. The rise of Christianity changed the meaning of Caesar's life, and so did the rise of Caesar's sawdust effigy, Benito Mussolini. But though great Caesar's provinces have themselves been overrun, Caesar's greatness remains. Man will ever

x. The Writing of Biography

be fascinated by those of his fellows who have changed the course of history. The biographer who can show us *Caesar* will be read when Gaul has been forgotten and when the seven hills of Rome have sunk beneath the blue Mediterranean.

Essay on Sources

Chapter I

THE NATURE OF BIOGRAPHY

There is a vast and scattered literature in English on the general nature of biography as a literary and historical form, but very few books have been entirely devoted to this subject. J. F. Stanfield's *An Essay on the Study and Composition of Biography* (Sunderland, Eng., 1813) is the oldest that I have located, while others are E. P. Hood, *The Uses of Biography: Romantic, Philosophic, and Didactic* (London, 1852); J. C. Johnston, *Biography: The Literature of Personality* (New York, 1927); André Maurois, *Aspects of Biography* (Cambridge, Eng., 1929); and Hesketh Pearson, *Ventilations: Being Biographical Asides* (Philadelphia, 1930). Although W. R. Thayer's *The Art of Biography* (New York, 1920) is primarily a brief history of biography, it contains a great deal of discussion of the nature of the biographical form. Edmund Gosse's article on "Biography" in the eleventh edition of the *Encyclopædia Britannica* (III, pp. 952–4) should also be mentioned.

It would be impractical to mention all the essays, articles, and casual comments by biographers and critics on the nature of biography, but the following are worth listing. Samuel Johnson's essays (*Rambler* #60, October 13, 1750, and *Idler* #84, November 24, 1759) make a good beginning, while Joseph Addison's "Of Modern Historians" (*Freeholder* #35, April 20, 1716) is also important. Others, listed chronologically, are Thomas Carlyle's many comments, collected in *Critical and Miscellaneous Essays* (Boston, 1838); an excellent anonymous article, "Biography," in the *Southern Literary Messenger* (1856), XXIII, pp. 282–8; Phillips Brooks, "Biography," a lecture delivered in 1886 and published in *Essays and Addresses*

(New York, 1895); H. H. Asquith, "Biography," a lecture delivered in 1901 and published in *Occasional Addresses: 1893–1916* (London, 1918); Wilfred Ward's biographical essays in *Problems and Places* (London, 1903) and *Last Lectures* (London, 1918); Leslie Stephen's introductory essay in his *Studies of a Biographer* (London, 1907); Sidney Lee, "Principles of Biography" (1911) and "The Perspective of Biography" (1918), published in *Elizabethan and Other Essays* (Oxford, 1929); Charles Whibley's article on the subject in his *Letters of an Englishman: Second Series* (London, 1912), pp. 76–82; E. T. Cook, "The Art of Biography," *National Review* (1914), LXIII, pp. 266–84; A. C. Benson, "The Art of the Biographer," *Transactions of the Royal Society of Literature* (1926) [n.s.] VI, pp. 139–64; Allan Nevins's chapter "Biography" in *The Gateway to History* (New York, 1938), as well as his "The Biographer and the Historian," *Humanities for Our Time* (Lawrence, Kansas, 1949) and his "How Shall One Write of a Man's Life?" *The New York Times Book Review* (July 15, 1951), pp. 1, 20; Philip Guedalla, "The Method of Biography," *Journal of the Royal Society of Arts* (1939), LXXXVII, pp. 925–35; Virginia Woolf, "The Art of Biography," *Atlantic Monthly* (1939), CLXIII, pp. 506–10; W. S. Weeden, "Concerning Biography," in *Humanistic Studies in Honor of John Calvin Metcalf* (Charlottesville, Va., 1941), a philosopher's view; Dumas Malone, "Biography and History," in J. R. Strayer, ed., *The Interpretation of History* (Princeton, 1943); A. L. Rowse, *The Use of History* (London, 1946), which contains some discussion of biography; G. M. Trevelyan, *Biography: A Readers' Guide* (Cambridge, Eng., 1947); and Leon Edel, "That One May Say This Was the Man," *The New York Times Book Review* (June 24, 1956), pp. 1, 12.

On the role of the individual in history, Sidney Hook, *The Hero in History* (Boston, 1955), is of primary importance. Herman Ausubel has analyzed the views of a number of professional historians on the subject in *Historians and Their Craft* (New York, 1950). Other important discussions are V. L. Aljberg, "History Through Biographical Lenses," *Social Studies* (1947), XXXVIII, pp. 243–6; Allan Nevins, "Is History Made By Heroes?" *Saturday Review* (November 5, 1955), XXXVIII, pp. 9–10, 42–5; and Oscar Handlin, "The History in Men's Lives," *Virginia Quarterly Review* (1954), XXX, pp. 534–41. The "great man" theory receives its strongest support in Thomas Carlyle, *On Heroes, Hero-Worship and the Heroic in History* (New York, 1891), in Ralph Waldo Emerson's introductory essay in *Representative Men* (Boston, 1903), and in William James, "Great Men and Their Environment" and "The Importance of Individuals," *The Will to Believe* (New York, 1927). Specific statements quoted or referred to in the text may be found in Joseph Schneider,

ESSAY ON SOURCES

"The Cultural Situation as a Condition for the Achievement of Fame," *American Sociological Review* (1937), II, pp. 480–91; V. F. Calverton, *The Newer Spirit* (New York, 1925), pp. 216, 239; Stephen Vincent Benét, "The Curfew Tolls," *Selected Works: Prose* (New York, 1942), pp. 383–98; Parke Godwin, ed., *The Auto-Biography of Goethe* (New York, 1846), I, pp. vii–viii; Ausubel, *Historians and Their Craft*, pp. 292 (Cheyney) and 288 (Thayer); Carlyle, *Critical and Miscellaneous Essays*, III, pp. 44–61; Lee, *Elizabethan Essays*, p. 44; W. E. Woodward, *George Washington: The Image and the Man* (New York, 1926), p. 33; Gilbert Chinard, *Thomas Jefferson: The Apostle of Americanism* (Boston, 1929), pp. 23–4; D. S. Muzzey, *James G. Blaine: A Political Idol of Other Days* (New York, 1934), p. v.

Most authorities on biography have stressed the importance of describing the personality of one's subject. Only a few of their writings can be listed here. "A Biographer at Work," *New Englander* (1866), XXV, pp. 218–27, is an interesting mid-Victorian account that emphasizes the *development* of personality; others are L. S. Portor, "Haunted Lives," *Atlantic Monthly* (1917), CXX, pp. 323–33; the introduction to Edmund Gosse's *Portraits and Sketches* (New York, 1914); Gamaliel Bradford, "The Art of Biography," *Saturday Review of Literature* (1925), I, pp. 769–70; André Maurois, "To Make a Man Come Alive Again," *The New York Times Book Review* (December 27, 1953), p. 1. For the opposite viewpoint see number eleven of Vicesimus Knox's *Lucubrations: Or Winter Evenings* (Dublin, 1788); "Modern Biography," *Blackwood's* (1849), LXV, pp. 219–34, which applies primarily to the biographies of literary figures; Charles Whibley, "The Indiscretions of Biography," *English Review* (1924), XXXIX, pp. 769–72, which advances the unique idea that it is permissible to discuss the personal life of a subject only if he himself was frank about his personal affairs; E. W. Adams, "On Polishing Windows—And Other Matters," *Contemporary Review* (1932), CXLI, pp. 88–93.

On the importance of literary artistry in biography see the already mentioned essays by Addison and Johnson, and Edmund Gosse, "The Custom of Biography," *Anglo-Saxon Review* (1901), VIII, pp. 195–208; Carl Van Doren, "Biography as a Literary Form," *Columbia University Quarterly* (1915), XVII, pp. 180–5; Arnold Bennett, *Things That Have Interested Me* (London, 1921), pp. 284–6; George Saintsbury, *Collected Essays and Papers* (London, 1923), I, pp. 409–33; C. K. Trueblood, "Biography," *Dial* (1927), LXXXIII, pp. 128–36; A. J. A. Symons, "Tradition in Biography," *Tradition and Experiment in Present-Day Literature* (London, 1929), pp. 147–60; Harold Nicolson, "Biography Old and New," *Living Age* (1937), CCCLII, pp. 265–8, and "The Practice of Biography," *American*

Scholar (1954), XXIII, pp. 151–61; J. T. Flexner, "Biography as a Juggler's Art," *Saturday Review of Literature* (October 9, 1943), pp. 3–4, 19. On the special importance of literary skill in describing personality see G. W. Allport, "Personality: A Problem for Science or a Problem for Art?" *Revista de Psihologie* (1938), I, p. 488–502; H. A. Murray, *Explorations in Personality* (New York, 1938), pp. 608–9; Allan Nevins, "The Struggle to Make the Past Alive," *The New York Times Book Review* (January 13, 1952), p. 14. Somerset Maugham's autobiography, *The Summing Up* (New York, 1938), contains many thoughtful comments on the problem of character delineation. Beard's comment is quoted by Nevins in *The Humanities for Our Time*, p. 45, and T. S. Eliot's lines are from *The Confidential Clerk* (New York, 1954), p. 18.

The power of the biographer to influence his portrait by his methods of selecting and interpreting evidence is discussed in John Chamberlain, "Walking the Tightrope: An Inquiry into the Art of Political Biography," *Modern Monthly* (1933), VII, pp. 105–9; N. I. White, "The Development, Use and Abuse of Interpretation in Biography," *English Institute Annual* (1942), pp. 29–58; W. S. Lewis, "The Difficult Art of Biography," *Yale Review* (1954), XLIV, p. 40; J. A. Garraty, "The Power of the Biographer," *Social Education* (1955), XIX, pp. 295–8. The quotation from the already noted article in the *Southern Literary Messenger* can be found in XXIII, p. 287.

For the Carnegie illustrations see Andrew Carnegie, *Autobiography* (Boston, 1920), pp. 41–4; J. K. Winkler, *Incredible Carnegie* (New York, 1931), pp. 22, 44, 48; B. J. Hendrick, *The Life of Andrew Carnegie* (Garden City, 1932), I, p. 58. Lloyd Lewis's statement is from his *Sherman: Fighting Prophet* (New York, 1932), p. 241. The Lincoln examples are from Emil Ludwig, *Lincoln* (Boston, 1929), p. 182; N. W. Stephenson, *Abraham Lincoln* (Indianapolis, 1922), p. 83; A. J. Beveridge, *Abraham Lincoln: 1809–1858* (Boston, 1928), II, p. 356; E. L. Masters, *Lincoln: The Man* (New York, 1931), p. 233. For Shelby Little's theory and practice see her *George Washington* (New York, 1929), pp. x, 23–4, 376. Desmond MacCarthy's comment is from *Memories* (London, 1953), p. 32.

On the importance of imagination in biography see Hilaire Belloc, *Selected Essays* (London, 1948), pp. 170–5; Odell Shepard, *Pedlar's Progress: The Life of Bronson Alcott* (Boston, 1937), pp. xii–xiii; Francis Hackett, "On Turning Historian," *Bookman* (1929), LXIX, pp. 575–87; Bradford Smith, "Biographer's Creed," *William and Mary Quarterly* (1953), X, pp. 190–4. On the restrictions that must be imposed on imagination see John Galsworthy, "The Creation of Character in Literature," *Bookman* (1931), LXXIII, pp. 561–9; Wallace Notestein, "History and the Biographer," *Yale Review* (1933), XXII, pp. 549–58; J. B. Frantz, "Adventuring in Biography," *Historian* (1953), XVI, pp. 45–61; F. B. Tolles, "The Biographer's Craft," *South Atlantic Quarterly* (1954), LIII, pp. 508–20. Strachey's distortions of Florence Nightingale have been exposed in Rosalind Nash, "Florence Nightingale According to Mr. Strachey," *Nineteenth Century* (1928), CIII, pp. 258–65. For similar attacks on other of Strachey's works see G. B. Harrison, "Elizabeth and Her Court," *Spectator* (1928), CXLI, p. 777; F. A. Simpson, "Methods of History," *Spectator* (1944), CLXXII, pp. 7–8. The quotations are from Lytton Strachey, *Eminent Victorians* (London, 1918), p. 136, and Sir Edward Cook, *The Life of Florence Nightingale* (London, 1914), I, pp. 13–14. Thomas's reconstruction of Lincoln's mood is from B. P. Thomas, *Abraham Lincoln* (New York, 1952), pp. 339–40. His explanation is from a speech delivered at the Mississippi Valley Historical Association meeting at St. Louis, April 28, 1955, a copy of which he kindly allowed me to use. Marchette Chute's comment is from her article "From 'Bad Risk' to Best Seller," *Library Journal* (1951), LXXVI, p. 1487.

Strachey's criticism of long artless biographies is from *Eminent Victorians*, p. viii; Johnson's comment is from *Rambler* #60, Addison's from *Freeholder* #35, Gosse's from *Anglo-Saxon Review*, VIII, p. 205. On the question of length in biography see Andrew Lang, *Sir Stafford Northcote, First Earl of Iddesleigh* (London, 1890), I, pp. xviii–ix and Allan Nevins, *The New York Times Book Review* (July 15, 1951), p. 20, favoring length, and S. T. Coleridge, *The Friend* (London, 1863), pp. 56–7; George Saintsbury, *Collected Essays*, I, p. 433; Robert Lynd, *Books and Authors* (New York, 1923), p. 114; C. V. Woodward, "Can We Believe Our Own History?" *Johns Hopkins Magazine* (1954), V, p. 16; H. S. Commager, "Among the World-Seekers and World-Forsakers," *The New York Times Book Review* (February 13, 1955), p. 3, arguing for brevity. Freeman's description of Washington's pre-natal life is in his *George Washington* (New York, 1948), I, pp. 46–7.

On the advantage of personal acquaintance with one's subject see the eighteenth-century biographer Roger North, quoted in W. H. Dunn, *English Biography* (London, 1916), p. 227; H. H. Asquith, *Occasional Addresses*, p. 45; W. S. Lewis, *Yale Review*, XLIV, pp. 33–4. For the opposite viewpoint see T. E. Kebble, *The Life of Lord Beaconsfield* (Philadelphia, 1888), p. ix, quoting Disraeli; Henry Adams to Sarah Hewitt, January 18, 1904, in H. D. Cater, ed., *Henry Adams and His Friends* (Boston, 1947), p. 549; Hesketh Pearson, *Thinking It Over* (London, 1938), p. 292. The quotations in the text are from F. S. Stevenson, *Historic Personality* (London, 1893), p. 16, quoting Voltaire; Georg Misch, *A History of Autobiography in Antiquity* (Cambridge, 1951), I, p. 63; Nicolson, *American Scholar*, XXIII, p. 158.

The difference between biography and autobiography is emphasized in the quoted statement of Wayne Shumaker, *English Autobiography: Its Emergence, Materials, and Form* (Berkeley, 1954), pp. 33–4, and in Leon Edel, *Henry James: The Untried Years* (Philadelphia, 1953), p. 337. But for a differing point of view see D. A. Stauffer, *The Art of Biography in Eighteenth Century England* (Princeton, 1941), p. 3.

Chapter II

BIOGRAPHY IN THE ANCIENT WORLD

The standard history of early biography is Friedrich Leo's *Die griechisch-römische Biographie nach ihrer litterarischen Form* (Leipzig, 1901). The fullest account in English is D. R. Stuart's *Epochs of Greek and Roman Biography* (Berkeley, 1928). For pre-Greek origins, Georg Misch, *A History of Autobiography in Antiquity* (Cambridge, 1951), contains a great deal of information, since all of the early "autobiographies" were actually biographical works. Misch also deals in passing with Greek and Roman biography *per se*. W. R. Thayer, *The Art of Biography* (New York, 1920) has some interesting comments on the classical biographers.

Quotations from Egyptian and Babylonian biographical fragments are from Misch, *Autobiography in Antiquity*, I, pp. 26, 19–20, 27, 38, 41–2.

The lines on Greek ideas about the influence of environment are from A. J. Toynbee, *Greek Historical Thought* (New York, 1952), pp. 143, 145. On the Greek view of funeral orations and self-praise see Stuart, *Epochs*, pp. 24–5, and Misch, *Autobiography in Antiquity*, I, p. 61.

Xenophon's encomium on Agesilaus has been translated in E. C. Marchant, ed., *Xenophon: Scripta Minora* (London, 1925). On the distortions in this work see p. xvii. The quotations from the *Memorabilia* are from Marchant's translation (London, 1923), pp. 45, 359.

For Plato's and Aristotle's contributions to the development of biography see Stuart, *Epochs*, pp. 124–5, and Misch, *Autobiography in Antiquity*, I, p. 292. The quotation from Isocrates' autobiography is from Misch, ibid., I, 159.

The quotations from Theophrastus are from W. H. D. Rouse, ed., *The Characters of Theophrastus* (London, 1928), pp. 71–2, 7–8. The best account of the Peripatetic and Alexandrian schools of biography is Stuart, *Epochs*, pp. 119–88.

On the *laudatio funebris* and the origins of Roman biography see Stuart, ibid., p. 200, 209–15; Misch, *Autobiography in Antiquity*, I,

ESSAY ON SOURCES [267

pp. 214–15; Alfred Duggan, *Julius Cæsar* (New York, 1955), p. 59. Cicero's comment is from Misch, ibid., I, p. 218n. Stuart, ibid., pp. 232–4, 247–8 describes Roman "authorized" lives and the relations of Roman to Greek biography. For Edward Gibbon's comment on Nepos, see his *Autobiography* (London, 1923), pp. 26–7.

The literature on Plutarch, of course, is extensive. The best English translation of his *Lives of Noble Grecians and Romans* is probably Bernadotte Perrin's in the Loeb Classical Library series (London, 1914–26); my quotations are from A. H. Clough's translation, reprinted in the handy Modern Library edition (New York, n.d.). For commentary on Plutarch see the Perrin and Clough introductions; Perrin's introductory essay in his *Plutarch's Themistocles and Aristides* (New York, 1901); R. C. Trench, *Plutarch: His Life, His Lives and His Morals* (London, 1873); G. T. Griffith, "The Greek Historians," in Maurice Platnauer, ed., *Fifty Years of Classical Scholarship* (Oxford, 1954), pp. 172, 188–9; and the introductory chapter of L. K. Barnett, *Writing on Life* (New York, 1951), which develops the idea that Plutarch anticipated all the techniques of the modern writers of "profiles." Also of interest is E. R. Dodds, "The Portrait of a Greek Gentleman," *Greece and Rome* (1933), II, pp. 97–107. For Plutarch's comment on Lucullus, see the Modern Library edition, p. 578; for his statement of his purpose in writing, ibid., p. 293; for the Alcibiades incident, ibid., p. 238; for his comparison of his work to that of portrait painters, ibid., p. 801; the anecdotes about Alexander are ibid., pp. 805, 822. The different "leads" employed by Plutarch are—in the order of their appearance in the text—ibid., pp. 678, 182, 449, 347.

The Modern Library edition of Suetonius' *Lives of the Twelve Caesars* (New York, 1931), edited by Joseph Gavorse, is the most recent of the many translations of this work. The quotations from Suetonius' lives of Caesar and Tiberius are from this edition, pp. 20–1, 145. For Plutarch's handling of Julius Caesar, see the Modern Library edition, pp. 854–95, especially pp. 863, 874, 892–3. Stuart's comment on Suetonius is in *Epochs*, p. 185. For the later influence of Suetonius see J. C. Rolfe, "Suetonius and His Biographers," American Philosophical Society *Proceedings* (1913), LII, pp. 206–25. Geneva Misener, "Iconistic Portraits," *Classical Philology* (1924), XIX, pp. 97–123, deals with the ways in which Plutarch and Suetonius (along with other classical biographers) made use of physical descriptions of their subjects. See especially pp. 110–11, 117–18.

On the *Scriptores Historiae Augustae*, see the introduction to the Loeb Classical Library edition, David Magie, ed. (London, 1921), especially pp. xv–xix.

Chapter III

THE DEVELOPMENT OF BIOGRAPHY

There is no comprehensive history of medieval and Renaissance biography, but all the histories of English biography cover the period. The fullest account is D. A. Stauffer, *English Biography Before 1700* (Cambridge, 1930). W. H. Dunn, *English Biography* (New York, 1916), pp. 1–80 is an excellent survey. Briefer accounts can be found in Harold Nicolson, *The Development of English Biography* (London, 1928), and W. R. Thayer, *The Art of Biography* (New York, 1920).

On saints' lives, see Stauffer, *Biography Before 1700*, pp. 4–22; Dunn, *English Biography*, pp. 1–45; G. H. Gerould, *Saints' Legends* (Boston, 1916), which stresses the legendary aspects of the subject; J. D. M. Ford, "The Saints' Lives in the Vernacular Literature of the Middle Ages," *Catholic Historical Review* (1931), XVII, pp. 268–77, a summary of the work of the German scholar Paul Meyer.

Alcuin's life of Willibrord has been translated by C. H. Talbot in *The Anglo-Saxon Missionaries in Germany* (New York, 1954). Talbot's introduction, pp. vii–xvii, is useful on saints' lives in general. There is an enthusiastic account of Adamnan's life of St. Columba in George Carver, *Alms for Oblivion* (Milwaukee, 1946), pp. 15–28. For the life of Columban by Jonas, see D. C. Munro, ed., "The Life of St. Columban by the Monk Jonas," *Translations and Reprints from the Original Sources of European History* (Philadelphia, n.d.), II, #7. Talbot, *Anglo-Saxon Missionaries*, pp. 25–62, translates Willibald's *Boniface*. On Eadmer's St. Anselm, see Stauffer, *Biography Before 1700*, pp. 12–14; Nicolson's comment is from his *English Biography*, p. 22. My account of Russian saints' lives is based on N. K. Gudzy, *History of Early Russian Literature* (New York, 1949), pp. 98–105, 213–16.

On medieval secular biography see Stauffer, *Biography Before 1700*, pp. 22–32. Einhard's *Charlemagne* has been translated by A. J. Grant in *Early Lives of Charlemagne* (London, 1905), pp. 4–50; for Joinville's *St. Louis*, see F. T. Marzials, ed., *Memoirs of the Crusades* (London, 1908), the quotation in the text being from p. 285; the comment of Jakob Burckhardt is from his *Civilization of the Renaissance in Italy* (New York, 1945), p. 200. For parallel trends not discussed in the text see P. J. Alexander, "Secular Biography at Byzantium," *Speculum* (1940), XV, pp. 194–209, and S. H. Chen, "An Innovation in Chinese Biographical Writing," *Far Eastern Quarterly* (1953), XIII, pp. 49–62, which provides a brief survey of the history of Chinese biography.

ESSAY ON SOURCES [269

Scattered materials on Italian Renaissance biography can be found in Burckhardt, *Renaissance*, J. A. Symonds, *Renaissance in Italy* (New York, 1888), H. O. Taylor, *Thought and Expression in the Sixteenth Century* (New York, 1930), and W. K. Ferguson, *The Renaissance in Historical Thought* (Boston, 1948). Boccaccio's *Dante* has been translated by J. R. Smith in *The Earliest Lives of Dante*, Yale Studies in English (New York, 1901), X. For Vasari see E. H. and E. W. Blashfield and A. A. Hopkins, eds., *Lives of Seventy of the Most Eminent Painters, Sculptors and Architects by Giorgio Vasari* (New York, 1887). Symonds's comments on the Italians are from his *Renaissance in Italy*, II, pp. 35, 38; Ferguson's statement about the importance of classical models is from his *Historical Thought*, pp. 17–18, his comment on Vasari from ibid., p. 61.

On the spread of the Renaissance throughout Europe see Taylor, *Thought and Expression* and Gilbert Highet, *The Classical Tradition* (New York, 1949). On Amyot's translation of Plutarch, see Taylor, ibid., p. 356, and Highet, ibid., p. 117. The many editions of Suetonius are noticed in J. C. Rolfe, "Suetonius and His Biographers," American Philosophical Society *Proceedings* (1913), LII, p. 206.

Useful summaries of French Renaissance biographical writings can be found in B. W. Bates, *Literary Portraiture in the Historical Narrative of the French Renaissance* (New York, 1945). My account of Matthieu and Brantôme is based on this work. The quotation from Brantôme's sketch of Elizabeth de Valois, however, is my own translation of Bates, p. 61.

Stauffer, *Biography Before 1700*, pp. 33–63, gives a good summary of the influence of the Renaissance on English biography. Stauffer's comment on Bede is from ibid., pp. 232–3; the quotation from More's *Richard III* is from ibid., pp. 40–1. On More and his biographers see P. S. and H. M. Allen, eds., *Sir Thomas More: Selections from His English Works and from the Lives by Erasmus & Roper* (Oxford, 1924), and Carver, *Alms for Oblivion*, pp. 29–49.

The development of the idea of biography is described by Stauffer, *Biography Before 1700*, pp. 235–55, the quotation from Bacon is from p. 249 of Stauffer; Marc Bloch's comment is from *The Historian's Craft* (New York, 1953), p. 168. For French trends see C. H. C. Wright, *French Classicism* (Cambridge, 1920); Arthur Tilley, *Decline of the Age of Louis XIV* (Cambridge, Eng., 1929); Henri Van Laun, ed., *The Characters Of Jean de la Bruyère* (London, 1952). On Fuller see S. C. Roberts, *Thomas Fuller: A Seventeenth Century Worthy* (Manchester, 1953); Carver, *Alms for Oblivion*, pp. 77–88; the quotations are from Stauffer, *Biography Before 1700*, pp. 238–9, and Nicolson, *English Biography*, p. 51. On Burnet see V. de S. Pinto, *English Biography in the Seventeenth Century* (London, 1951), especially pp. 39–40. Pinto provides a convenient

270] ESSAY ON SOURCES

printing of Burnet's *Life and Death of Rochester* and of other seventeenth-century biographies. Johnson's comment is from James Boswell, *The Life of Samuel Johnson* (Oxford, 1927), II, p. 147.

There is an excellent brief analysis of Aubrey in Edgar Johnson, *One Mighty Torrent* (New York, 1937), pp. 70–4. There are many editions of Aubrey's *Lives*, perhaps the best of which is Andrew Clark's (Oxford, 1898).

On Izaak Walton see his *Lives* (Oxford, 1927); Stauffer, *Biography Before 1700*, pp. 91–120; Johnson, *One Mighty Torrent*, pp. 74–84; Carver, *Alms for Oblivion*, pp. 57–76; John Butt, "Izaak Walton's Methods in Biography," *English Association Essays* (1933), XIX, pp. 67–84.

Chapter IV

BIOGRAPHY REACHES MATURITY

The great work on eighteenth-century biography is D. A. Stauffer, *The Art of Biography in Eighteenth Century England* (Princeton, 1941). Together with its bibliographic supplementary volume it provides a definitive treatment of English biography of the period and in addition it is the best available commentary on European trends. The other general histories of English biography devote ample space to the eighteenth century, and Mark Longaker, *English Biography in the Eighteenth Century* (Philadelphia, 1931), is also useful. Stauffer, however, is the main source for this chapter, and all quotations from the minor works referred to herein are, unless otherwise noted, from *The Art of Biography*. The opening quotation, summarizing Stauffer's view of the period, is from p. 553.

W. H. Dunn, *English Biography* (New York, 1916), pp. 85–6, is particularly useful on Defoe and the relation of biography to the novel. On Fénelon, see Arthur Tilley, *Decline of the Age of Louis XIV* (Cambridge, Eng., 1929), pp. 253–4. Longaker, *Biography in the Eighteenth Century*, is particularly good on the development of scholarship. See especially pp. 208–9, 218–19, 228–30, dealing with Middleton and Malone. Voltaire's comments are from John Morley, *Voltaire* (London, 1923), pp. 298, 305.

Wayne Shumaker's comment on the origins of introspective autobiography is from his *English Autobiography: Its Emergence, Materials and Form* (Berkeley, 1954), p. 29; Addison's comments are from *Freeholder*, #35; Knox's are quoted by Dunn, *English Biography*, p. 120.

Samuel Johnson's views on biography are to be found in his *Rambler* #60 and *Idler* #84 papers; there are also many scattered references to his views on the subject in James Boswell, *Life of Samuel*

ESSAY ON SOURCES [271

Johnson (Oxford, 1927). J. W. Krutch, *Samuel Johnson* (New York, 1944), is an excellent biography. All historians of the biography of the period deal extensively with Johnson, but see especially Sir Walter Raleigh, *Six Essays on Johnson* (Oxford, 1910). For the *Lives of the Poets* see the edition of Arthur Waugh (New York, 1897), and for a convenient selection, including the *Life of Savage*, see W. L. Fleischauer, ed., *Samuel Johnson: Lives of the English Poets* (Chicago, 1955). Quotations in the text are from this edition, pp. 231, 233. On the reviews of the *Lives of the Poets* see Stauffer, *Art of Biography*, p. 392.

The remarkable introduction to Conyers Middleton, *History of the Life and Times of Marcus Tullius Cicero* (London, 1876) provides the information on Middleton's methods of writing biography.

With Boswell, as with Johnson, all the authorities already noted have extensive comments to offer. Boswell's introduction to the biography affords him an opportunity to expound upon his theory and practice. A study of Boswell's journal entries about Johnson and the comparable passages in the biography throws a good deal of light on his methods. See also George Mallory, *Boswell the Biographer* (London, 1912).

Chapter V

NINETEENTH-CENTURY TRENDS

There is no general history of nineteenth-century biography. W. H. Dunn, *English Biography* (New York, 1916), pp. 157–99 is the best survey; W. R. Thayer, *The Art of Biography* (New York, 1920), pp. 101–47, and Harold Nicolson, *The Development of English Biography* (London, 1928), pp. 109–31 are also useful. E. H. O'Neill, *A History of American Biography: 1800–1935* (Philadelphia, 1935) is comprehensive but lacking in critical judgment, while D. K. Merrill, *The Development of American Biography* (Portland, Me., 1932) is sound but rather brief. E. H. O'Neill, ed., *Biography By Americans—1658–1936: A Subject Bibliography* (Philadelphia, 1939) is a useful listing of biographies written by American authors, and Marion Dargan, ed., *Guide to American Biography: 1607–1933* (Albuquerque, 1949, 1952) is a bibliography of biographies about Americans which also contains brief excerpts from reviews.

On Lockhart's *Scott* see Nicolson, *English Biography*, pp. 117–25, for a particularly favorable view; Edgar Johnson, *One Mighty Torrent* (New York, 1937), pp. 307–20; George Carver, *Alms for Oblivion* (Milwaukee, 1946), pp. 200–12; Dunn, *English Biography*, pp. 160–7, containing excerpts from the estimates of many other critics;

Sir Robert Rait, "Boswell and Lockhart," Royal Society of Literature *Transactions* (1933), XII, pp. 105–27. Carlyle's criticisms of Lockhart and of other nineteenth-century biographers can be found in the many reviews included in his *Critical and Miscellaneous Essays* (Boston, 1838).

There was much discussion, even at the time, of the reticence of Victorian biographers. Defenses of reticence include an anonymous article on "Modern Biography," *Blackwood's* (1849), LXV, pp. 219–34; M. A. Dodge ("Gail Hamilton"), "The New School of Biography," *Atlantic Monthly* (1864), XIV, pp. 579–89; S. T. Coleridge, *The Friend* (London, 1863), II, pp. 56–61; William Wordsworth, *Prose Works* (London, 1876), II, pp. 1–24. The opposite point of view is advanced in "Biographies of Great Men," *New York Review* (1842), X, pp. 358–75; "The Duty of a Biographer," *Democratic Review* (1851), XXVIII, pp. 254–8; C. A. Collins, "Biography at a Discount," *Macmillan's* (1864), X, pp. 158–63. Dickens's comment is quoted in Godfrey Davies, "Biography and History," *Modern Language Quarterly* (1940), I, pp. 79–94; Baudelaire's is from Charles Baudelaire, *My Heart Laid Bare* (New York, 1951), pp. 203–4. On Hamilton Fish and Tom Moore as censors see Allan Nevins, *Gateway to History* (New York, 1938), p. 171. The quotation from "Parson" Weems is quoted by D. S. Freeman in *George Washington: A Biography* (New York, 1948), I, p. 538; for Sparks as an editor see Nevins, *Gateway*, pp. 161–3. The Carlyle quotation about "the inward springs" is from *Critical and Miscellaneous Essays*, I, p. 289; Whitman's remarks are quoted in André Maurois, *Aspects of Biography* (Cambridge, Eng., 1929), p. 26; the Lincoln quotation is from J. B. Frantz, "Adventuring in Biography," *Historian* (1953), XVI, p. 59.

The quotation about the popularity of biography in 1821 is from Dunn, *English Biography*, p. 157, quoting John Watkins; Smith's comment on Nollekens is from *Nollekens and His Times* (London, 1828), I, p. 6.

On Froude's *Carlyle*, in addition to the general surveys, see Johnson, *One Mighty Torrent*, pp. 393–404; Carver, *Alms for Oblivion*, pp. 254–67; J. A. Froude, *My Relations with Carlyle* (London, 1901); James Crichton-Browne and Alexander Carlyle, *The Nemesis of Froude* (London, 1903); W. H. Dunn, *Froude and Carlyle* (New York, 1930). Froude's comment on the purpose of biography is from his *Relations with Carlyle*, p. 40; Carlyle's view on publishing unflattering comments is quoted in Johnson, *One Mighty Torrent*, p. 393.

The controversy provoked by Froude produced a large body of argument on both sides. The conservative, or anti-Froude position can be seen in anonymous articles in the *Spectator* (1882), LV, pp.

ESSAY ON SOURCES [273

988–90 and *Cornhill Magazine* (1883), XLVII, pp. 601–7; M. O. W. Oliphant, "The Ethics of Biography," *Living Age* (1883), CLVIII, pp. 323–33; George Tyrrell, "The Ethics of Suppression in Biography," *Month* (1896), pp. 360–7; Agnes Repplier, "Memoirs and Biographies," in Henry Van Dyke, ed., *Counsel upon the Reading of Books* (Boston, 1900), pp. 95–135; "Concerning Biography," *Academy* (1901), LX, pp. 167–8; R. H. Hutton, *Brief Literary Criticisms* (London, 1906), pp. 226–33. For the other side of the argument see Walter Lewin, "Bowdlerized Biography," *Forum* (1891), X, pp. 658–66; E. S. Purcell, "On the Ethics of Suppression in Biography," *Nineteenth Century* (1896), XL, pp. 533–42; P. L. Ford, *The True George Washington* (Philadelphia, 1896), p. 6; Edmund Gosse, "The Custom of Biography," *Anglo-Saxon Review* (1901), VIII, pp. 195–208. Gosse's 1910 lecture is quoted in *Atlantic Monthly* (1910), CV, p. 716.

On the impact of psychology on biography see J. A. Garraty, "The Interrelations of Psychology and Biography," *Psychological Bulletin* (1954), LI, pp. 569–82. Quotations in the text are from Francis Galton, *Hereditary Genius* (London, 1869), p. 43; John Fiske, "Sociology and Hero-Worship," *Atlantic Monthly* (1881), XLVII, p. 81; Havelock Ellis, *Views and Reviews* (London, 1932), pp. 96–8, 143.

Freud's *Leonardo da Vinci: A Study in Psychosexuality* is most easily available in the Modern Library edition (New York, 1947). The quotations in the text are from pp. 14–15, 33–4, 88, 91, 109, 117–18, 121. For commentary on the soundness of Freud's interpretation of Leonardo see R. R. Wohl and Richard Trossman, "A Retrospect of Freud's *Leonardo*," *Psychiatry* (1955), XVIII, pp. 27–39.

Froude's comment on "imaginative" historians is quoted in Nevins, *Gateway to History*, p. 173; Brett is quoted in Gertrude Atherton, *Adventures of a Novelist* (New York, 1932), p. 344. On Belloc see Nevins, ibid., p. 173; A. C. Ward, *Twentieth Century Literature* (London, 1931), pp. 194–5; and Belloc's essay "On Footnotes," in J. B. Morton, ed., *Selected Essays of Hilaire Belloc* (London, 1948), pp. 170–5. Gertrude Atherton's description of her work on Hamilton is in her *Adventures*, pp. 315–25, 340.

Chapter VI

THE "NEW" BIOGRAPHY AND THE MODERN SYNTHESIS

The literature on Lytton Strachey is enormous; only a few of the most important studies can be listed here. There are essays on Strachey in Edgar Johnson, *One Mighty Torrent* (New York, 1937), pp. 503–23; George Carver, *Alms for Oblivion* (Milwaukee, 1946), pp. 287–301; Mark Longaker, *Contemporary Biography* (Philadelphia, 1934), pp. 29–63; Cyril Clemens, *Lytton Strachey* (Webster Groves, Mo., 1942) is valuable for the many comments by authors and critics which Clemens has collected. The most scholarly studies of Strachey have been made by C. R. Sanders, but his approach is, I believe, much too sympathetic toward Strachey. "Lytton Strachey's Conception of Biography," *PMLA* (1951), LXVI, pp. 295–315 is typical of Sanders's work. For other articles and essays see D. S. Mirsky, "Mr. Lytton Strachey," *London Mercury* (1923), VIII, pp. 175–84; Desmond MacCarthy, "Lytton Strachey as a Biographer," *Life and Letters* (1932), VIII, pp. 90–102; Guy Boas, "Lytton Strachey," *English Association Pamphlets* (1935), #93; Leonard Bacon, "An Eminent Post-Victorian," *Yale Review* (1941), XXX, pp. 310–24; Max Beerbohm, *Lytton Strachey: The Rede Lecture* (Cambridge, Eng., 1943); George Gordon, *The Lives of Authors* (London, 1950), pp. 12–22. For criticisms of Strachey on specific points see the articles by Rosalind Nash, F. A. Simpson, and G. B. Harrison listed in the sources for Chapter I. The Bertrand Russell story is from Bertrand Russell, "Portraits from Memory II, Maynard Keynes and Lytton Strachey," *Harper's* (1953), CCVI, p. 71; Hesketh Pearson's reaction to *Eminent Victorians* is from his *Thinking It Over* (London, 1938), pp. 203–4. Strachey's comment on Livy is from a review of Ferrero's *Greatness and Decline of Rome*, quoted by Guy Boas, "Lytton Strachey—Reviewer," *Spectator* (1950), CLXXXIV, p. 456; the other quotation is from Strachey's *Portraits in Miniature* (New York, 1931), p. 158. Virginia Woolf's comment is from her "Art of Biography," *Atlantic Monthly* (1939), CLXIII, p. 507.

On the popularity of biography in the twenties and thirties see the editorial "Biographies," *Saturday Evening Post* (July 12, 1920), CCIII, p. 20; James Barrie, "Courage," *Rectoral Address at St. Andrews University* (New York, 1926), p. 27; J. C. Johnston, *Biography: The Literature of Personality* (New York, 1927), pp. 14–15; *Saturday Review of Literature* (1928), V, p. 33; ibid. (1929), VI, p. 337; D. K. Merrill, *The Development of American Biography* (Portland, Me., 1932), p. 84; L. M. Field, "Biography Boom," *North American Review* (1930), CCXXX, pp. 433–40; Orlo Williams, "The Subject of Biography," *National Review* (1933), C, p. 693; J. C. Long, "Biography Now and Tomorrow," *Saturday Review of Literature* (May 18, 1946), XXIX, pp. 16–17. Dunn's comment is from his *English Biography* (New York, 1916), pp. 225–8; J. T. Adams's is from his "New Modes in Biography," *Current History* (1929), XXXI, p. 259; Lewis's remark was quoted in *Literary Digest* (June 15, 1929), CI, p. 25. The statement about "the present passion for biography" is from Orlo Williams's above-mentioned article in the *Na-*

ESSAY ON SOURCES [275

tional Review; Harold Nicolson's comment is from his "Biographies Old and New," *Living Age* (1937), CCCLII, p. 265.

On the origins of the "new biography" see the opening chapter of Longaker, *Contemporary Biography*; Agnes Repplier, "Strayed Sympathies," *Atlantic Monthly* (1921), CXXVIII, pp. 798–805; J. T. Adams, "Biography as an Art," *Saturday Review of Literature* (1927), IV, pp. 297–9; L. M. Gelber, "History and the New Biography," *Queen's Quarterly* (1930), XXXVII, pp. 127–44; S. A. Rhodes, "Marcel Schwob and the Art of Biography," *Romantic Review* (1934), XXV, pp. 112–17. General discussions of the "new" biography can be found in Longaker, *Contemporary Biography*, and in S. McC. Crothers, "Satan Among the Biographers," *Atlantic Monthly* (1923), CXXI, pp. 289–97; G. F. Bowerman, *The New Biography* (Washington, 1929); Bonamy Dobrée, "Modern Biography," *National Review* (1932), XCIX, pp. 121–9; Liddell Hart, "Neo-Georgian Biography," *Cornhill Magazine* (1934), CLXIX, pp. 155–63; Harold Nicolson, *Living Age*, CCCLII, pp. 265–8; Edgar Johnson, "American Biography and the Modern World," *North American Review* (1938), CCLXV, pp. 364–80; Townshend Scudder, "Biography in America," *English Institute Annual* (1939), pp. 116–29; J. A. Garraty, "Biographers Are Only Human," *Saturday Review* (March 20, 1954), XXXVI, pp. 11–13, 55–7. Discussions that take an especially favorable view include M. A. deW. Howe, "Biography Drifts toward the Novel," *Independent* (1925), CXV, pp. 359–61; André Maurois, "The Modern Biographer," *Yale Review* (1928), XVII, pp. 227–45; Osbert Burdett, "Experiment in Biography," *Tradition and Experiment in Present-Day Literature* (London, 1929), pp. 161–78; G. G. Benjamin, "The New Biography," *Southwestern Social Science Quarterly* (1934), XIV, pp. 291–301, a particularly naïve and pretentious article worth noting only in that it reflects the spirit of much of the literature on the subject. By far the best analysis of the weaknesses of the "new" biography is H. M. Jones, "Methods in Contemporary Biography," *English Journal* (1932), XXI, pp. 113–22, but two other articles deserve special mention, S. V. Benét's witty and incisive "A Defense of Mrs. Anonymous," *Bookman* (1926), LXIV, pp. 168–70, and Bernard DeVoto's thunderous denunciation, "The Skeptical Biographer," *Harper's* (1933), CLXVI, pp. 181–92.

On fictional biography see Dunn, *English Biography*, p. 194; Lewis Mumford, "The Task of Modern Biography," *English Journal* (1934), XXIII, pp. 1–9; W. E. Wilson, "On Writing Historical Fiction," *Western Humanities Review* (1951), VI, pp. 15–21; M. E. Mason, "The Vogue for Biography," *Writer* (1950), LXIII, pp. 14–19; Irving Stone, "Speaking of Books," *The New York Times Book Review* (February 10, 1957), p. 2. The quotations in the text are from

L. A. Beck ("E. Barrington"), *Glorious Apollo* (New York, 1925), preface, n.p.; Francis Steegmuller ("Byron Steel"), *O Rare Ben Jonson* (New York, 1928), pp. 88–93; Francis Gribble, *Seen in Passing: A Volume of Personal Reminiscences* (London, 1929), pp. 246–52; Hesketh Pearson, *Ventilations: Being Biographical Asides* (Philadelphia, 1930), pp. 132, 134, 182, 211; Mumford, *English Journal*, XXIII, pp. 2–3.

On the origins of "intuitive" biography see J. F. Kearney, "The Psychological Biography," *Catholic World* (1929), CXXIX, pp. 96–8; C. K. Trueblood, "Sainte-Beuve and the Psychology of Personality," *Character and Personality* (1939), VIII, pp. 120–43; Merrill, *American Biography*, pp. 85–6; Gamaliel Bradford, "The Art of Psychography," *New York Post Literary Review* (1923), III, pp. 641–2 and "The Art of Biography," *Saturday Review of Literature* (1925), I, pp. 769–70. On Ludwig see the introductory essay in his *Genius and Character* (New York, 1927) and his autobiography, *Gifts of Life* (Boston, 1931), pp. 371–81. On Maurois see Georges Lemaitre, *André Maurois* (Palo Alto, Calif., 1939), pp. 51–72; André Maurois, *Aspects of Biography* (Cambridge, Eng., 1929), "The Modern Biographer," *Yale Review* (1928), XVII, pp. 239–45, "To Make a Man Come Alive Again," *The New York Times Book Review* (December 27, 1953), p. 1; Longaker, *Contemporary Biography*, pp. 91–124. On Zweig see scattered comments in his autobiography, *The World of Yesterday* (New York, 1943), and Friderike Zweig, *Stefan Zweig* (New York, 1946), p. 156.

There is a great mass of literature on the psychological biography. For a convenient summary see J. A. Garraty, "The Interrelations of Psychology and Biography," *Psychological Bulletin* (1954), LI, pp. 569–82. For a summary of the early work of Freud's disciples see Lucile Dooley, "Psychoanalytic Studies of Genius," *American Journal of Psychology* (1916), XXVII, pp. 363–416; Franklin Fearing, "Psychological Studies of Historical Personalities," *Psychological Bulletin* (1927), XXIV, pp. 521–39. On the early flirtations of historians with psychoanalysis see J. A. Garraty, "Preserved Smith, Ralph Volney Harlow, and Psychology," *Journal of the History of Ideas* (1954), XV, pp. 456–65. General discussions of the technique may be found in H. E. Barnes, "Psychology and History," *American Journal of Psychology* (1919), XXX, pp. 337–76, and "Some Reflections on the Possible Services of Analytical Psychology to History," *Psychological Review* (1921), VIII, pp. 22–37; Matthew Josephson, "Historians and Mythmakers," *Virginia Quarterly Review* (1940), XVI, pp. 92–109; Franz Alexander, "Psychology and the Interpretation of History," in C. F. Ware, ed., *The Cultural Approach to History* (New York, 1940), pp. 48–57; Goodwin Watson, "Clio and Psyche: Some Interrelations of History and Psychology," *ibid.*, pp. 34–47; E. M.

Forster, *The Development of English Prose between 1918 and 1939* (Glasgow, 1945), pp. 9–10, 20–1; Lionel Trilling, "Freud and Literature," and "Art and Neurosis," *The Liberal Imagination* (New York, 1953), pp. 44–64, 159–78; E. N. Saveth, "The Historian and the Freudian Approach to History," *The New York Times Book Review*, January 1, 1956, p. 7. The quotations in the text are from *Hamlet*, III, iv; J. R. Lowell, *My Study Windows* (Boston, 1871), pp. 200, 205; Trueblood, *Character and Personality*, VIII, p. 131; Preserved Smith, "Luther's Early Development in the Light of Psycho Analysis," *American Journal of Psychology* (1913), XXIV, p. 360; Barnes, *Psychological Review*, VIII, p. 27; L. P. Clark, "Unconscious Motives Underlying the Personalities of Great Statesmen," *Psychological Review* (1921), VIII, p. 2, (1923), X, p. 56; Josephson, *Virginia Quarterly Review*, XVI, p. 100; J. W. Krutch, *Edgar Allan Poe* (New York, 1926), pp. 18–19; Clement Wood, *Amy Lowell* (New York, 1926), p. 12; Mumford, *English Journal*, XXIII, p. 5.

For an excellent article on the origins and nature of the debunkers see Frank Klement, "Debunking the Debunkers," *Social Studies* (1947), XXXVIII, pp. 366–9. Other discussions include Edmund Pearson, "Plutarch *et Fils*," *Outlook* (1927), CXLVI, pp. 54–6; C. M. Fuess, "Debunkery and Biography," *Atlantic Monthly* (1933), CLI, pp. 347–56; Rupert Hughes, "Pitfalls of the Biographer," *Pacific Historical Review* (1933), II, pp. 1–33. The Hughes quotation is from pp. 13–14; the lines from Hughes's *George Washington* are quoted in Dixon Wecter, *The Hero in America* (New York, 1941), p. 144.

On the decline of the "new" biography see Norman Cousins, "Back Seat Drivers' Department," *Saturday Review of Literature* (February 22, 1941), XXIII, p. 10; J. C. Long, ibid. (May 18, 1946), XXIX, pp. 16–17; H. H. Lyons, "Books," *Holiday* (February, 1949), p. 23; V. S. Pritchett, "A Literary Letter from London," *The New York Times Book Review* (January 25, 1953), p. 26.

Foster's criticism of conservative biography is from John Foster, *Critical Essays Contributed to the Eclectic Review* (London, 1856), II, p. 194; Carlyle's is quoted in Sidney Lee, *Elizabethan and Other Essays* (Oxford, 1929), p. 65; Stephen's is quoted in ibid., p. 33; Saintsbury's is from George Saintsbury, *Collected Essays and Papers* (London, 1923), I, p. 411.

The quotations in the text on the conservative counterattack are from DeVoto, *Harper's*, CLXVI, p. 183; Allan Nevins, *Gateway to History* (New York, 1938), p. 335; Gelber, *Queen's Quarterly*, XXXVII, p. 131. The Peter Wright case is discussed in *Saturday Review* (1926), CXLII, p. 89–90, and in *The New York Times*, July 14, 16, 1926, January 27, 28, February 4, 1927; Hughes's difficulties are described in *Pacific Historical Review*, II, p. 23; the "iconoclast" quotation is from G. C. Knight, *James Lane Allen and the Genteel Tradition* (Chapel Hill, N. C., 1935), p. ix; Fuess's remark is from C. M. Fuess, "The Biographer and His Victims," *Atlantic Monthly* (1932), CXLIX, p. 62; Nevins's comment on Winkler is quoted in Klement, *Social Studies*, XXXVIII, pp. 368-9; for Jones's view see his "Patriotism—But How?" *Atlantic Monthly* (1938), CLXII, pp. 589-91.

The sources of the comments quoted in the text are a good sample of the large body of antipsychoanalytic literature. See Charles Whibley, "The Indiscretions of Biography," *English Review* (1924), XXXIX, pp. 769-72; W. C. Abbott, "Some 'New' History and Historians," *Massachusetts Historical Society Proceedings* (1931), LXIV, pp. 286-93; Philip Guedalla, "The Future of Biography," *Week-End Review* (1931), III, p. 115; Jones, *English Journal*, XXI, pp. 113-22; Benét, *Bookman*, LXIV, pp. 168-70. Maurois's comment on Russell is from *Aspects of Biography*, p. 90. The other quotations are from J. T. Adams, *Current History*, XXXI, p. 260; DeVoto, *Harper's*, CLXVI, p. 185.

On the female "synthesizers" see M. B. Stern, "Approaches to Biography," *South Atlantic Quarterly* (1946), XLV, pp. 362-71, and C. D. Bowen, *The Writing of Biography* (Boston, 1950). For the quotations in the text see L. H. Tharp, *Until Victory: Horace Mann and Mary Peabody* (Boston, 1953), pp. 3, 321; M. B. Stern, *The Life of Margaret Fuller* (New York, 1942), p. 3; Stern, *South Atlantic Quarterly*, XLV, p. 367; Bowen, *Writing Biography*, pp. 17, 19. The quotations from Mrs. Bowen's book on Adams are in C. D. Bowen, *John Adams and the American Revolution* (Boston, 1950), pp. 642, 153-4. The comparison with Adams's journal is from a review by D. C. Steiner in *New England Quarterly* (1953), XXVI, pp. 133.

For Maurois's developing "conservatism" see *The New York Times Book Review* (December 27, 1953), p. 1; for Pearson's see Hesketh Pearson, "Warts and All," *Saturday Review of Literature* (October 12, 1946), XXIX, pp. 13-14. For Marquis James's remark see his *Life of Andrew Jackson* (Indianapolis, 1938), p. 910. On the *Dictionary of American Biography* see the prefaces to volume I (New York, 1928), pp. vii-viii, and volume XX (New York, 1936), pp. vii-xvi; H. J. Carman, "The Dictionary of American Biography: An Appreciation," *Historical Outlook* (1930), XXI, pp. 211-12; R. F. Nichols, "The Dictionary of American Biography," *Pennsylvania Magazine of History and Biography* (1936), LX, pp. 323-8. For a criticism of some of its articles see H. K. Beale, "The Professional Historian: His Theory and His Practice," *Pacific Historical Review* (1953), XXII, pp. 241-3. The changing attitude of scholars toward biography is discussed in Dumas Malone, "Biography and History," in J. R. Strayer, ed., *The Interpretation of History* (Princeton, 1943), pp. 121–48. Tolles's view of the "modern synthesis" appears in F. B. Tolles, "The Biographer's Craft," *South Atlantic Quarterly* (1954), LIII, pp. 508–20. For other discussions of recent trends in biography see Cleveland Amory, "Trade Winds," *Saturday Review* (October 2, 1954), XXXVII, pp. 6–11; the introductory chapter of Lincoln Barnett's *Writing on Life* (New York, 1951); Ivor Brown, "Speaking of Books," *The New York Times Book Review* (July 25, 1954), p. 2; J. W. Dodds, "New Territories in Victorian Biography," in J. E. Baker, ed., *The Reinterpretation of Victorian Literature* (Princeton, 1950), pp. 197–206; Oscar Handlin, "The History in Men's Lives," *Virginia Quarterly Review* (1954), XXX, pp. 534–41; A. S. Link, "A Decade of Biographical Contributions to Recent American History," *Mississippi Valley Historical Review* (1948), XXXIV, pp. 637–52; Robert Partin, "Biography as an Instrument of Moral Instruction," *American Quarterly* (1956), VIII, pp. 303–15; V. S. Pritchett, *The New York Times Book Review* (January 25, 1953), p. 26; R. E. Riegel, "Changing Fashions in American Biography," *New England Social Studies Bulletin* (1953), IX, pp. 8–14; C. V. Woodward, "Can We Believe Our Own History?" *Johns Hopkins Magazine* (1954), V, pp. 2–6.

Chapter VII

CHOOSING A SUBJECT

The introductory quotation is from Allan Nevins, "How Shall One Write of a Man's Life?" *The New York Times Book Review* (July 15, 1951), p. 20; Cecil Woodham-Smith's is from her article "Biographies I'd Like to Write and Never Shall," ibid. (July 24, 1955), p. 7, which is an interesting discussion of the whole problem discussed in this chapter.

The literature on biography by contemporaries listed in Chapter I is pertinent to the question of biography by relatives, but see also Edmund Gosse, "The Custom of Biography," *Anglo-Saxon Review* (1901), VIII, pp. 205–6; Wallace Notestein, "Retrospective Reviews: Recent British Biographies and Memoirs," *American Historical Review* (1926), XXXII, pp. 22–33. A. R. Burr's comment is from *The Autobiography* (Boston, 1909), pp. 18–19; Josephus Daniels's is from his *The Wilson Era* (Chapel Hill, 1944), p. 483. For the J. W. Alexander quotation see his *The Life of Archibald Alexander* (New York, 1856), pp. iii–iv.

On biographers' identification with their subjects see André Maurois, *Aspects of Biography* (Cambridge, Eng., 1929), pp. 119–21; Sigmund Freud, *Leonardo da Vinci: A Study in Psychosexuality*

(New York, 1947), p. 116; W. E. Wilson, "On Writing Historical Fiction," *Western Humanities Review* (1951), VI, p. 18; C. D. Hazen, ed., *Letters of William Roscoe Thayer* (Boston, 1926), pp. 182–3; Ida M. Tarbell, *All in the Day's Work* (New York, 1939), pp. 142–3. Elizabeth Stevenson, *Henry Adams* (New York, 1955), pp. 164–9, provides an interesting suggestion that Adams's biography of Albert Gallatin is an example of an author's identification with his subject.

For the quotations from Lytton Strachey's *Elizabeth and Essex* (New York, 1929), see pp. 24–5, 263. At the request of the author of the "oilman's" biography I am refraining from publishing the names of the persons involved. Dumas Malone's statement is from his "Biography and History," in J. R. Strayer, ed., *The Interpretation of History* (Princeton, 1943), p. 130. Allan Nevins's statement on the importance of a sympathetic approach is from *The New York Times Book Review* (July 15, 1951), p. 20.

Johnson's views on biographies of unimportant persons are from his *Rambler* #60; Phillips Brooks's are from his lecture on "Biography," *Essays and Addresses* (New York, 1895), p. 428; the Rembrandt quotation is from F. F. Bond, *Breaking into Print* (New York, 1933), p. 166. See also W. H. Dunn, *English Biography* (New York, 1916), pp. 104–6; E. T. Cook, "The Art of Biography," *National Review* (1914), LXIII, pp. 282–3. For a contradictory opinion see G. B. Shaw, *Sixteen Self Sketches* (New York, 1949), pp. 17–18.

Marchette Chute's statement is from her "From 'Bad Risk' to Best Seller," *Library Journal* (1951), LXXVI, p. 1486. Godfrey Davies's warning about overemphasizing "new" material is from his "Biography and History," *Modern Language Quarterly* (1940), I, p. 82.

On the importance of special knowledge of one's subject's profession and times see Joseph Addison, *Freeholder* #35; Arthur Bryant, "The Art of Biography," *London Mercury* (1934), XXX, pp. 242–3; Cecil Woodham-Smith, *The New York Times Book Review* (July 24, 1955), p. 7. Lincoln Barnett's contradictory opinion is to be found in his *Writing on Life* (New York, 1951), pp. 13, 348.

For a statement of the dangers involved in using papers controlled by relatives see H. K. Beale, "The Professional Historian: His Theory and His Practice," *Pacific Historical Review* (1953), XXII, p. 243. William Allen White's remark on widows was made to Walter Johnson; my source is a letter from Johnson, December 5, 1956. On Robert T. Lincoln's battles with the Lincoln biographers see B. P. Thomas, *Portrait for Posterity* (New Brunswick, N. J., 1947), *passim;* D. C. Mearns, *The Lincoln Papers* (Garden City, 1948), *passim;* Tarbell, *Day's Work*, pp. 169–70. The quotations are from Thomas, ibid., pp. 111–12; Mearns ibid., I, pp. 45–6, 134.

W. R. Thayer's *The Art of Biography* (New York, 1920), pp. 111–

ESSAY ON SOURCES [281

12, presents a good statement of the proper policy for relatives of biographical subjects to adopt. For the policies of the Roosevelt and Taft families regarding Pringle see H. F. Pringle, *Theodore Roosevelt: A Biography* (New York, 1931), p. 605, and *The Life and Times of William Howard Taft* (New York, 1939), I, p. vii. Compare also Tyler Dennett, *John Hay: From Poetry to Politics* (New York, 1933), p. v, with N. W. Stephenson, *Nelson W. Aldrich: A Leader in American Politics* (New York, 1930), p. viii. Randall's experiences with the Jefferson family are described in F. J. and F. W. Klingberg, eds., *The Correspondence of Henry Stephens Randall and Hugh Blair Grigsby* (Berkeley, 1952), pp. 15, 65, 110–11; Borden Company policy is described in J. B. Frantz, "Adventuring in Biography," *Historian* (1953), XVI, pp. 56–7.

For Parton's comments on the financial side of biography see C. E. Norton, "Parton's Biographical Writings," *North American Review* (1867), CIV, p. 600; C. E. L. Wingate, "Boston Letter," *Critic* (1891), XIX, p. 218.

Chapter VIII

THE MATERIALS OF BIOGRAPHY

Most of the materials of biography discussed in this chapter are "personal documents." For this reason the most useful general survey of the subject is G. W. Allport's brilliant study "The Use of Personal Documents in Psychological Science," *Social Science Research Council Bulletin* #49 (New York, 1942). Louis Gottschalk's "The Use of Personal Documents in History," ibid., #53 (New York, 1945) is also useful for its differing emphasis, reflecting as it does the subtle difference in approach between the historian and the biographer.

In the introductory section, the Coolidge and Roosevelt statements are from E. E. Morison, ed., *The Letters of Theodore Roosevelt* (Cambridge, 1951–4), III, p. 150, and W. A. White, *A Puritan in Babylon* (New York, 1938), p. 246; the comment on the difference between a biographer and an autobiographer is from F. S. Stevenson, *Historic Personality* (London, 1893), p. 42; Maugham's comment is from W. S. Maugham, *The Summing Up* (New York, 1938), p. 10; Spencer's is quoted in André Maurois, *Aspects of Biography* (Cambridge, Eng., 1929), p. 157. On Roosevelt's posterity letters see Tyler Dennett, *John Hay: From Poetry to Politics* (New York, 1939), p. 349; Morison, *Roosevelt Letters*, VI, p. 1490; H. F. Pringle, *Theodore Roosevelt: A Biography* (New York, 1931), pp. 452–4. The quotations on the fallibility of memory are from Nikolai Berdyaev, *Dream and Reality: An Essay in Autobiography* (New York,

1951), pp. ix–x; W. H. Dunn, *English Biography* (New York, 1916), pp. 261–2, quoting Lewes; J. D. Adams, "Speaking of Books," *The New York Times Book Review* (March 1, 1953), p. 2, quoting Boring. For the problem of Melville's *Redburn* see W. H. Gilman, *Melville's Early Life and Redburn* (New York, 1951). The pioneering work on the nature of the autobiography is A. R. Burr, *The Autobiography* (Boston, 1909). Other basic studies are Wayne Shumaker, *English Autobiography: Its Emergence, Materials, and Form* (Berkeley, 1954); A. M. Clark, *Autobiography: Its Genesis and Phases* (London, 1935); Georg Misch, *A History of Autobiography in Antiquity* (Cambridge, 1951); William Matthews, ed., *British Autobiographies: An Annotated Bibliography* (Berkeley, 1955). See also Samuel Johnson, *Idler* #84; W. R. Inge, *Lay Thoughts of a Dean* (Garden City, n.d.), pp. 71–5; R. G. Lillard, *American Life in Autobiography* (Stanford, Calif., 1956), pp. 1–13. The general histories of English biography contain many references to autobiographies.

Cowley's statement on the difficulty of writing honestly about one's self is quoted by Harold Nicolson, *The Development of English Biography* (London, 1928), p. 16; for Freeman's remarks see D. S. Freeman, *R. E. Lee: A Biography* (New York, 1934), I, p. xii. The analysis of Lodge's autobiography is based on H. C. Lodge, *Early Memories* (New York, 1913), pp. vii, 14, 235–7, and *passim*. The Roosevelt-Churchill story is from Frank Freidel, *Franklin D. Roosevelt: The Apprenticeship* (Boston, 1952), p. 354. The A. R. Burr quotation is from *The Autobiograhy*, p. 46.

On diaries see the introductions in Arthur Ponsonby, *English Diaries* (London, 1922), and *More English Diaries* (London, 1927); William Matthews, ed., *British Diaries: An Annotated Bibliography* (Berkeley, 1950), and *American Diaries: An Annotated Bibliography* (Berkeley, 1945). See also Kate O'Brien, *English Diaries and Journals* (London 1947); Inge, *Lay Thoughts*, pp. 75–7.

The quotations on the inevitability of self-revelation in diaries are from Ponsonby, *Diaries*, p. 31; Matthews, *English Diaries*, p. x. Bernard Berenson's comment is from his *Rumor and Reflection* (New York, 1952), pp. ix–x; W. E. Woodward's description of Washington's diary is from his *George Washington: The Image and the Man* (New York, 1926), p. 106; the "Public Man" controversy is described in R. N. Lokken, "Has the Mystery of 'A Public Man' Been Solved?" *Mississippi Valley Historical Review* (1953), XL, pp. 419–40; the murderer's diary is described in Ponsonby, *More Diaries*, p. 29; the Henry James story is from Rebecca West, *Ending in Earnest* (New York, 1931), pp. 163–6; Creel's story is from George Creel, *Rebel at Large* (New York, 1947), p. 245; Gladstone's comment is quoted in Ponsonby, *Diaries*, p. 11.

ESSAY ON SOURCES [283

The quotations on the editing of diaries are from Ponsonby, *Diaries*, p. 5; Leonard Woolf, ed., *A Writer's Diary* (New York, 1954), p. vii, and the review of that work in *The New York Times Book Review* (February 21, 1954), p. 1; Josephus Daniels, *The Wilson Era* (Chapel Hill, 1946), p. 24; H. K. Beale, *American Historical Review* (1951), LVII, p. 185.

Jefferson's statement is from a letter to Robert Walsh, April 5, 1823, printed in Adrienne Koch and William Peden, *The Life and Selected Writings of Thomas Jefferson* (New York, 1944), p. 705; Morley's comment is quoted by A. F. Pollard, "Biographers and Historians," *History* (1929), XIII, p. 318; Robert Rait's opinion is from his "Boswell and Lockhart," *Transactions* of the Royal Society of Literature (1933), XII, pp. 114–15. Rodell's analysis of the Holmes-Laski letters is from *Saturday Review* (March 14, 1953), p. 48; Jones's is from Ernest Jones, *The Life and Work of Sigmund Freud: Years of Maturity* (New York, 1955), p. 155. Maurois's comments on De Musset's letters are from *Aspects of Biography*, p. 86. On the value of a long series of letters see John Stuart Mill, quoted in Shumaker, *English Autobiography*, p. 104. The information on Senator Lehman's correspondence is from S. K. Bailey and H. D. Samuel, *Congress at Work* (New York, 1952), p. 101; on Theodore Roosevelt's see Morison, *Roosevelt Letters*, I, p. xv; on F.D.R.'s see Freidel, *Apprenticeship*, p. 373. Edel's comment is from Leon Edel, *Henry James: The Untried Years* (Philadelphia, 1953), p. 17.

On the decline of the importance of letters as biographical sources see George Saintsbury, *Collected Essays and Papers* (London, 1923), I, p. 432; G. R. Agassiz, *Letters and Recollections of Alexander Agassiz* (Boston, 1913), p. vi. Freidel's comment on the communications speed-up is from a personal letter to me, March 2, 1954.

Ernest Newman's comment is from his *The Life of Richard Wagner* (New York, 1933), I, p. ix.

The relation of an author and his work is a two-sided problem. One can learn about the man from what he writes and about his works from the study of his life. See W. H. Crawshaw, *Literary Interpretation of Life* (New York, 1900); R. P. Basler, *Sex, Symbolism and Psychology in Literature* (New Brunswick, 1948); G. E. Bentley, "The Critical Significance of Biographical Evidence," *English Institute Essays: 1946* (New York, 1947); F. F. Browne, "A New Theory of Biography," *Dial* (1898), XXIV, pp. 281–3. A sampling of the many less systematic discussions of this question would include George Brandes, *William Shakespeare: A Critical Study* (New York, 1898), II, p. 413; Robert Lynd, *Books and Authors* (New York, 1923), p. 85; J. C. Johnston, *Biography: The Literature of Personality* (New York, 1927), pp. 256–9; W. S. Maugham, *The Summing Up* (New York, 1938), p. 191; Leon Edel, "Hugh Walpole and

Henry James," *American Imago* (1951), VIII, pp. 3–21; Lionel Trilling, *The Liberal Imagination* (New York, 1953), p. 167; Marvin Magalaner and R. M. Kain, *Joyce: The Man, the Work, the Reputation* (New York, 1956), p. 27. The quotations in the text are from Maurois, *Aspects of Biography*, pp. 90–1; René Wellek, *History of Modern Criticism: The Romantic Age* (New York, 1955), p. 236.

On the use of paintings and photographs in biography see Emil Ludwig, *Gifts of Life* (Boston, 1931), p. 374, *Of Life and Love* (New York, 1946), p. 166; Godfrey Davies, "Biography and History," *Modern Language Quarterly* (1940), I, p. 86, quoting Carlyle; C. D. Bowen, *The Writing of Biography* (Boston, 1950), p. 13. Maugham's statement is from *The Summing Up*, p. 215; Allport's is from *Personal Documents*, p. 120. See also P. F. Dunne's comment, quoted in Elmer Ellis, *Mr. Dooley's America* (New York, 1941), p. 288.

The statement about the editing of Charles Francis Adams is from Stewart Mitchell, ed., *New Letters of Abigail Adams* (Boston, 1947), p. xxiv; Hoar's remark is from G. F. Hoar, *Autobiography of Seventy Years* (New York, 1903), I, p. 329; Voltaire is quoted in Marston Balch, ed., *Modern Short Biographies and Autobiographies* (New York, 1940), p. v.

The quotations on conflicting testimony of contemporaries are from V. W. Brooks, *Opinions of Oliver Allston* (New York, 1941), p. 304; M. A. deW. Howe, *Barrett Wendell and His Letters* (Boston, 1924), p. 239; J. A. Garraty, *Henry Cabot Lodge: A Biography* (New York, 1953), p. 28, quoting Eliot; Guy Chapman, *Beckford* (New York, 1937), p. 11. See also Magalaner and Kain, *Joyce*, p. 15.

Mrs. Bowen's interviewing technique is described in C. D. Bowen, "The Magnificence of Age," *Harper's* (April, 1953), CCVI, p. 61; Freidel's comment is from a personal letter to me, January 15, 1954. Miss Burney's account of Boswell is quoted in Sir Walter Raleigh, *Six Essays on Johnson* (Oxford, 1910), pp. 46–7; Boswell's statement is quoted in Mark Longaker, *English Biography in the Seventeenth Century* (Philadelphia, 1931), p. 434; Froude's is quoted in Dunn, *English Biography*, p. 173. Hay's is from Dennett, *Hay*, p. 137.

Chapter IX

THE PROBLEM OF PERSONALITY

The introductory quotations are from Dumas Malone, "Biography and History," in J. R. Strayer, ed., *The Interpretation of History* (Princeton, 1943), p. 134, and Eleanor Ruggles, as quoted in *The New York Times Book Review* (March 8, 1953), p. 14. The Wilson

ESSAY ON SOURCES [285

quotations are from R. S. Baker, *Woodrow Wilson: Life and Letters* (Garden City, 1927), I, p. 110, II, pp. 242, 243.

More biographers make use of legendary materials than are willing to admit it, but I have located a few comments on the subject in prefaces. See Waldo Frank, *Birth of a World: Bolivar in Terms of His Peoples* (Boston, 1951), pp. vi–vii; C. A. Robinson, Jr., *Alexander the Great* (New York, 1947), p. 14; Winthrop Sargent, *The Life and Career of Major John André* (Boston, 1861), p. vii.

The comments on Wilson by contemporaries are taken from Josephus Daniels, *The Wilson Era* (Chapel Hill, 1946), pp. 3–4; David Lawrence, *The True Story of Woodrow Wilson* (New York, 1924), p. 13; A. S. Link, *Woodrow Wilson and the Progressive Era* (New York, 1954), p. 186n. B. P. Thomas's imaginative reconstruction is from his *Abraham Lincoln* (New York, 1952), p. 93; his explanation is from a personal letter to me, January 30, 1953. N. I. White's criticism of Maurois is from "The Development, Use and Abuse of Interpretation in Biography," *English Institute Annual* (1942), p. 48.

DeVoto's comment on psychoanalytical biography is from "The Skeptical Biographer," *Harper's* (1933), CLXVI, p. 188; Louis Gottschalk's statement is from his *The Use of Personal Documents in History* (New York, 1945), p. 6. The Maurois quotation is from "To Make a Man Come Alive Again," *The New York Times Book Review* (December 27, 1953), p. 1. The statement from the *Dial* is from F. F. Browne, "A New Theory of Biography," *Dial* (1898), XXIV, p. 281.

On handwriting see M. W. Thewlis and I. C. Swezy, *Handwriting and the Emotions* (New York, 1954); H. H. and G. L. Anderson, *Projective Techniques* (New York, 1951), pp. 416–43; Alfred Binet, *Les Révélations de l'Écriture* (Paris, 1906); G. W. Allport and P. E. Vernon, *Studies in Expressive Movement* (New York, 1933), pp. 185–7; G. R. Pascal, "The Analysis of Handwriting," *Character and Personality* (1943), XII, pp. 123–44.

Boder's experiments are described in D. P. Boder, "The Adjective-Verb Quotient: A Contribution to the Psychology of Language," *Psychological Record* (1940), III, pp. 310–43. For a general survey of similar literature see F. H. Sandford, "Speech and Personality," *Psychological Bulletin* (1942), XXXIX, pp. 811–45.

On the DRQ see John Dollard and O. H. Mowrer, "A Method of Measuring Tension in Personal Documents," *Journal of Abnormal and Social Psychology* (1947), XLII, pp. 3–32. White's value-analysis is described in "*Black Boy*: A Value-Analysis," ibid., (1947), XLII, pp. 440–61; for a fuller account see White's *Value Analysis: The Nature and Use of the Method* (Glen Gardner, N. J., 1951).

Baldwin's method is described in A. L. Baldwin, "Personal Structure Analysis: A Statistical Method for Investigating the Single Personality," *Journal of Abnormal and Social Psychology* (1942), XXXVII, pp. 163–83. The "Jenny letters" are to be found in G. W. Allport, "Letters from Jenny," ibid. (1946), XLI, pp. 315–50, 449–80.

The quotations on style are from F. V. Lucas, *Style* (New York, 1955), pp. 49–51.

For the study of political "types," see H. D. Lasswell, *Power and Personality* (New York, 1948), especially Chapter III, and A. L. and J. L. George, *Woodrow Wilson and Colonel House: A Personality Study* (New York, 1956). For a related study see Alex Gottfried, "The Use of Psychosomatic Categories in a Study of Political Personality," *Western Political Quarterly* (1955), VIII, pp. 234–47, which analyzes the Chicago politico Anton Cermak.

The contributions of the social psychologists can be studied in the volumes mentioned in the text, G. M. Gilbert, *Psychology of Dictatorship* (New York, 1950), and Hadley Cantril, *The Psychology of Social Movements* (New York, 1941). For a summary of "national character" studies, see Margaret Mead, "The Study of National Character," in Daniel Lerner and H. D. Lasswell, eds., *The Policy Sciences* (Stanford, Calif., 1951), pp. 70–85.

The quotation about the complexity of man is from André Maurois, *Aspects of Biography* (Cambridge, Eng., 1929), p. 27; for Roosevelt's contradictions see J. M. Burns, *Roosevelt: the Lion and the Fox* (New York, 1956), pp. 472–3; Baldwin's comment is from *Journal of Abnormal and Social Psychology*, XXXVII, p. 163.

Chapter X

THE WRITING OF BIOGRAPHY

A good deal of the material in this chapter has appeared in my article "How to Write a Biography," *South Atlantic Quarterly* (1956), LV, pp. 73–86.

On Buehler see Charlotte Buehler, "The Curve of Life as Studied in Biographies," *Journal of Applied Psychology* (1935), XIX, pp. 405–9; Else Frenkel, "Studies in Biographical Psychology," *Character and Personality* (1936), V, pp. 1–34; Olga Rubinow, "The Course of Man's Life—A Psychological Problem," *Journal of Abnormal and Social Psychology* (1933), XXVIII, pp. 207–15.

On Irving and his methods see D. G. Mitchell, *Bound Together* (New York, 1884), pp. 12–13; S. T. Williams, *Life of Washington Irving* (New York, 1935), *passim*.

There is an excellent biography of Parton, M. E. Flower's *James*

ESSAY ON SOURCES [287

Parton: The Father of American Biography (Durham, N. C., 1951). For Parton's "rules" see "James Parton's Rules of Biography," *McClure's Magazine* (1893), I, pp. 59–62. Henry Adams's method is described in his letters to Sarah Hewitt, printed in H. D. Cater, ed., *Henry Adams and His Friends* (Boston, 1947), pp. 547–9; Joseph Hergesheimer described his experiences in "Biography and Bibliographies," in Elmer Adler, ed., *Breaking into Print* (New York, 1937), pp. 75–83; Holmes Alexander did the same in "Wrong Ways to Write Biography," in A. S. Burack, ed., *The Writer's Handbook* (Boston, 1941), pp. 274–83.

Nicolson's method is described in Harold Nicolson, "How I Write Biography," *Saturday Review of Literature* (1934), X, pp. 709–11, and in *The Development of English Biography* (London, 1927), pp. 10–11. For Pearson's see Hesketh Pearson, *Thinking It Over* (London, 1938), p. 322; for Mrs. Bowen's see C. D. Bowen, *The Writing of Biography* (Boston, 1950), pp. 1–28, and "The Magnificence of Age," *Harper's* (April, 1953), CCVI, p. 59; for Sandburg's see B. P. Thomas, *Portrait for Posterity* (New Brunswick, N. J., 1947), pp. 295–6; for Freeman see Dumas Malone, "The Pen of Douglas Southall Freeman," in D. S. Freeman, *George Washington: A Biography* (New York, 1954), VI, pp. ix–xxxi. G. W. Allport's outline is from "A Tentative Set of Rules for the Presentation and Evaluation of Life Histories and Case Studies," an unpublished manuscript used with the permission of the author.

In addition to these accounts, there are many other descriptions of method available. These vary a great deal in specificity, length, and interest. The following, listed alphabetically, are samples of these accounts:

Katharine Anthony, "Writing Biography," in Helen Hull, ed., *The Writer's Book* (New York, 1950), pp. 220–6. A discussion of general principles without much stress on specific methods. Emphasizes interpretation, imagination, and organization, and is very critical of academic scholars.

Gertrude Atherton. In her autobiography, *Adventures of a Novelist* (New York, 1932), pp. 309–21, 340–44, and *passim*, she describes very specifically her work in writing *The Conqueror*.

R. S. Baker. In his *American Chronicle* (New York, 1945), pp. 487–91, 510–14, he discussed his methods and motives in writing his life of Wilson.

Jacques Barzun, "Truth in Biography: Berlioz," *University Review* (1939), V, pp. 275–80. A general discussion of principles and problems involved in writing a life of Berlioz.

A. J. Beveridge. His method can be reconstructed from Thomas, *Portrait for Posterity*, pp. 245–6, and from Elizabeth Donnan and L. F. Stock, eds., "Senator Beveridge, J. Franklin Jameson, and

Abraham Lincoln," *Mississippi Valley Historical Review* (1949), XXXV, pp. 639–73.

Gamaliel Bradford. Of his many writings about biography, his "Confessions of a Biographer," *Wives* (New York, 1925), pp. 3–14, comes closest to describing his methods. On his philosophy of biography, which places great stress on portraying personality, see "The Art of Biography," *Saturday Review of Literature* (1925), I, pp. 769–70.

J. B. Frantz, "Adventuring in Biography," *Historian* (1953), XVI, pp. 45–61. A discussion of some of the problems connected with his writing a life of Gail Borden.

Francis Hackett, "On Turning Historian," *Bookman* (1929), LXIX, pp. 575–87. This is an account of the problems of using old manuscripts, and of the supposed impossibility of combining careful analysis of complicated historical problems with readability.

John Hay. Tyler Dennett, *John Hay: From Poetry to Politics* (New York, 1933), pp. 135–41, contains interesting material on Nicolay and Hay's methods in their life of Lincoln.

Emil Ludwig, *Gifts of Life* (Boston, 1931), pp. 371–81. A discussion in quite specific terms of his method of research and writing, stressing the fact that he decided upon his basic interpretation before beginning his research.

Marthe McKenna, *Write Your Own Best Seller* (London, 1946), pp. 158–68. A practical discussion of how to write popular biography.

M. L. Robinson, "On Writing Biography," *Writer* (1940), LIII, pp. 72–3. Practical advice that stresses the "potential drama" in men's lives.

Bradford Smith, "Biographer's Creed," *William and Mary Quarterly* (1953), 3d series, X, pp. 190–5. A description of the author's method that places great stress on using the techniques of the novelist.

M. B. Stern, "Approaches to Biography," *South Atlantic Quarterly* (1946) XLV, pp. 362–71, and *The Life of Margaret Fuller* (New York, 1942), pp. xv–xvi. A description of her technique, similar to C. D. Bowen's.

F. B. Tolles, "The Biographer's Craft," *South Atlantic Quarterly* (1954), LIII, pp. 508–20. A discussion of the author's life of George Logan that stresses the importance of chronology and the imaginative but scholarly reconstruction of events.

Mallory Trent, "Blueprint for Biography," *Writer* (1943), LVI, pp. 117–18. A hack-biographer's "formula."

Stefan Zweig, *The World of Yesterday* (New York, 1943), pp. 319–20. An account of his methods that stresses intuition and severe pruning of successive drafts of the manuscript.

ESSAY ON SOURCES

Although I have not discussed them in the text, there are some interesting articles on biographies written for children that might well be included here. See M. E. Mason, "The Vogue for Biography," *Writer* (1950), LXIII, pp. 14–19; H. H. Peckham, "Historical Writing for Children," *William and Mary Quarterly* (1952), 3d series, IX, pp. 401–10, a description of a professional scholar's experience in writing a child's life of William Henry Harrison; R. A. and M. R. Brown, "Biography in the Social Studies: Changing Concepts," *Social Education* (1954), XVIII, pp. 30–2, containing a useful bibliography of literature on the use of biography as a teaching device; Brown and Brown, "Biography and the Social Studies: Another Harvest of American Lives," ibid. (1955), XIX, pp. 213–17; H. F. Graff, "For Younger Readers," *The New York Times Book Review* (November 6, 1955), p. 48, a discussion of recent trends in biographies for children; Marchette Chute, "Shakespeare of London," *Hornbook* (1955), XXXI, pp. 28–35, an explanation of the author's experiences in writing a child's life of Shakespeare.

INDEX

Abbott, Wilbur C., 142
Abraham, Karl, 197
Abraham Lincoln (Sandburg), 252–3
Abraham Lincoln (Thomas), 19–21
Acts and Monuments (Foxe), 68
Adamnan, 58
Adams, Abigail, 206
Adams, C. F., 206 n
Adams, Henry: *Education*, 183, 247; on method, 246–7
Adams, James Truslow, 125, 144
Adams, John, 146–7, 172, 206, 252
Adams, John Q., 173
Addison, Joseph, 23, 87–8, 169
adjective-verb quotient, 224–5
Admiral of the Ocean Sea (Morison), 205
Adventures of Peregrine Pickle (Smollett), 77
Aeschylus, 36
Agassiz, Alexander, 201
Agassiz, G. R., 201
Agesilaus, 36, 37
Agricola, Gnaeus, 49
Ahuramadzda, 33
Albert, Prince, 243
Alcibiades, 45–6, 47
Alcuin, 57
Alexander (the Great), 43, 47, 118
Alexander, Archibald, 158
Alexander, Holmes, 256; on method, 249–50
Alexander, James W.: *Archibald Alexander*, 158
Alexander Hamilton (Lodge), 13
Alexander Hamilton (Warshow), 13
Alexandrian biography, 41–2, 49
Alfred, 62
Allport, Gordon W.: on describing character, 9; on personal re-
Allport, Gordon W. (*continued*) mains, 204; *Psychology of Rumor*, 211 n; *Personal Documents*, 220–1; on method, 254–6
Altgeld, John Peter, 127
Always the Young Strangers (Sandburg), 183
Amenhotep IV, 133
American Historical Association, 5
America's Last King (Guttmacher), 219
Amyot, Jacques, 65–6
-ana, 84–5
Anabasis (Xenophon), 37
Anabasis of Alexander the Great (Arrian), 118
And Keep Your Powder Dry (Mead), 238
Anderson, F. M., 191
Andrew Carnegie (Hendrick), 161
Andrew Jackson (James), 149
anecdotes, use in biography, 38, 45–8, 62, 65, 84
Anne of Brittany, 67
Anthony, Katherine, 145–6; *Margaret Fuller*, 134
Antidosis (Isocrates), 38
Antigonus of Carystus: *Lives of the Philosophers*, 41
Archibald Alexander (Alexander), 158
Ariel (Maurois), 203, 219
Aristotle, 35, 37–40, 47, 128, 136
Aristoxenus of Tarentum, 39–40, 136
Armenian Magazine, 82
Armitage, Angus: *Sun, Stand Thou Still*, 8
Arrian: *Anabasis of Alexander*, 118
Aspects of Biography (Maurois), 144, 198
Asquith, H. H., 156

INDEX

Asser, Bishop, 62
Assurmasipal, 33
Athenae Oxoniensis (Wood), 72–3
Atherton, Gertrude, 118, 119–20; *Conqueror*, 120
Atticus, Pomponius, 43
Aubrey, John, 73–4
Authentic Narrative (Scott), 83
"authorized" biography, 99, 161–2
Autobiography: relation to biography, 26, 82–3, 177–89; classical examples really biographies, 31–2; 18th-century religious, 82; editing of, 157; self-revelation in, 179–82, 227–8; motives for writing, 183; reliability of, 184–9; of members of the family, 205–6
Autobiography, The (Burr), 189

Bach, Johann Sebastian, 24
Bacon, Francis, 70
Baldwin, A. L., 230–5, 240
Barnes, H. E., 133–4, 135
Barnett, Lincoln, 48, 169
Barrie, James, 124–5
Barton, W. E., 171
Barzun, Jacques, 142–3
Bashkirtsev, Marie: *Journal*, 190
Bath Club, 141 n
Baudelaire, Charles, 100
Beale, H. K., 194; *Bates Diary*, 194 n
Beard, Charles A., 11
Beaumont, Francis, 128
Beck, Lily Adams: *Glorious Apollo*, 127
Beckford, William, 208
Bede, 58; *Ecclesiastical History*, 68–9
Beecher, Henry Ward, 137
Beer, Clifford: *A Mind That Found Itself*, 183
Beethoven, Ludwig van, 131
Belloc, Hilaire, 118–19, 123; *Danton*, 119; *Marie Antoinette*, 119
Bemis, S. F., 173
Benedict, Ruth: *Chrysanthemum and Sword*, 238
Benét, Stephen Vincent: "The Curfew Tolls," 5; criticism of "new" biography, 143

Berdyaev, Nikolai: *Dream and Reality*, 181
Berenson, Bernard, 190
Beveridge, Albert J., 17, 171–2
Binet, Alfred, 221–2
Biographia Britannica, 79
Biographical dictionaries, 79, 102, 111
Biography: definition, 3, 69–71, 138–9; relation to history, 3–8, 68–71, 86–7; role of the individual in, 4–8, 34, 108–9, 238–9; description of character in, 8–21, 27–8, 46–8, 59, 73–5, 115, 129–31, 215–40; popularity, 8, 69, 77, 101, 118, 120, 124–6, 139, 149; relation to imaginative literature, 9–11, 69–70, 77–8, 82, 85–6, 117–20, 219; as an art, 9–11, 22–3, 40–1, 74, 86, 107, 165, 240, 258; length of, 23–4, 107; personal knowledge of subject, 24–7, 156–9; relation to autobiography, 26, 82–3; relation to religion, 35, 50, 51, 54–60; impartiality and objectivity, 18–19, 44–5, 49, 87, 89, 115–16, 155–9, 164; motives for writing, 31–2, 35, 54–6, 64, 71, 77, 84, 86–91, 105–6, 115–16, 155–63; scholarship, 41–2, 46, 49, 73, 74–5, 80–1, 85–6, 91–3, 101–2, 108, 117–18, 126, 147–50; critical literature on, 77, 86–9, 101–3, 139–44, 219–21; use of personal documents in writing, 83–4, 177–206, 220–37; physical descriptions in, 67, 85; style and organization, 35–6, 41, 44, 55, 85, 92–3, 94–5, 166–8, 241–59; reticence in biography, 98–101, 103–8, 112, 170, 206–7; use of portraits in, 131, 204, 219; rules for writing, 153, 176; relation of subject and author, 155–9; subsidized, 161–2; source materials for, 170, 177–214; restrictions, 169–74; visiting subject's haunts, 204–5; opinions of contemporaries in, 206–12; oral sources, 208–11; content analysis in,

INDEX

Biography (*continued*) 223–37; importance of chronology, 257
Biography, history of: Egyptian, 31–2, 34, 36; Assyrian, 32–3, 34; Greek, 34–42; Roman, 42–53; in Middle Ages, 54–62; in Renaissance, 49, 62–75; English, 59, 62, 66–108, 122–6; Russian, 59–60; Italian, 63–5; French, 65–7, 69–70, 78; in 18th century, 76–96; in 19th century, 97–112; American, 100–2, 125–6; since 1900, 112–51; present status of, 149–51; accounts of method, 241–7
Biography of a Business (James), 3
Biography of the Earth (Gamow), 3
Bismarck (Ludwig), 130
Black Boy (Wright), 227–30
Blake, William, 166
Bloch, Marc, 70
Boccaccio, Giovanni, 63–4
Boder, D. P., 224–5
Borden, Gail, 174
Borden Company, 173–4
Boring, Edwin G., 182
Boris, 60
Boswell, James, 28, 47, 72, 84, 88, 89, 97–9, 105, 210–11, 241; *Life of Johnson*, 25–7, 93–6; use of journal, 95, 210; as culmination of history of biography, 94, 96
Bourdeilles, Pierre de, 67
Bowen, Catherine Drinker: *John Adams*, 145–7; personal interviewing, 209; on method, 252
Bowers, Claude: *Jefferson and Hamilton*, 149
Braddock, Edward, 18
Bradford, Gamaliel, 4, 126; *Types of American Character*, 130; *Damaged Souls*, 130; *Saints and Sinners*, 130; *The Quick and the Dead*, 130
Brandeis, Louis D., 209
Brantômes, *see* Bourdeilles, Pierre de
Brett, George, 118

British Diaries (Matthews), 190
Brooks, Phillips, 164–5
Brooks, Van Wyck, 207
Brougham, Lord, 110
Bryan, William Jennings, 134, 137
Bryce, James, 22
Buehler, Charlotte, 243
Buffon, Comte de, 236
Burke, Edmund, 94, 102, 103
Burkhardt, Jakob, 62
Burnet, Gilbert: *Lives of Dukes of Hamilton and Castleherald*, 71–2; *History of His Own Time*, 72; *Life and Death of Rochester*, 72
Burney, Fanny, 210
Burns, James M.: *Roosevelt*, 239–40
Burr, Aaron, 175, 213, 249–50
Burr, Anna R., 157; *The Autobiography*, 189
Busemann, A., 224
Butler, Benjamin F., 206
Butler, Samuel, 107
Byron, Lord, 99, 125, 127, 131, 160, 166, 198

Caesar, Julius, 43, 48, 49–52, 66, 258–9
Calverton, V. F.: *The Newer Spirit*, 4–5
Cantril, Hadley: *Psychology of Social Movements*, 238
Cardan, Jerome, 82
Carlyle, Jane Welsh, 105
Carlyle, Thomas, 5, 6, 27, 98, 101, 103, 104–5, 108, 109, 140, 163, 211; *Sterling*, 165
Carlyle (Froude), 104–6
Carnegie, Andrew, 14–16, 137, 142; *Autobiography*, 14–15, 183
Carnegie Foundation, 175 n
Caruso, Dorothy, 157–8
Caruso, Enrico, 157–8
Casca, Publius, 52
Cato Major, 48
Cavendish, George, 68
Chance or Destiny? (Handlin), 6
Chandler, Colonel, 147
Chapman, Guy, 208
Charlemagne (Einhard), 24, 60–1

Charles XII (Voltaire), 79
Charnwood, Lord, 171
Chateaubriand, François de, 203
Châtelet, Mme du, 81
Chaucer, Geoffrey, 21
Chesterfield, Lord, 79
Cheyney, Edward P., 5
Chinard, Gilbert: *Thomas Jefferson*, 7
Christopher Columbus (Irving), 102
Chrysanthemum and Sword (Benedict), 238
Churchill, Lord Randolph, 156
Churchill, Winston, 156, 189
Chute, Marchette, 21, 165–6, 212
Cicero, Marcus Tullius, 43, 81, 91–3, 151
Clark, L. P., 134–5; *Lincoln*, 134
Clodius, Publius, 50
Cobden, William, 169
Colet, John, 66
Columbia University, 211
Columbian Centinel, 145
Columbus, Christopher, 205
Comte, Auguste, 108
Condorcet, Marquis de: *Voltaire*, 83
Confessions (Rousseau), 179
Confidential Clerk (Eliot), 11
Congreve, William, 107
Conkling, Alfred R., 244–6
Conkling, Roscoe, 244–6
Conqueror (Atherton), 120
content analysis in biography, 223–37
Cook, Sir Edward: *Florence Nightingale*, 20, 124
Coolidge, Calvin, 171 n; as letter-writer, 178
Coolidge, Mrs. Calvin, 171 n
Copernicus, Nicolaus, 8
Cordus, Junius, 53
Cousins, Norman, 139
Cowley, Abraham, 184
Creel, George, 192
Crockett, David, 13
Cromwell, Oliver, 27, 98, 164, 169
Crusade in Europe (Eisenhower), 236

Cushing, Dr. Harvey, 160
Cyclopaedia of American Biography, 102
Cyrus, 34

Damaged Souls (Bradford), 130
Daniels, Josephus, 156–7, 194, 217
Dante, 63–4
Danton (Belloc), 119
Darius (the Great), 33
Darius III, 47
Darwin, Charles, 109; *Origin of Species*, 110
Davies, Godfrey, 168 n
Death Be Not Proud (Gunther), 165
debunking biography, 39–40, 136–8, 141–2
Defoe, Daniel, 77–8, 85, 117, 128
Demosthenes, 43
Dennett, Tyler, 181
determinism, 4–5, 108–9, 116–17
De Thou, Jacques, 72
DeVoto, Bernard, 203; criticism of "new" biography, 140, 144, 220
Diaghilev, Sergei, 156
Dial, 221
Dialogues des Mortes (Fénelon), 78
diaries, 83–4, 99 101, 177; as biographical sources, 189–95, 206; editing of, 193–4
Diary of a Public Man, 190–1
Diary of Edward Bates (Beale), 194 n
Dichtung und Wahrheit (Goethe), 181–2
Dickens, Charles, 99, 125
Dictionary of American Biography, 149
Dictionary of National Biography, 102, 111, 140
Diderot, Denis, 102
Discomfort-Relief Quotient, 226–7
Disraeli, Benjamin, 126
Disraeli (Maurois), 131
Divine, "Father," 238
Dollard, John, 226–7
Donald, David, 167
Donne, John, 74–5, 107, 128
Douglas, Stephen A., 217

INDEX

Dream and Reality (Berdyaev), 181
Dryden, John, 70, 80
Dunn, Waldo H., 25, 55, 124

Eadmer of Canterbury, 59
Ecclesiastical History (Bede), 68–9
Edel, Leon, 200 n
Edgar Allan Poe (Griswold), 104
Education (Adams), 183
Einhard, 62; *Charlemagne*, 24, 60–1
Einstein, Alfred, 169
Eisenhower, Dwight D.: *Crusade in Europe*, 236
Eliot, Charles W., 186, 207
Eliot, T. S.: *Confidential Clerk*, 11
Elizabeth I, 124, 161
Elizabeth and Essex (Strachey), 122, 123, 161
Ellis, Havelock, 111–12; *British Genius*, 111
Emerson, R. W., 224–5
Eminent Victorians (Strachey), 22, 121–4, 136
encomium, 36, 37, 38, 43, 44
English Men of Letters (Morley), 102
Erasmus, Desiderius, 66
Essay on Biography (Stanfield), 242–3
Euripides, 41
Evagoras of Salamis, 36

Famous Americans of Recent Times (Parton), 22
Fast, Howard, 127
Father and Son (Gosse), 107
Fénelon, François, 78; *Dialogues des Mortes*, 78
Ferenczi, Sandor, 197
Ferguson, Wallace K., 63 n, 65
Fiction: influence on biography, 9–11, 77–8, 82, 85–6, 117–20, 126–9, 146–7; as source for biography, 178, 182–3, 203
Fielding, Henry: *Joseph Andrews*, 84
Fish, Hamilton, 101

Fiske, John, 111
Flaminius, Titus, 48
Fletcher, John, 128
Florence Nightingale (Cook), 20, 124
Ford, Paul Leicester: *True George Washington*, 106–7, 136
Forster, John, 102
Foster, John, 139–40
Foxe, John, 68
Francis Bacon (Mallet), 79
Franklin, Benjamin, 175, 213
Frantz, Joe B., 173–4
Frederick II (of Prussia), 24, 27, 98
Freeman, Douglas Southall, 252, 253; *George Washington*, 4, 24, 175 n, 254; *R. E. Lee*, 24, 185; on reliability of evidence, 185
Freidel, Frank, 24, 188–9, 202 n, 209
French Revolution (Carlyle), 98
Freud, Sigmund, 122, 142, 159, 197, 219–20; *Interpretation of Dreams*, 112; *Leonardo da Vinci*, 112–17, 144; *General Introduction to Psychoanalysis*, 133
Froude, James Anthony, 108, 118, 210–11; *Carlyle*, 104–6
Fuess, Claude M., 142
Fuller, Thomas: *Worthies*, 71
Fuller, Timothy, 145

Galton, Francis: *Hereditary Genius*, 110
Gamow, George: *Biography of the Earth*, 3
Gandhi, Mohandas, 169
Garrison, L. M., 217
Gateway to History (Nevins), 141
Gauguin, Paul, 127
Gelber, Lionel M., 141
George II, 24
George III, 219
George V, 162
George, Alexander: *Wilson and House*, 237–8
George, Juliette: *Wilson and House*, 237–8
George Washington (Freeman), 4, 24, 175 n

INDEX

Gerould, Gordon H., 56
Gertrude, Queen, 132
Gibbon, Edward, 43, 83, 236
Gilbert, G. M.: *Psychology of Dictatorship*, 238
Gilman, W. H., 183
Giotto, 65
Gladstone, Lord, 141 n
Gladstone, William E., 24, 102, 137, 141, 169, 193
Gladstone (Morley), 24
Gleb, 60
Goethe, Johann Wolfgang von, 5, 102, 181–2, 184
Goethe (Lewes), 102, 181–2, 184
Goethe (Ludwig), 130
Goldsmith, Oliver, 87
Gordon, Charles George, 124
Gosse, Edmund, 23, 107–8, 122, 139; *Father and Son*, 107; on biographies by relatives, 156
Gosse, Philip Henry, 107
Gottschalk, Louis, 220–1
Grand Cyrus (Scudery), 69
Grant, U. S., 101, 137, 183
Gray, Thomas, 83, 94, 107
Gregg, William, 160
Greville, Charles, 190
Gribble, Francis, 128
Griswold, Rufus W.: *Poe*, 104
Grover Cleveland (Nevins), 149
Guedalla, Philip, 126, 143
Guggenheim Foundation, 175 n
Gunther, John, 165
Guttmacher, M. S.: *America's Last King*, 219

Hackett, Francis, 126
Hadrian, 49
Hale, W. B., 159; *Story of a Style*, 223–4
Hall, G. Stanley, 111
Hamilton, Alexander, 13, 18, 101, 120, 134, 157
Hamilton, John C., 101, 157
Hamlet, 132
Handel, George Frideric, 24
Handlin, Oscar: *Chance or Destiny?*, 6
handwriting and biography, 221–3
Harding, W. G., 178

Hardy, Thomas, 203
Harlow, R. V., 134
Harriman, E. H., 181
Harris, William: *James I*, 80
Harrod, R. F., 170
Harvard College, 186–7, 207
Hay, John, 171–2, 180–1, 211
Haywood, John, 69
Hegel, G. W. F., 109
Hendrick, Burton J.: *Carnegie*, 15, 161
Henri de Guise, 66
Herbert, George, 74
Hereditary Genius (Galton), 110
Hergesheimer, Joseph, 250; on method, 247–9
Hermippus of Smyrna, 41
Herndon, William, 103, 167, 172
Herodotus, 9, 34
Hewitt, Abram S., 246–7
Hewitt, Sarah, 246–7
Hippocrates, 34
Histoire des derniers troubles de France (Matthieu), 66
Historia sui temporis (De Thou), 72
Historic Personality (Seymour), 109
History of His Own Time (Burnet), 72
History of King Richard III (More), 67
Hitler, Adolf, 238; *Mein Kampf*, 183
Hoar, George F., 206–7
Hobbes, Thomas, 73
Hogg, Thomas J., 159
Holmes, O. W., Jr., 196–7, 209
House, E. M., 214, 237
Hughes, Rupert, 138, 141–2
Hugo, Victor, 148
humanism, 62–4

Ickes, Harold L., 193
Inni, 31–2
Interpretation of Dreams (Freud), 112
Intimate Papers of Colonel House (Seymour), 214
"intuitive" biography, 129–31
Ion of Chios, 36

INDEX

Irving, Washington: *Christopher Columbus*, 102; on method, 243–4
Isocrates, 36, 43; *Antidosis*, 38

Jackson, Andrew, 13, 148 n, 175
James, Henry, 192
James, Marquis, 148 n, 244; *Biography of a Business*, 3; *Jackson*, 149
James, William, 110–11, 225
Jastrow, Joseph, 111
Jefferson, Thomas, 7, 24, 134, 150, 173, 175, 195, 198, 213, 227
Jefferson and Hamilton (Bowers), 149
John Adams (Bowen), 145–7, 252
John Sterling (Carlyle), 165
Johnson, Samuel, 25–8, 72, 75, 77, 79–80, 87, 93–5, 98–9, 105, 107, 123, 139, 164, 210, 241; on art in biography, 23, 102; on knowledge of subject, 25; *Lives of the Poets*, 27, 89–90; *Life of Savage*, 80, 124; on motives of biographers, 88–91
Johnson, Walter, 170–1
Joinville, Jean de, *St. Louis*, 61–2
Jonas, 58–9
Jones, Ernest: *Life of Freud*, 25, 160, 197; on letters as biographical sources, 197
Jones, H. M.: criticism of "new" biography, 142, 143
Jonson, Ben, 73, 128
Joseph Andrews (Fielding), 84
Josephson, Matthew, 135
Journal of a Young Artist (Bashkirtsev), 190

Kant, Immanuel, 24
Kendall, Amos, 13
Keynes, J. M., 170
Klement, Frank, 137
Knox, Vicesimus, 87
Korzybski, Alfred, 225–6
Krutch, J. W., 135

La Bruyère, Jean de, 70, 78
La Rochefoucauld, François de, 69

Lamon, Ward Hill, 171; *Recollections of Abraham Lincoln*, 17
landatio funebris, 42–3, 44
Langtry, Lily, 141 n
Laski, Harold, 196–7
Lasswell, H. D., 238; *Power and Personality*, 237
Lawrence, David, 217
Lee, R. E., 185
Lee, Sidney, 5
Lehman, Herbert, 200
Leland, John, 68, 150
Leonardo da Vinci (Freud), 112–17, 144
letters, as source material, 83, 100–1, 178, 195–202, 230–5; over supply of, 199–201
Lewes, George Henry: *Goethe*, 102, 181–2, 184
Lewis, Lloyd, 16
Lewis, Wyndham, 125
Library of American Biography (Sparks), 102
Library of Congress, 172, 175, 248
Life and Death of Rochester (Burnet), 72
Life and raigne of Henrie IIII (Haywood), 69
Life and Works of Washington (Sparks), 100–1
Life of Christ (Papini), 126
Life of James I (Harris), 80
Life of Marcus Tullius Cicero (Middleton), 79, 83, 91–3
Lincoln, Abraham, 17–18, 19–21, 131, 137, 142, 160, 167, 171–2, 183, 211, 216–17, 218–19; on biography, 108
Lincoln, Robert T., 171–2
Lincoln, Thomas, 171
Lincoln (Clark), 134
Link, A. S., 24
Little, Shelby, 18–19
Little Flowers of St. Francis, 59
Lives of Dukes of Hamilton and Castleherald (Burnet), 71–2
Lives of Illustrious Florentines (Villani), 64
Lives of the Caesars (Suetonius), 49–53, 66
Lives of the Judges (Foss), 110

Lives of the Noble Grecians and Romans (Plutarch), 43–52, 65–6
Lives of the Painters (Vasari), 25, 65
Lives of the Philosophers (Antigonus), 41
Lives of the Poets (Johnson), 27, 89–90
Livy, 50, 122, 123
Lockhart, John, 98–9, 103; *Scott*, 98–9
Lodge, Henry Cabot, 160, 178, 191, 207; *Alexander Hamilton*, 13; *Early Memories*, 186–8; reliability of, as autobiographer, 186–8
Lodovico, 258
Logan, George, 149–50
Long, J. C., 125–6
Longfellow, Henry Wadsworth, 137
Look Homeward, Angel (Wolfe), 203
Lowell, Amy, 135
Lowell, James Russell, 132
Lucas, F. L., 236
Lucullus, Lucius, 45
Ludwig, Emil: *Lincoln*, 17; *Napoleon*, 126; *Goethe*, 130; *Bismarck*, 130; on use of portraits, 131, 204, 219; criticism of psychoanalysis, 144
Lust for Life (Stone), 127
Luther, Martin, 133–4, 220

Macaulay, Thomas B., 9, 103
MacCarthy, Desmond, 19
Macfadden, Mrs. Bernarr, 205 n
Machiavelli, Niccolò, 64
Macmillan and Co., 118
Madame de Maintenon (La Beaumelle), 83
Madison, Dolly, 145–6
Mallet, David: *Francis Bacon*, 79, 81
Malone, Dumas, 24, 162–3, 175 n, 215, 253
Malone, Edward, 80, 85
Mann, Horace, 145
Manning, Henry Cardinal, 106, 124

Margaret Fuller (Anthony), 134
Margaret Fuller (Stern), 145
Margaret of Anjou (Prévost), 86
Marie Antoinette, 160
Marie Antoinette (Belloc), 119
Mark Twain (Paine), 24
Marlowe, Christopher, 125
Marx, Karl, 109
Mason, William, 83, 94
Masson, David, 102
Masters, Edgar Lee: *Lincoln: the Man*, 17–18
Matthews, William: *British Diaries*, 190
Matthieu, Pierre: *Histoire des derniers troubles de France*, 66
Maugham, W. Somerset: *Moon and Sixpence*, 127; *Summing Up*, 179; on self-portraiture, 179; on physical factors in personality, 204
Maurois, André, 126, 147–8, 221; *Disraeli*, 131; criticism of psychoanalytical biography, 144; *Aspects of Biography*, 144, 198; identification with subject, 158–9; on letters, 198; *Ariel*, 203, 219
Maximus, Marius, 53
McCargo, David, 15
McKinley, William, 178
Mead, Margaret: *And Keep Your Powder Dry*, 238
Mein Kampf (Hitler), 183
Melville, Herman: *Redburn*, 135
Memorabilia (Xenophon), 37, 127
memory, fallibility of, 181–2, 209–11
menologies, 54
Merezhkovski, Dmitri: *Da Vinci*, 119
Methodism, 82
Middleton, Conyers, 88, 95, 150, 241; *Cicero*, 79, 81, 83, 91–3
Milton, John, 73, 102
Mind That Found Itself, A (Beer), 183
Minstrels, 55
Misch, Georg, 25, 32
Mitchell, Broadus, 160 n
Montesquieu, 24

INDEX

Moon and Sixpence (Maugham), 127
Moore, Tom, 99
More, Sir Thomas, 66, 68; *History of King Richard III*, 67
Morgenthau, Henry, 201
Morison, S. E.: *Admiral of Ocean Sea*, 205
Morland, W. C., 15
Morley, John, 22, 169, 195 n; *Gladstone*, 24, 102; *Men of Letters*, 102
Mowrer, O. H., 226–7
Mumford, Lewis: on fiction in biography, 129; on psychological biography, 135
Münsterberg, Hugo, 111
Murray, Henry A., 10
Musset, Alfred de, 198
Mussolini, Benito, 258
Muzzey, David S., 7–8
My Memoir (Wilson), 205

Napoleon, 5, 160, 204, 220
Napoleon (Ludwig), 126
Nepos, Cornelius, 43
Nevins, Allan, 142, 147; on describing character, 9; criticism of "new" biography, 141, 144; *Gateway to History*, 141; *Grover Cleveland*, 149; on lack of biographical rules, 153; on sympathy in biography, 164; oral history, 211
Nevsky, Alexander, 60
"new" biography, 122–44
New Kingdom, 31–2
New Yorker, 150
Newer Spirit (Calverton), 4–5
Newman, Ernest, 160, 202
News and Observer (Raleigh, N.C.), 156
Nicolay, J. G., 171–2, 211
Nicolson, Harold, 59, 99, 126, 162; on knowledge of subject, 25; on method, 251
Nietzsche, Friedrich, 250
Nightingale, Florence, 19–20, 124
Nijinsky, Romola, 156
Nijinsky, Waslaw, 156
Nineteenth Century, 106

Nollekens, Joseph, 104
North, Roger, 88
North, Sir Thomas, 66
Norton, C. E., 171

O Rare Ben Jonson (Steegmuler), 127–8
Oliphant, Margaret, 106
Olivet, H. W., 15
Oral History Project, 211
Origin of Species (Darwin), 110
Osler, Sir William, 160
Othello, 258
Oxford University, 73

Paine, Albert B.: *Mark Twain*, 24
Paine, Tom, 127
Pamela (Richardson), 77
Papini, Giovanni, 125–6; *Christ*, 126
Parkman, Francis, 9
Parmenio, 47
Parton, James, 102, 213; *Famous Americans of Recent Times*, 22; on difficulty of writing biography, 174–5; on method, 244–6
Pascal, G. R., 222
Pearson, Edmund, 137–8
Pearson, Hesketh, 121, 126; on fiction in biography, 128–9; on method, 251–2
Pendergast, Thomas J., 12
Pepys, Samuel, 98
Pericles, 35, 36, 38
Peripatetic biography, 39–42, 44
personal documents in biography, 83–4, 177–206, 220–37
personal interviews, 208–11
personal structure analysis, 230–5
Petrarch, 63
Pharsalia, battle of, 122, 123
Pitcairn, Robert, 15
Pitt, William, 24
Plato, 37, 38, 136; *Republic*, 40
Plutarch, 41, 61, 64, 71, 75, 78, 81, 84–5, 94, 111, 115, 116, 127, 136, 150, 159, 169; *Lives*, 43–52, 111; translations, 65–6, 70, 87
Poe, Edgar Allan, 135
Polycrates, 36

Pompeia, 50
Pompey, 122
Ponsonby, Sir Arthur, 84, 190, 191 n, 193
Pope, Alexander, 76–7
Portraits and Criticisms (Wright), 141 n
Positivism, influence on biography, 108
Postman, L., 211 n
Power and Personality (Lasswell), 237
Praxiteles, 35
Prévost, Abbe: *Margaret of Anjou*, 86
Prince (Machiavelli), 64
Princeton Theological Seminary, 158
Pringle, H. F.: *Theodore Roosevelt*, 149, 173; *Taft*, 173
Pritchett, V. S., 139
profile, 48, 150
psychoanalytical biography, 112–17, 133–5, 142–4, 219–20
"psychography," 4, 130
psychology, influence on biography, 109–17, 132–5, 181, 220–40
Psychology of Dictatorship (Gilbert), 238
Psychology of Rumor (Allport and Postman), 211 n
Psychology of Social Movements (Cantril), 238
Pulitzer Prize (biography), 173
Purcell, Edmund S., 106
Putnam, General Israel, 101
Pythagoras, 40

Quakerism, 82
Queen Victoria (Strachey), 123
Quick and the Dead (Bradford), 130

R. E. Lee (Freeman), 24
Rait, Sir Robert, 196
Raleigh, Sir Walter, 73
Raleigh, Sir Walter (critic), 95
Rambler, 88
Randall, Henry S., 173
Randall, J. G., 160

Ranke, Leopold von, 108
Recollections (Taft), 205
Redburn (Melville), 135, 182–3
religion, influence on biography, 35, 50, 51, 54–60, 82–3, 100
Rembrandt, 165
Repplier, Agnes, 107–8
Republic (Plato), 40
Republican Party, 17, 188
Retz, Cardinal de, 69
Richard III, 67
Richard Savage (Johnson), 80, 89–90, 124
Richardson, Samuel: *Pamela*, 77
Riethmuller, C. J., 13
Rise of Cotton Mills in South (Mitchell), 160 n
Robinson, J. H., 133, 135
Robinson Crusoe (Defoe), 78
Rockefeller, John D., 137
Rockefeller Foundation, 175 n
Rodell, Fred, 196–7
Rodman, Selden, 257
Romance of Leonardo da Vinci (Merezhkovski), 119
Romanticism, 76, 97–8
Roosevelt, Eleanor, 205
Roosevelt, Franklin D., 12, 24, 160, 188–9, 200, 202 n, 205, 227, 239
Roosevelt, Theodore, 214; as letter-writer, 178, 180–1, 195, 200
Roosevelt: Lion and Fox (Burns), 239–40
Roper, William, 68
Rorschach test, 224
Rossetti, Dante Gabriel, 125
Rousseau, Jean Jacques, 83, 102
Ruggles, Eleanor, 215
Russell, Bertrand, 121, 144

St. Andrews University, 124
St. Anselm, 59
St. Augustine, 82
St. Boniface, 59
St. Columba, 58
St. Columban, 58–9
St. Cuthbert, 58, 68
St. Louis (Joinville), 61–2
St. Willibrord, 57–8
Sainte-Beuve, Charles Augustin, 102–3, 130, 132–3

INDEX [xi

Saints and Sinners (Bradford), 130
saints' lives, 54–60, 68, 72
Saintsbury, George, 104, 200–1
Samuel Adams (Harlow), 134
Samuel Johnson (Boswell), 25–7, 83, 93–6
Sand, George, 148, 198
Sandburg, Carl, 167, 257; *Always the Young Strangers*, 183; *Lincoln*, 252–3; on method, 252–3
Sanford, F. H., 226
Saturday Evening Post, 124
Satyrus, 41, 42
Savage, Richard, 27, 89–91
Schneider, Joseph, 4
Scott, Thomas: *Authentic Narrative*, 83
Scott, Sir Walter, 98–9, 103
Scripps College, 252 n
Scriptores Historiae Augustae, 53, 57
Scudéry, Madame de, 69
Seymour, Charles: *Intimate Papers*, 214
Seymour, Francis S.: *Historic Personality*, 109
Shahn, Ben, 257
Shakespeare, William, 5, 21, 78, 128, 132, 212, 239, 258
Shelley, Percy Bysshe, 33, 126, 131, 158–9, 166, 203, 219
Sheridan, Philip H., 247–8
Sherman, Ellen, 16
Sherman, William T., 16
Shumaker, Wayne, 26 n, 82
Sigmund Freud (Jones), 25, 160
Simpson, M. H., 188
Sir Walter Scott (Lockhart), 98–9
Smith, John Thomas, 104
Smith, Preserved, 133–5
Smollett, Tobias: *Peregrine Pickle*, 77
Social Science Research Council, 220
Socrates, 37, 38, 40, 127, 136
Sophocles, 36
Southern Literary Messenger, 12
Sparks, Jared, 243–4; *Life and Works of Washington*, 100–1; *Library of American Biography*, 102

Spencer, Herbert, 179–80
Stanfield, J. M.: *Essay on Biography*, 242–3
Statesmen of the Reign of George III (Brougham), 110
Stauffer, Donald A., 69, 76, 79
Steegmuller, Francis: *O Rare Ben Jonson*, 127–8
Steele, Richard, 78
Stephen, Sir Leslie, 140
Stephenson, Nathaniel W., 17
Sterling, John, 27, 98
Stern, Madeleine B., 144–6; *Margaret Fuller*, 145
Stone, Irving: *Lust for Life*, 127
Story of a Style (Hale), 223–4
Strachey, Giles Lytton, 19–22, 107, 120–4, 126, 139, 244; criticisms of Victorian biography, 22; *Eminent Victorians*, 22, 121–4, 136; on art of biography, 122; *Elizabeth and Essex*, 122, 123, 161; contributions to biography, 22, 123; *Son of Heaven*, 123; *Queen Victoria*, 123
Stuart, D. R., 49
Study of British Genius (Ellis), 111
subsidized biography, 161–2
Suetonius (Gaius Suetonius Tranquillus), 64–6; *Lives of the Caesars*, 49–53; translations, 66
Sulla, 43
Sun, Stand Thou Still (Armitage), 8
Symonds, John A., 64

Tacitus, Cornelius, 49, 66, 81
Taft, W. H., 173
Taft, Mrs. W. H.: *Recollections*, 205
Taft (Pringle), 173
Talbot, C. H., 56
Tarbell, Ida M., 171
Tariff of Abominations, 23
Tatler, 78
Tennyson, Alfred, Lord, 105, 217
Tharp, Louise Hall, 144–5
Thayer, William Roscoe: on role of individual in history, 5–6
Theodore Roosevelt (Pringle), 149

INDEX

Theophrastus, 44, 64, 70, 78, 136; *Characters*, 38–9
Thomas, Benjamin P., *Abraham Lincoln*, 19–21, 218–19
Thomas Jefferson (Chinard), 7
Thoreau, Henry David, 132
Thucydides, 9, 35
Timoleon, 44, 48
Tiro, 43
Tolles, F. B., 149–50
Tree, Herbert, 129
True George Washington (Ford), 106–7, 136
Truman, Harry S., 12–13, 200
Tullius, Manius, 43
Twain, Mark, 203
Types of American Character (Bradford), 130
Tyrrell, George, 106

Use of Personal Documents (Allport), 220–1

Valois, Marguerite de, 67
Value-analysis, 227–30, 236
Van Buren, Martin, 183, 249
Van Gogh, Vincent, 127
Vandenberg, Arthur, 13
Vasari, Giorgio: *Lives of the Painters*, 25, 65
Victoria, Queen, 98, 243
Victorian biography, 22, 98–108, 120, 136
Villani, Filippo, 64
Vinci, Leonardo da, 112–17, 133, 219
Vladimir, 60
Voltaire, 22, 79, 102, 169, 175; on knowledge of subject, 25; on scholarship, 81; on respect for dead, 207
Voltaire (Condorcet), 83

Wagner, Richard, 133, 160, 202, 220
Walpole, Sir Robert, 24
Walton, Izaak, 74–5
Warshow, Robert: *Alexander Hamilton*, 13
Washington, George, 5, 6, 18–19, 24, 100–1, 106, 134, 137, 138, 175 n, 190, 243, 254

Way of All Flesh (Butler), 107
Webster, Daniel, 160
Weems, Mason Locke, 100
Wendell, Barrett, 207
Wesley, John, 82
West, Rebecca, 192
Whibley, Charles, 142
White, N. I., 219
White, R. K., 227–30, 236
White, W. A., 170–1
Whitman, Walt, 103
Wilkes, John, 94
Willard, Nahum, 147
William, Kaiser (Wilhelm II), 130–1
William Gregg (Mitchell), 160 n
Willibald, 59
Wilson, William E., 159
Wilson, Woodrow, 24, 134, 171 n, 194, 198, 214, 216–17, 223, 237
Wilson, Mrs. Woodrow, 171 n; *My Memoir*, 205
Wilson and House (George), 237–8
Winkler, J. K., 14–16, 142
Wolfe, Thomas: *Look Homeward, Angel*, 203
Wolsey, Thomas, 68
Wood, Anthony, 73–4, 80, 150
Wood, Clement, 135
Woodham-Smith, Cecil, 155, 169
Woodward, William E., 6; *Bunk*, 137
Woolf, Leonard, 193–4
Woolf, Virginia, 123, 193
Worthies of England (Fuller), 71
Wotton, Henry, 75
Wright, Peter, 141
Wright, Richard: *Black Boy*, 227–30
Wright, Silas, 212–13
Wundt, Wilhelm, 111

Xenophilus, 40
Xenophon, 36, 43; *Anabasis*, 37; *Memorabilia*, 37, 127

Yale University, 214

Zweig, Stefan, 126, 131

JOHN ARTHUR GARRATY

was born in Brooklyn on July 4, 1920. He attended Brooklyn College and began his graduate studies at Columbia University, from which he received his M.A. in 1942. After some years as an instructor in the United States Maritime Service, Mr. Garraty returned to Columbia, where he was awarded a Ph.D. in 1948. After studying psychology at Harvard University on a Ford Foundation Fellowship, Mr. Garraty returned to teaching at Michigan State University, where he is an associate professor of history. He is the author of *Henry Cabot Lodge: A Biography* (1953) and *Woodrow Wilson: A Great Life in Brief* (1956). He is married and lives in East Lansing, Michigan.

A NOTE ON THE TYPE AND PRODUCTION

The text of this book is set in Caledonia, a Linotype face designed by W. A. Dwiggins (1880–1956), who was responsible for so much that is good in contemporary book design. Though much of his early work was in advertising and he was the author of the standard volume Layout in Advertising, Mr. Dwiggins later devoted his prolific talents to book typography and type design, and worked with great distinction in both fields. In addition to his designs for Caledonia, he created the Metro, Electra, and Eldorado series of type faces, as well as a number of experimental cuttings that have never been issued commercially.

Caledonia belongs to the family of printing types called "modern face" by printers—a term used to mark the change in style of typeletters that occurred at the end of the eighteenth century. It is best evidenced in the letter shapes designed by Baskerville, Martin, Bodoni, and the Didots.

This book was composed, printed, and bound by The Plimpton Press, Norwood, Mass. The paper was made by S. D. Warren Company, Boston. Typography by Sidney R. Jacobs.

TITLES IN THIS SERIES

1 Harry Elmer Barnes. *Historical Sociology: Its Origins and Development.* 1948.
2 Jacob Burckhardt. *Judgments on History and Historians.* 1958.
3 Herbert Butterfield. *Herbert Butterfield on History. Christianity and History.* 1949. *The Discontinuities between the Generations in History.* 1971. *The Present State of Historical Scholarship.* 1965.
4 Courtland Canby, Nancy E. Gross, eds. *The World of History.* 1954.
5 G. Kitson Clark. *The Critical Historian.* 1967. bound with *Guide For Research Students Working on Historical Subjects.* 1958.
6 Robin G. Collingwood. *Essays in the Philosophy of History.* 1965.
7 Henry Steele Commager. *The Nature and the Study of History.* 1965.
8 L. P. Curtis, Jr., ed. *The Historians Workshop: Original Essays by Sixteen Historians.* 1970.
9 Folke Dovring. *History as a Social Science.* 1960.
10 Martin Duberman. *The Uncompleted Past.* 1969.
11 Mircea Eliade. *Cosmos and History: The Myth of the Eternal Return.* 1954.

12 G. R. Elton. *Political History: Principles and Practices.* 1970.
13 Martin Feldman, Eli Seifman, eds. *The Social Studies: Structure, Models, and Strategies.* 1969.
14 John A. Garraty. *The Nature of Biography.* 1957.
15 John Higham, Leonard Krieger, Felix Gilbert. *History.* 1965.
16 H. Stuart Hughes. *History as Art and as Science.* 1964.
17 Paul Murray Kendall. *The Art of Biography.* 1965.
18 William Leo Lucey. *History: Methods and Interpretation.* 1958.
19 Raymond G. McInnis, James W. Scott, eds. *Social Science and Research Handbook.* 1974.
20 John Madge. *The Tools of Social Science.* 1953.
21 Arthur Marwick. *The Nature of History.* 1981.
22 Hans Meyerhoff, ed. *The Philosophy of History in Our Time.* 1959.
23 A. D. Momigliano. *Studies in Historiography.* 1966.
24 Herbert J. Muller. *The Uses of the Past.* 1953.
25 Allan Nevins. *The Gateway to History.* 1938.
26 Roy Pascal. *Design and Truth in Autobiography.* 1960.
27 A. L. Rowse. *The Use of History.* 1946.
28 Robert Allen Skotheim, ed. *The Historian and the Climate of Opinion.* 1969.
29 Robert Stover. *The Nature of Historical Thinking.* 1967.
30 Pardon E. Tillinghast. *The Specious Past: Historians and Others.* 1972.
31 Ludwig von Mises. *Theory and History.* 1957.